I0130940

Experiments in Recreation Research

First published in 1971, *Experiments in Recreation Research* examines critically the techniques of assessment, measurement, and projection for use in studies of the supply and demand aspects of sport and recreation. The research was carried out in two main parts—first, a desk study of previous social research relating to recreation, covering such areas as questionnaire and interview surveys, time budget diaries, non-survey methods of data collection and forecasting techniques; and second, a series of experimental studies which seek to throw more light on the usefulness of particular techniques and concepts for the future planning of recreation opportunities.

The merit of the book lies in its application of social research and statistical methods to recreation planning problems. Many of the experimental studies—such as those employing cluster and factor analyses and gravity models—have direct and immediate relevance to the solution of specific planning problems. Because of this, the book will be of vital concern to town planners as well as to those persons involved in the planning and management of urban and rural recreation facilities of many kinds. It should also be of interest to research workers and teachers in other fields where techniques of this kind might be applicable.

Experiments in Recreation Research

Thomas L. Burton

Routledge
Taylor & Francis Group

First published in 1971
by George Allen & Unwin Ltd

This edition first published in 2025 by Routledge
4 Park Square, Milton Park, Abingdon, Oxon, OX14 4RN

and by Routledge
605 Third Avenue, New York, NY 10158

Routledge is an imprint of the Taylor & Francis Group, an informa business

Publisher's Note
The publisher has gone to great lengths to ensure the quality of this reprint but points
out that some imperfections in the original copies may be apparent.

Disclaimer
The publisher has made every effort to trace copyright holders and welcomes
correspondence from those they have been unable to contact.

A Library of Congress record exists under LCCN: 72192274

ISBN: 978-1-041-14690-2 (hbk)
ISBN: 978-1-003-67567-9 (ebk)
ISBN: 978-1-041-14693-3 (pbk)

Book DOI 10.4324/9781003675679

Experiments in Recreation Research

BY THOMAS L. BURTON

Associate Professor of Urban and Regional Planning
University of Waterloo, Ontario
Previously Centre for Urban and Regional Studies
University of Birmingham

LONDON · GEORGE ALLEN & UNWIN LTD

First published in 1971

ISBN 0 04 790003 2

Printed in Great Britain
in 10 point Times Roman
by Alden & Mowbray Ltd
Oxford

It matters little how wrong we are with our existing theories, if we are honest and careful with our observations.

WILLIAM BEVERIDGE
in his Farewell Address as Director of the London School of Economics, June 24, 1937

Acknowledgements

The talents and efforts of many people have gone into the planning and conduct of the research studies that are reported in this book. I should like to acknowledge here my great debt to these people. Without their constant and unequivocal support, it is doubtful that the enterprise would ever have reached fruition. Not all of the people who have given of their time and energies can be mentioned here, but they may rest assured that their contributions have been appreciated. Some persons, however, merit particular mention.

My greatest debt has undoubtedly been to my colleagues on the research team—Cilla Noad, who served from November 1967 to September 1968, and Tony Veal, who served from September 1968 to the completion of this report. Both have carried the responsibility for a significant portion of the work. Miss Noad played a major role in the preparation of the methodological review of recent recreation studies. Mr Veal conceived and carried through the fourth of the experimental studies that were undertaken. He, alone, is the author of Chapters 13 to 15 of this book. In addition, I have found his knowledge of statistical method a continual source of help during the analytical stages of the other experimental studies.

Others who have contributed directly to the study are Phillippa Rahtz and Don Curtis who carried out most of the interviews for the Pilot Household Survey; Helen Parsons who played a major part in the coding of the questionnaires from both the Household and Site Surveys; Ann Massey who undertook the awesome task of coding the Time Budget Diaries; Tony Hinxman, of the University of Birmingham's Computer Services, who somehow made statistical sense out of many of my most outrageous requests; and Mr A. McCready of Bordesley College of Education, and his students, without whom the interviews in public libraries could not have been carried out.

There are various other people who, though they did not contribute directly to the study, nonetheless provided invaluable and, often, essential aid. Foremost among these are the City of Birmingham's Deputy Librarian, Mr Hargreaves, and the Librarians of Handsworth and Yardley Wood Branch Libraries, Miss Hathaway and Mr Cash, respectively. Without their co-operation, the library surveys could not have taken place. Mention should also be made here of the unceasing encouragement and support of Denis Molyneux at the Sports Council. His faith in the value of the research has been surpassed only by his patience in waiting for the long-overdue results.

Various people have read all or part of the manuscript of this book. Chief among them have been Professor Barry Cullingworth, the Director of the Centre for Urban and Regional Studies; Gordon Cherry, the Deputy Director; Dr Jack Ellis of the University of Waterloo, Ontario; and Professor Louis Twardzik, Chairman of the Department of Park and Recreation Resources at Michigan State University. To each of them, I offer my sincere thanks.

The final debt which I must acknowledge is, perhaps, the most important of all. It is to the Sports Council, and in particular to the members of its Study Group on Sociological Surveys. That the study was possible at all is due in no small measure to the enthusiastic support of this body, while its successful conclusion owes much to the Group's thoughtful and constructive comments. Any errors are, of course, entirely my own responsibility.

THOMAS L. BURTON

Preface

This series of *Urban and Regional Studies* is intended to be a vehicle for the publication of the final reports of major studies undertaken in the Centre for Urban and Regional Studies at the University of Birmingham. It complements the series of *Occasional Papers* and *Research Memoranda* (published by the Centre) which typically present interim reports or more restricted studies.

The present volume outlines the findings of the *Recreation Planning Study* carried out between 1967 and 1969, with the support of the Department of Education and Science and the Sports Council. The terms of reference of the study were: 'To examine critically techniques of assessment, measurement and projection for use in studies of the supply and demand aspects of sport and recreation which could provide a basic methodology for future studies at the regional and subregional levels.' These terms of reference were deliberately formulated in broad and rather vague terms, the intent being to allow the research team freedom to investigate any methodological approaches which might appear, in the course of study, to offer potentially useful tools for recreation planning. The scope was intended to be essentially exploratory, with the objective of providing guidelines for wider studies at the national, regional and subregional levels, rather than an attempt to lay down precise and definite rules of procedure to be followed in all future research studies.

The book is in five parts. Part One, comprising four chapters, constitutes a methodological review of recent research, based primarily upon an analysis of about fifty major recreation studies in this country and the United States. As a result of this review, four experimental studies were undertaken, the results of which are outlined in the remainder of the book. The first of these, described in Part Two, was based upon a large-scale household and activities survey. The objectives of this were first, to test the relative values of alternative methods of collecting recreation data; second, to identify 'recreation types' through the use of cluster and factor analysis techniques; and third, to establish the relative importance of various socio-economic characteristics as 'determinants' of recreation behaviour. The results are outlined in Chapters 5 to 9.

The third part of the book (Chapters 10 and 11) is concerned with methods of measuring recreation supply and with an examination of demand–supply relationships in the area in which the household and activities survey took place. It is followed, in Part Four, by a single chapter in which some major problems of recreation demand forecasting are discussed.

The final section of the book, consisting of Chapters 13 to 15, is considerably different from the other parts in that it puts forward a theory for the provision of recreation facilities which the ensuing studies were then designed to test. The theory is derived from the adaptation of a gravity model of the kind used in transportation studies.

The data employed in the experimental studies were obtained through questionnaire surveys in the homes of respondents and at selected recreation sites. Five documents were employed in the household survey, as follows: (1) a pilot household questionnaire, (2) instructions to interviewers for the main survey, (3) a household questionnaire, (4) a recreation activities questionnaire, with covering letter, and (5) a time budget diary, also with covering letter. The site surveys used three documents: (1) instructions to interviewers, (2) a questionnaire, and (3) a counting sheet for enumerators. Copies of these documents have not been reproduced in this book. They have, however, been reproduced, with some explanatory notes, in a separate publication, Research Memorandum No. 3, obtainable from the Centre for Urban and Regional Studies, University of Birmingham, price £0·75p.

The Centre for Urban and Regional Studies was established as an experiment designed to overcome some of the problems created by the traditional organizational structure of Universities and, at the same time, to bridge the gap between research and policy. Its success must, therefore, be judged not only on the criterion of academic excellence but also on the contribution which it can make to the problems facing policy-makers, administrators and planners. The merits, or otherwise, of this book should be judged by the same criteria.

University of Waterloo, Ontario   THOMAS L. BURTON
  July 1970

Contents

Tables

Figures

Prologue

Recreation is not an easily defined, homogeneous entity. Indeed, it is much easier to define what it is *not* than to say what it *is*. It does not include work. Nor does it include certain personal and social obligations that all people have, such as sleeping and washing. Beyond this, however, it is impossible to speak with any great certainty. It is easier, and perhaps more useful, to consider the *functions* of recreation in modern society and, then, to outline the more important ways in which these functions are carried out—more important, that is, in a planning sense.

One point is clear. The notion that life today consists of 'eight hours of work, eight hours of sleep and eight hours of recreation in each day' simply cannot be sustained in the light of the empirical evidence that is increasingly becoming available to us. Instead, the concept of recreation and of the role which it occupies within contemporary society needs to be considered in positive terms. It can no longer be conceived solely as a residual—as something which happens to be left over to each person after work and other necessary chores have been completed.

In fact, there would appear to be three main positive functions which recreation performs: it provides relaxation; it provides entertainment; and it provides a means for personal and social development. These three functions were first outlined systematically by *Dumazedier* [24].* (He, however, did not draw a distinction between positive and negative functions. Yet recreation can have negative functions: that is, negative in terms of motivation—as when, for example, a person watches television merely to fill in time between two positive, or chosen, activities.) No particular recreation pursuit will necessarily perform all of these three functions: but all pursuits will usually satisfy at least one of them and many will encompass more than one. Thus, a visit to the cinema may give a person relaxation, or it may provide him with entertainment; or it may produce a combination of both of these elements. Between them these three functions seem to embody the central positive characteristic of recreation: it is not the residual of work, but its antithesis or complement. Far from being an alternative to work, recreation

* References are collated in the Bibliography, page 355 *et seq.*

19

pre-supposes the existence of work, so as to provide a contrast or complement to it. Thus, current trends towards a reduction of weekly working hours and an increase of free time represent a *redistribution* of the balance of time between work and recreation rather than a trend towards the replacement of work by recreation. This viewpoint seems to be supported by empirical evidence from the United States, where recent reductions in the length of the standard working week in various occupations, to thirty hours or less, have resulted in the growth of moonlighting—that is, the taking of an additional regular job [93]. If this concept of recreation is at all realistic, then it has considerable implications for the future development of patterns of recreation. It could be argued, for example, that there is a certain minimum level below which the length of the working week will not fall—or, rather, below which workers will not want it to fall.

Recreation, *as relaxation*, provides a respite from work; a period in which the individual can rest mentally and physically from the demands of work and other necessary chores. *As entertainment*, it provides an antidote to the boredom and repetition that are often involved in work, in personal and domestic chores, and in retirement. And, *as a means of personal and social development*, it serves to allow the individual to develop along lines which may contrast significantly with the often restrictive thoughts and actions that work and other chores may permit. In short, then, recreation may be defined as participation, in its broadest sense, in any pursuits—other than those associated with work and necessary tasks of a personal and social nature—which a person undertakes freely for purposes of relaxation or entertainment or for his own personal or social development.

At this point, it is worth considering briefly the relationship between recreation and a word which is often taken to have a similar, though wider, meaning: leisure. Recreation, in its widest sense, is identical with leisure. In narrower sense, it has often been qualified by reference to such factors as location and timing: for example, *outdoor* and *indoor* recreation, the *day trip* and the *annual holiday*. It has sometimes been suggested that recreation and leisure can be clearly distinguished according to function. Broadly, recreation is said to encompass the functions of relaxation and entertainment, while leisure is concerned chiefly with personal and social development. Such a distinction is, however, of very limited value—if only because many pursuits can be undertaken for two or more of these purposes at the same time. A visit to the opera, for example, may provide entertainment, relaxation and intellectual stimulus all at one time. Is this, then, leisure or recreation? Another—more objective —distinction has been made by Clawson and Knetsch [18]. They suggest that 'leisure is *time* of a special kind; recreation is *activity* (or inactivity) of special kinds'. Leisure is free, or discretionary, time: that is, time over the use of which a person may exercise choice. Recreation is then the use that is made of this time. This distinction is more systematic than the previous one, and potentially more useful. It has the major disadvantage, however, that it is not a distinction which is ordinarily understood. The fact is that, for the majority of people, recreation and leisure are more or less synonymous terms for things which are done during free time. It seems simplest, therefore, to consider the two terms as being identical, referring to those pursuits that people undertake during their free time.

Although interest throughout this study has been concerned with the whole range of possible recreation pursuits, particular attention has been focused upon sport as a form of recreation. The chief characteristic of sport is competition—whether against other participants in teams (for example, soccer and cricket), or as individuals (boxing and fencing); or whether against natural and artificial obstacles (mountaineering and motor rallying). It has two significant dimensions: those who take part in sports and those who watch them. It does, in fact, occupy an important place in the general pattern of recreation activity in this country. About two thirds of the total population, for example, expresses an interest of some kind in association football [35]. Moreover, sport has an important place in our schools' curricula. And, perhaps most important, it has far-reaching land use implications. All of this suggests that the provision of facilities for sport needs to be planned in a more comprehensive and systematic way than for many other recreation pursuits.

The wide range in the types and numbers of pursuits that fall within the scope of the term *recreation* has induced almost all research investigators in this field to attempt to classify pursuits into groups of various kinds. This grouping has sometimes been done at the data collection stage of a study, as in the *Pilot National Recreation Survey* [6]; and sometimes at the data analysis stage, as in the *Household Activity Systems Study* [17]. It has been done on the basis of several different criteria. The study by Proctor [43] hypothesized that certain kinds of pursuits naturally 'go together'—that pursuits can be grouped in such a way that those who take part in one pursuit within a defined group will be more likely to take part in other pursuits within that same group than in pursuits in other groups. Thus, one group consisted of 'winter sports'; a second of 'water

21

sports'; and a third of 'backwoods recreation'. Burton [8], on the other hand, classified activities on the basis of the impact which the demands for them had upon the use of land and other resources. This led to a threefold classification—by type of pursuits, by their timing and by their location. There have been other classifications based upon a similar kind of reasoning, notably by Coppock [19] and Wolfe [48].

But why classify pursuits at all? A major reason is that classification helps the investigator to establish different *recreation types*, on the basis of which it may be possible to predict future demands for various kinds of facilities. If participation in any particular pursuit can be linked by correlation and other methods to participation in other pursuits, and to certain socio-economic characteristics, then, as the socio-economic characteristics of a given population change, it should become possible to predict, at least in general terms, how participation in given pursuits and groups of pursuits will change. The particular reason for employing groups of pursuits rather than individual pursuits is the hypothesis that correlations between the former and socio-economic variables—the presumed causal factors—will be more accurate and more stable over time than correlations for the latter.

A major problem with classification is to decide at which stage of a study it is to be carried out. Should it be left as an exercise to be carried out at the data analysis stage or should it be done earlier, at the data collection stage? The latter makes the conduct of a study very much easier than the former. On the other hand, classification at the analysis stage ensures that the groupings are based upon objective analytical procedures and do not incorporate value-judgments by the investigator. An examination of recent recreation studies indicates clearly that there is no obvious standard classification. Indeed, as Cullingworth [22] has noted, 'the usefulness of any particular classification will depend upon the purpose for which it is required . . . no one classification with suffice for all purposes . . . and classifications are not mutually exclusive'. In particular, there have been few attempts, beyond those mentioned above, to formulate criteria upon which to base classifications.

However, even if classification is not undertaken until the analysis stage of a study (and thus after the data about individual pursuits have been collected), there is still a major problem of definition. Should respondents in an interview survey, for example, be requested to provide data about their participation in a given predetermined set of activities, or should they be asked to provide data pertaining to pursuits which they can define themselves? The former procedure has the disadvantages that it may omit certain pursuits which are significant for some individuals but not for the population generally, and that it could lead to ambiguities in definition for some pursuits. Thus, one person who has been for a Sunday afternoon drive and taken sandwiches with him may decide that this comes into the category of a 'picnic', while another may consider it as 'driving for pleasure', and a third may count it as both. The definition of a pursuit is here in the hand of the respondent not the investigator. This is not so where individuals simply record pursuits in their own words. The investigator is then free to decide into which category of pursuit this best belongs. The disadvantage of this procedure is, however, that it involves a large amount of laborious office work before analysis can be carried out. Predefined pursuits, on the other hand, can be precoded for easy statistical analysis. Undefined pursuits have to be coded later. Most recent studies have utilized predetermined and precoded pursuits, but have attempted to make certain that these have covered a wide range of possibilities. Two notable exceptions to this were the *Household Activity Systems Study* [17] and the American part of the *Cross National Time Budget Study* [44]. Both studies, by their nature, required that respondents record their activities in their own words. Both, as a result, involved complicated and laborious coding exercises.

The nature of recreation is not the only problem which we face: demand is also a concept which requires clarification. Demand is, essentially, an economic concept. It is the technical term used to describe the relationship between the quantities of a product that people will purchase and prices. It refers to a desire which is backed up by ability and willingness to pay for the product which is desired. At any given price people will purchase a certain quantity of a product; and, as this price changes, so the quantity purchased is likely to change. Thus, demand refers to *a relationship between quantities and prices*. Demand is often confused, however, with consumption (or quantity demand). Consumption refers to *the quantity which is actually purchased, or consumed, at any given price*. Usually, non-economists will use the term demand to mean what is technically consumption. In Figure 1, for example, the economists' concept of demand is represented by the line *DD*, which shows a relationship between a range of prices, measured on the vertical axis, and a range of quantities, measured on the horizontal axis. The actual, or equilibrium, price which reigns in the market at any given time will be determined by the interaction of this demand schedule with a supply schedule, *SS*, which shows a relationship between quantities supplied and price: in Figure 1, this equilibrium price is *OP*, at which point *OM* units of the product will be consumed. This latter value is usually what is meant by the term demand among non-economists—the quantity demanded, or consumed, at a particular price. In a market system, however, this quantity can change with changes in price.

It is not difficult to understand why the layman will often use the term demand to mean consumption in respect of recreation facilities. Many recreation facilities are available for general public use at no direct cost to the user: there is no fee or charge. Hence, there is no

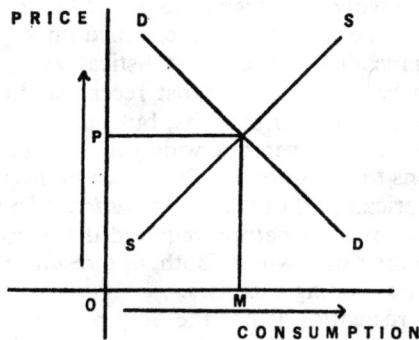

Figure 1. The nature of economic demand

schedule which shows a relationship between prices and consumption, since there is only ever one price—zero! Changes in consumption will reflect, primarily, changes in supply.* Thus, in Figure 2, the quantity consumed at zero price, *OM*, is determined by the point at which the supply schedule, *SS*, intersects the horizontal axis. This quantity is increased to *ON* when the supply is increased to $S^1 S^1$. In this situation, consumption is, effectively, the only measure of demand. Thus, the numbers of people who visit an urban park provide the only measure of demand for that park, and changes in these numbers will usually reflect changes in one or more elements of supply—for example, improved access to the park or improved weather conditions.

In making a distinction between demand and consumption in this

* This, of course, is extremely simplified: in the long term, consumption may change with changes in other factors—for example, total population, numbers of persons within particular age-groups, and so on.

way, we are not simply being pedantic. The numbers of users of an urban park certainly reflect a demand for it. But they also reflect *supply*. It is very likely, for instance, that the numbers of visitors to parks in South-West Birmingham will be considerably higher than in the North-West part of the city. This does not necessarily imply, however, that the demand for parks is greater in the former area than in the latter. It could equally indicate that the supply of parks is greater in the former area. (This was, in fact, found to be the case in respect of the two areas employed for the experimental studies described in later chapters.) The figures in both areas are measures of consumption, which derive from the interaction of supply and demand

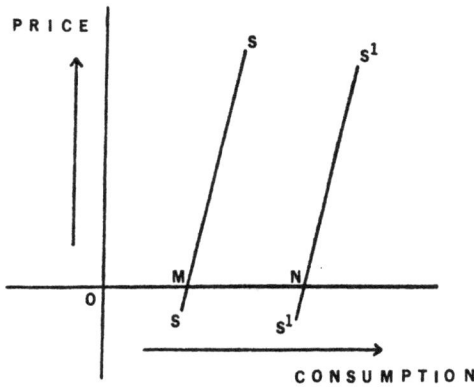

Figure 2. Consumption in a non-price system

factors. Figures of use or attendance are the direct effect of existing demand and existing supply. In the case of many public recreation facilities the measurement of demand is complicated by the fact that a relationship cannot be established between quantities demanded and price, since there is only one price—zero. Thus, figures of consumption include an implicit relationship between supply and demand. The economist's concept of demand, on the other hand, as represented by the demand schedule, *DD*, in Figure 1, takes no account of supply, which is assumed to be a wholly independent variable.

The interest in this study is primarily with supply and consumption and, particularly, with the interrelationships between them. The concern has been to discover ways of measuring and projecting rates

25

of consumption of recreation activities, given certain assumptions about the availability of facilities and about the background factors affecting consumption—for example, income levels and leisure time. Equally, we are concerned to investigate and measure the ways in which supply generates consumption: how the establishment of a new facility within an area creates its own pattern of consumption and affects levels of consumption of other facilities within the area. The economist's concept will not be totally ignored, if only because there are certain kinds of (commercial) recreation facilities for which this kind of analysis is appropriate. The major concern will be, however, with consumption and supply, and especially with the interrelationships between them. To the layman, however, consumption is demand. It is proposed, therefore, to use the word demand in this sense, and to continue to refer to the study as being concerned with 'the demand and supply aspects of sport and recreation'. Should it be necessary to refer specifically to the economist's concept of demand, then it will be designated as *economic demand*.

The demand for recreation can be considered in five dimensions: existing demand, latent demand, induced demand, diverted demand and substitute demand. *Existing demand* refers simply to a demand which currently exists. It is measured in terms of, for example, the use which is made of tennis courts in a public park, throughout a season, or the total numbers of tennis balls sold in a particular area during a season. *Latent demand* is one which, for some reason, is not effective, but which would be so in other circumstances. It is a demand which is frustrated by such factors as the nonexistence of facilities. Induced, diverted and substitute demands are all supply-related concepts. *Induced demand* is one which is created as a direct result of the provision of a supply of facilities. That is, if a new recreation facility is made available, an entirely new demand may be generated for it, in addition to any latent demand which was previously unsatisfied. One of the biggest single problems in recreation planning at the present time stems from our complete lack of understanding of the nature of induced demand for recreation facilities and of its size. *Diverted demand* refers to a demand for a certain kind of facility which is diverted from one source of supply to another as a result of the provision of a new supply. Thus, for example, the provision of a swimming pool in a district which was previously without one will cause some residents of that district to stop using a pool in a nearby district and to use the new pool in their own district instead. Their demand has been diverted from the existing pool to the new one. Finally, *substitute demand* is similar to diverted demand, but refers to completely different recreation facilities. Thus, to continue with the above example, the construction of a new swimming pool in a district can cause some residents to take up swimming in place of another activity, such as tennis, in which they previously took part. They have substituted a demand for swimming for a demand for tennis.

Most recent studies of recreation demands have been concerned with demand in its popular sense (that is consumption); and all have considered existing demands. Few, however, have attempted to seek information about latent demands and about the three categories of supply-related demands. This stems, in part, from the major difficulties inherent in finding a satisfactory method of assessing such demands, which would be meaningful for policy. Simply to ask people about which activities they would like to take up is inadequate, since experience has shown that most people will make statements which give no consideration to the impact that this will have upon the amount of money and time which they have available for recreation. The *Pilot National Recreation Survey* [6] attempted to avoid some of the difficulties inherent in this approach by asking respondents about both those activities which they would like to take up and those which they positively planned to take up. The latter question, it was felt, would provide a much more reasonable indicator of latent demand. The relatively small size of the sample restricted the value of the resulting data: but, as expected, the figures were lower for all activities in response to the question about positive planning than for the question which simply asked about likes. The *Household Activity Systems Study* [17] developed a *game* approach. The study sought information about all activities undertaken by respondents by means of a time budget diary which they were asked to complete. Each respondent was then also requested to indicate how he (or she) would use an additional four hours of leisure time per week if this were available to him. This approach attempted to provide the investigator with strict time and income restraints to build into respondents' aspirations, thereby reducing the degree of idealism which respondents could include in their statements about future activities. Both of these studies were first attempts at tackling a very complicated problem. Neither method has received sufficient testing and the measurement of latent demand remains an open field for research. This is even more true of induced, diverted and substitute demands. At present, there has been no research at all into possible methods of measuring these categories of demand. Some attempt will be made in this study to investigate these aspects of demand, but the major concern will be with the more immediate problems of measuring and forecasting existing demand.

Supply, like demand, is a concept which needs clarification in the context of recreation studies. It has two dimensions: present (or existing) supply and future (or potential) supply. *Present supply* refers to the existing supply of facilities, including both facilities made available through the market, such as cinemas and ice rinks, and those made available by other means, such as public libraries. *Potential supply* refers to future supplies of facilities, which are financed on various bases, according to whether or not they are to be provided through the market or otherwise. Most recent studies have been concerned with the measurement of existing supply, although there have been some general studies which have pointed to the potential supply available in given areas, such as the *Lea Valley Study* [23].

Perhaps more important than this distinction between existing and potential supply is the conceptual distinction between supply itself and opportunity. *Supply* is usually taken simply to refer to the resources—land and facilities—available for recreation. *Opportunity*, on the other hand, is a demand-related concept. It is analogous to the economist's concept of *effective supply*: that is, a supply which is capable of satisfying a demand. The demand for recreation facilities is one which is constrained in space and time. Recreation facilities are demanded within a given location, that location being determined, in large measure, by the ease or difficulty of obtaining access in time and distance. Supply is effective only if its location is such that it provides an opportunity for the satisfaction of demand. The effect of this distinction between the simple concept of supply and the more meaningful one of opportunity has been most clearly illustrated by the O.R.R.C. studies of recreation in America: 'public areas designated for outdoor recreation include one-eighth of the total land of the country, but . . . for reasons of location (or management) much of the vast acreage nominally designated for recreation is now not available for general public recreation use' [38].

Location is not, of course, the only feature which distinguishes opportunity from supply. The O.R.R.C. studies also noted the importance of management. Moreover, the effects of management can be manifested at both the policy level and the operational level. Thus, for example, a policy which makes educational facilities available for the recreational use of only recognized organizations ensures that such facilities do not constitute an effective supply for persons who do not belong to these organizations. In a similar way, facilities which, for operational reasons, are made available only between the hours of, say, 8 a.m. and 6 p.m. do not constitute an effective supply for persons whose time is wholly committed for this period—for example, those at work or engaged in travel to and from work during these hours.

Thus supply, like demand, is a concept which requires clear definition in the context of the present study. The concern will be, in fact, with recreation opportunity—in particular, with alternative methods of measuring and assessing opportunity for any given population and within any given area.

A knowledge of the nature and scope of the different kinds of recreation demand is a first prerequisite of planning. Recreation planning can be manifested, broadly, in two ways. On the one hand, it can be deterministic: that is, it can be concerned to provide recreation facilities of a kind which it is thought, by policy-makers, that the population *ought to have*. On the other hand it can be directed towards the provision of those facilities which it has been shown (or which it is believed) that the population *wants*. This is not the place to enter into a discussion of the relative merits of the two philosophies. It is sufficient merely to say that, while much educational and social policy in Britain is directed towards persuading people to take part in those recreation pursuits which somehow make them 'better people', planning policies are increasingly being directed towards the provision of those facilities for which there is a known, or assumed, public demand. And, moreover, since planning is, by its nature, occupied with provision for the future, an increasing concern is being expressed for forecasts of likely future demands for recreation facilities. Thus, the need is not simply to measure existing demand and to reduce latent, induced, diverted and substitute demands to forms which can be expressed quantitatively. There is also a more important need to discover reliable ways of forecasting how all of these demands will change in the future.

The purpose of this study is threefold: firstly, to examine critically techniques of measuring demand for recreation facilities; secondly, to examine alternative methods of forecasting recreation demands so that these may be useful for planning; and finally, to consider alternative ways of compiling inventories of supplies of recreation facilities. The object is to discover, test and improve methods and techniques, rather than to extend our knowledge of demands and supplies themselves, either nationally or locally. The study has been undertaken in two parts. Firstly, major methodological problems were identified through an exhaustive review of recent major recreation studies and by means of consultations with other research investigators involved in recreation studies. The findings of this part of the study were incorporated in a report, published early in 1969, which also included outline proposals for the second part of the study which was to follow [14]. This was to consist of a series of experimental studies aimed at finding solutions to some of the problems identified in the first part of the study. The term experimental is not used here in its strictly scientific sense of an investigation which allows one to observe 'the effect on a dependent variable of the manipulation of an independent variable under controlled conditions' [67]. This, in the social sciences, is impossible to achieve. The defining characteristic of the experiment is control; control over the application of the independent variable to the dependent variable; and control of the conditions in which this application is carried out. Such control can never be totally obtained in behavioural studies. The term experiment is used here in a much broader sense—to mean investigations which utilize experimental methods, such as matching, even though these investigations cannot be undertaken in a situation which is totally controlled.

Both the review of previous research and the experimental studies have been tackled in three broad sections, concerned, respectively, with techniques of data collection, techniques of analysis, and techniques of forecasting. The scope of the study was intended to be essentially exploratory, with the objective of providing guidelines for wider studies at the national and, more particularly, the regional and subregional levels. It was not expected that the study would provide complete and detailed solutions to major methodological problems. The purpose was much less ambitious, but perhaps more immediately useful. It was to identify basic problems and to investigate possible solutions to these by means of some experimental studies.

Part One

A Methodological Review of Recent Recreation Studies

Chapter 1
Collection of Recreation Data

Six methods of collecting data about recreation will be considered in this chapter: interview surveys; self-administered and, particularly, postal surveys; observation; documents which have been compiled for purposes other than the immediate one for which it is intended to use them; physical evidence; and mechanical and electronic devices. All of these are established social research techniques and all have been utilized, at least to some extent, in recreation research. This review of their merits and limitations is based upon an analysis of more than a hundred papers relating to social sicence research methods generally and more than fifty recent recreation studies. In addition, consultations have been held with about twenty persons engaged in recreation research, either currently or at some time in the recent past.

No review of research, in any field of study, whether of methods or findings, can be complete without at least a brief examination of the objectives and scope of this research; for there is no doubt that methods and findings will be conditioned, at least in part, by objectives. Thus, for example, the type of sampling method that can be used for a study of the recreational use of urban parks will differ considerably if the objective is to obtain a picture of the proportion of the total population which makes use of such parks (requiring a household survey) rather than to obtain a profile of *only* those who use them (requiring a survey in the parks themselves).

Most recent recreation studies in Britain have been limited in objectives and severely restricted in scope. Generally, the objective has been to provide improved background data about current trends in recreation habits, for the use of planners and others concerned with the provision of facilities:

'As our society becomes increasingly leisure-orientated there is a growing need for more basic information about the factors governing recreation activities. The demand for facilities is increasing at an accelerating rate as proportions of available time and disposable income become larger. Recreation activities create a demand for land and specialized facilities, but the planning authorities and commercial organizations responsible for their development are not helped to make adequate plans for the future by the lack of information about both the present situation and the precise nature of future demand' [6].

Statements of this kind abound in recent studies, but rarely has there been much attempt to go beyond such generalizations and to outline, more precisely, the ways in which such data can be utilized by planners. By and large, recent studies have simply provided better and more reliable data, on the basis of which planners have had to continue to make *informed judgments* about what facilities to provide. Virtually no recent studies have attempted to formulate criteria, based upon the findings of research, which planners and others can utilize in the formulation and implementation of plans. Recreation planning in Britain has not really advanced beyond the stage of making inventories of supplies and surveys of demands.* This is not, of course, to decry the importance of inventories and surveys. On the contrary, one of the main purposes of this study is to examine ways in which the data obtained from such inventories and surveys may be made more accurate, comprehensive and useful for planning purposes. The kinds of data obtained from social research studies constitute the basic foundations upon which planning policies can be constructed. There is a need, however, to distinguish between the mere recognition of the importance of research as a basis for planning and the purposeful design of research studies to obtain data which seek to provide answers to specific planning questions. Too often the objectives of recreation studies have been expressed in very broad and general terms—such as 'to provide detailed information on the use of (demand for) recreation facilities which will serve as a basis for planning'. Perhaps there is now a need to devote less attention to the collection of data and more attention to improvements in the use that can be made of data in the formulation of policies and plans. But, prior to this, there is an even greater need to systematize methods of collecting and analysing data so that the latter is in a form which can be utilized by planners. We start, therefore, with a critical review of methods of collecting data about recreation.

Interview Surveys

The major advantage of interview surveys over other research techniques is, of course, their flexibility. The skilled interviewer can make

* Every generalization of this kind has its exceptions, as does this one. In particular, there is B. Cracknell's 'Access to the Countryside as a Factor in Planning for Leisure' [20]. Another notable exception is the Sports Council's *Planning for Sport* [45].

34

sure that the respondent fully understands the nature of the information that is being sought; he can probe more deeply into the subject's responses; he can show the respondent cards, lists and similar material and so focus his attention more completely on the subject of interest; above all, he can establish rapport with the respondent and thereby maintain the latter's interest and participation in the study.*

There are, broadly, two groupings into which interview surveys can be divided:

(i) the interview technique that is used—*standardized, semi-standardized* or *non-standardized;*

(ii) the location of the interview—in the *household,* or on *site* (by on site is meant at the place where the subject matter of the survey generally occurs—for example, a shopping centre or public park). Site surveys may relate to either the users of facilities and services, or to the suppliers, or to both.

These two categories are, of course, not mutually exclusive.

The standardized (or structured) interview is used when the same, or similar, information is to be collected from each respondent. This means that the answers of all respondents must be comparable and classifiable; differences in responses must reflect actual differences among respondents, and not differences arising from the different questions asked or the differences in meaning which respondents have attributed to the same questions. The wording and sequence of questions are determined in advance and these are asked of all respondents in exactly the same way. The semi-standardized interview, in contrast, is based upon a list of required information which is given to the interviewer. In its simplest form it utilizes a schedule or questionnaire which the interviewer may present to the respondent in any sequence of questions. At its most refined level, the interviewer operates only with a list of the data which he must obtain.

Standardized and semi-standardized interviews are, basically, the required techniques for situations in which the same categories of information are sought from all respondents. The objectives of the non-standardized interview are quite contrary to this. The user of the non-standardized interview makes no attempt to obtain the same categories of information from each respondent, and there is no necessity for the unit of analysis to be the individual (although it

---

* This flexibility in the interview situation has both advantages and disadvantages. For a discussion of these, see M. B. Parten, *Survey, Polls and Samples* [74].

usually is). The essence of the non-standardized interview is that the questions can be varied from one respondent to another. Hence, there is no predetermined schedule or questionnaire and often no check-list of required information. Usually, there is no predetermined population sample for study. At its most formal, it approaches the semi-standardized interview. This is called the guided or focused interview, which covers a predetermined set of topics but allows the interviewer total freedom in the methods he uses to obtain data relating to these topics. At its most informal, it consists of conversation and entirely non-directive interviewing. It has been likened in this respect to the psychoanalyst's couch! There is no predetermined set of topics to be covered and the approach is entirely free.

All forms of the non-standardized interview require highly skilled interviewers. The interviewer has very great freedom in the formulation of the content of the interview and in the questioning procedures. The questioning will therefore stem from the interviewer's understanding of the overall objectives of the inquiry. Hence, non-standardized interviews will generally be conducted by the researchers themselves.

Household surveys may involve only one individual in each household, or all members of the household—or, indeed, selected members only (for example, those within a particular age-group). They may be on any scale from a single neighbourhood to a national inquiry. *Site* surveys may be made of the users or the suppliers of facilities and services. User surveys yield information about the users of a facility, particularly the intensity of use (non-users are, of course, automatically excluded). They can be carried out by interviews with individuals and groups of individuals, or by reference to organized clubs and other bodies. The major limitation of the latter lies, however, in the fact that large numbers of users of certain facilities may not be members of clubs and organizations. Site surveys of suppliers may be made by reference to the observation of facilities actually available, or by interviews with the persons responsible for the provision of facilities.

The interview survey has become the most popular method of obtaining data about recreation demands in recent years. All major national and regional demand studies during the past decade have employed it (with the few exceptions discussed later in this chapter). Most have been by household interview; although Burton [17], the Greater London Council [25], and the British Travel Association [5] have all conducted large-scale site interviews. Generally, there have been few problems encountered in the conduct of these surveys.

The major difficulties have been in the planning and analysis of them, and have been broadly twofold. The first problem has been to identify and obtain an adequate sample of respondents; the second, to ensure comparability of data between surveys. In general, the attention of investigators has been focused chiefly upon the former problem, while the latter has been largely ignored.

Sampling is defined as the selection of part of an aggregate of material to represent the whole aggregate. All rigorous sampling requires the subdivision of the material to be sampled into sampling units. These may be natural units (e.g. individuals) or aggregates of these (e.g. families and households), or artificial units (e.g. areas on maps). These units must be capable of clear and unambiguous definition. Clear definition demands the construction of a frame: that is, if households are to be the sampling unit, there must be available a list of households, and any that are selected must be capable of unambiguous location. A typical and commonly-used sampling frame is the Electoral Register.

The major problem in sampling is, of course, to avoid bias. The latter can arise in two main ways: through errors in the selection of the sample, and through chance differences between the members of a 'population' that are included within a sample and those that are not included. Bias arising from errors in selection forms a constant component of total error, which does not decrease as the size of the sample is increased. True sampling error—that is, error arising from chance differences—does decrease with increasing size of sample. It is not appropriate here to discuss different sampling methods and alternative sampling frames. Yates [78] and Kish [71] have both made excellent surveys of these, which are standard texts on the subject. The former is a British study and is useful therefore for those seeking information about sampling frames that are readily available in this country. The latter is an American text which takes its examples from conditions in that country.

From the point of view of recreation studies, however, there are two particular problems which occur frequently in drawing samples: first, determining the size of the sample that is required; and second, securing a sample which is 'representative' of the larger population that is the subject of the study. The former problem arises from the nature of recreation itself—a collective term embracing a wide range of diverse pursuits. The size of the sample required to achieve a given accuracy depends upon the variability of the material and upon the extent to which it is possible to eliminate the different components of this variability from the sampling error. The variability in the case of recreation surveys lies in the numbers of different pursuits that the subject incorporates. We know from previous studies that levels of participation in any particular recreation activity are not very high, in terms of the proportion of the total population taking part. There is a large number of pursuits in which only 1 per cent or less of the population takes part. Further, there are many pursuits for which participation is restricted to specific groups in the population: many sports for example are largely the province of young persons between the ages of about 12 and 25 years. Thus, unless the sample is relatively large, a household survey on recreation habits generally is unlikely to pick up sufficient numbers of persons who take part in *minority pursuits* to make statistical analysis worthwhile and meaningful.

An example of this problem is seen in the *Pilot National Recreation Survey* [6]. This is probably the most comprehensive study of general recreation habits that has yet been undertaken in this country. The object of the study was to secure at least tentative answers to questions about how patterns of recreation demands are changing: which are majority activities, which are minority ones, which have a potentially broader appeal, and so on. Emphasis was directed towards outdoor pursuits, and especially to those which had obvious planning implications, such as the recreational use of the motor car. Team games were, however, treated as a single group on the grounds that they were unlikely to be growing rapidly in popularity and, anyway, had been adequately considered in other studies. The concern was therefore with informal pursuits which generate substantial demands for land and thereby are important in physical planning terms. The survey was conducted by means of household interviews of the standardized type. These interviews were held with 3,167 respondents: 2,839 adults aged 17 years and over, and 328 children aged between 12 and 16 years. A random sample was attempted, intended to be representative of the total population of the country, both urban and rural, and spread across the Registrar-General's standard regions of England and Wales, plus Scotland. At least twenty sampling points were selected within each region, with approximately equal regional sub-samples, to ensure that each region provided sufficient data for at least a simple regional analysis to be undertaken. Addresses at which interviews were to be held were selected at each sampling point by the choice of a random starting point on the Electoral Register and instructions to interviewers to call at every tenth address thereafter. No substitutes were permitted, either for the households or the selected individuals within them. At each address the selected respondent was to be the youngest person over the age of twelve years who was present in the household at the time of the call. This was intended to guard against the under-representation of young people, those most commonly away from home.

The investigators' attempt to avoid a particular sample bias was, in fact, rather too successful. Though the proportion of respondents in each of the youngest age-groups (12–16 years and 17–24 years) corresponded almost exactly to the proportions of persons in these age-groups in the national population, some of the older age-groups were under-represented: the age-group 65 years and over included only 10 per cent of respondents, but represents 15 per cent of the national population. (The extent to which these proportions were affected by non-response is unknown.) However, though the attempt to avoid bias in the structure of the sample was moderately successful, the total size of the sample proved to be inadequate. It was large enough for simple descriptive analysis and the statement of broad conclusions. But analytical work involving the division of the sample into sub-samples by age, income, occupation and community size was only just permissible for the national sample, and certainly not for the regional sub-samples. Even the full national sample was insufficient to give adequate data about minority activities. Thus, respondents were asked to indicate which of thirty activities they had ever undertaken during 1965: for only ten of the thirty activities was the proportion of respondents who had participated greater than 1 per cent; indeed, the most popular activity of all (swimming) was undertaken by only 11 per cent of respondents. It was considered by the investigators that a tenfold increase in the size of the sample would have been necessary to pick up sufficient numbers of participants in minority activities to make possible a meaningful analysis of their characteristics.

The same problem—that of securing adequate data about minority activities—was also encountered in the two other national recreation studies which have been carried out in recent years: the British Broadcasting Corporation's study of *The People's Activities* [1], and the Government Social Survey's *Leisure and Planning Inquiry* [109]. The former study was, however, concerned chiefly with radio and television habits, and utilized a time-diary in addition to an interview. The fact that it failed to obtain much data about minority activities was of little direct concern, since both listening to the radio and watching television are large-scale majority activities. The experiences of the Government Social Survey's study are, as yet, unknown in detail, since the analysis is not completed. It is understood, however, that it experienced similar problems to those encountered in the *Pilot National Recreation Survey* in respect of minority activities.

One possible way of avoiding the difficulties of obtaining sufficient data about minority recreation activities in interview surveys is, of course, to carry out surveys at the sites of these activities: that is, in theatres and cinemas, at sports grounds, in parks and open spaces, and so on. Several studies of this kind have been undertaken in recent years. The Central Council of Physical Recreation examined the *Non-residential Use of the Crystal Palace National Recreation Centre* in this way [16]. Burton did the same for the use of *Windsor Great Park* [11] during summer weekends. The Greater London Council employed both site and household interviews in its study of the use of urban parks and open spaces. [25] The chief advantage of site surveys is, of course, that they limit the survey 'population' to those persons who are known to take part in the activities in which the investigator is interested or to use the facilities which are the focus of his concern. The major problem lies in the difficulty of obtaining an unbiased sample. This is due largely to the fact that there is no list of the population from which a strictly random sample can be drawn—except in the case of club facilities when a list of members could be used.

The interviewers in the Windsor Great Park study were stationed at selected entrances to the park and instructed to carry out interviews continuously. When they had finished interviewing one group they were to choose the next group to enter the park for interview. In the Greater London Council surveys, interviewers were also stationed at selected entrances to parks, but were instructed to interview, at fifteen-minute intervals, the first person entering or leaving the park, or the person nearest the gate. In the study of *Weekend Motorists in the Peak District National Park* [5] interviewers were stationed at selected parking places and cars entering the parking place were chosen for interview. The driver was interviewed in the first car to enter the park, any other adult aged 16 years or more in the next car; this sequence was then repeated for all cars entering the park.

Each of these methods is likely to produce a biased sample. They have three sources of bias in common. Firstly, the choice of entrances or parking places may not be representative ones. Secondly, interviewing on particular days of the week at particular times of the year may produce a sample which is not representative of users on the other days and at other times of the year. (The seriousness of this bias will depend, of course, on the purpose of the survey.) Thirdly, visitors to parks are unlikely to arrive at a steady rate. By interviewing at a constant rate, undue emphasis is given to those arriving during slack periods. This can be overcome to a certain extent by counting the rate at which people are entering and weighting the sample accordingly. It is evident that none of these sources of bias is likely to be reduced merely by increasing the size of the sample—indeed some could be made worse.

The second major difficulty in recent recreation studies has been to ensure comparability of data between studies. This has two aspects: the type and quantity of data which is sought about recreation activities, and the range of data which is sought about the 'background' characteristics of respondents—that is, the profile data. The first problem is partly one of definition. As was noted earlier, recreation is a collective term embracing a wide range of diverse pursuits. In some cases there is no generally accepted definition of what pursuits constitute recreation—especially in the case of informal outdoor pursuits such as driving for pleasure, walking for pleasure, nature walks, hiking and rambling. When, for example, does hill-walking become climbing? In one survey hill-walking may be classified as climbing; in a second, it may be included in walking; and in a third, it may be classed as a distinct activity in itself. A lack of comparability of this kind is often irritating but, fortunately, not too serious—as long as each individual definition is clear and unambiguous. Lack of comparability in the types and quantities of profile data about respondents, and in the ways in which these data are collected, is, however, more serious, since these are the background characteristics which form the basis of comparisons between the findings of different studies.

Little attention has been given to the kinds of profile data that ought to be collected in social surveys, and the ways in which they should be collected. The British Sociological Association has recently set up a working party to investigate comparability of data, and this has produced a series of 'first appraisals', relating to age, sex, marital status and birth place [65], education [85], family and household [81], income [68], and occupation [64].* These have proved to be a useful starting point for the consideration of the types of profile data that should be obtained in recreation surveys. The present situation is chaotic. An analysis of six recent major recreation surveys in Britain has shown that they can be compared on only four items of profile data: whether or not the respondent was employed; if he

* Some of this material has now been published as *Comparability in Social Research*, Heinemann Educational Books, 1969.

Table 1. *Profile Data Obtained for Six Recent Recreation Studies*

	1 PILOT NATIONAL RECREATION SURVEY (B.T.A.)	2 THE PEOPLE'S ACTIVITIES (B.B.C.)	3 SURVEY OF MAJOR COUNTY CRICKET (N.O.P.)	4 SURVEYS OF USE OF OPEN SPACE (G.L.C.)	5 LEISURE AND PLANNING INQUIRY (G.S.S.)	VILLAGE LIFE IN HAMPSHIRE
OCCUPATION						
Employed or unemployed	×	×	×	×	×	×
What firm (name)						
Type of firm	×	×	×	×	×	×
Job actually done	× ×		×	× ×		
Any qualifications	× ×					
Length of official working week						
Any overtime						
Paid weekly or monthly						
INCOME						
Actual income	×					
Income groups	× ×	×			× ×	
SOCIAL CLASS						
Self-rating						
Rating by interviewer	× ×	×	×		×	
Other method						
EDUCATION						
Type of school attended	×					
Operator of school						
Co-educational or single sex						
Age left school	×	×	×	×	×	×
Any further education						
Any qualifications						
CAR						
Ownership	× ×		× ×		×	
Use made of it	× × ×					×
HOUSEHOLD GOODS						
Television						
Washing machine						
Refrigerator						
Telephone						

42

×× × ××

×××× × × × ×

××× × × × × ×

× ×

× ×

× × ×× × × × ×

HOUSING
  Type of dwelling
  Garden/no garden
  Owned or rented
  Length of residence
  Previous place of residence
  Age of present dwelling
SEX
AGE
  Date of birth
  Actual age
  Age-group
MARITAL STATUS
  Two groups
  Three groups
  Four groups
  Five groups
HOUSEHOLD COMPOSITION
HOLIDAYS
  Length of paid holidays p.a.

was employed, what job he actually did; whether or not he owned or had the use of a car; and the composition of his household. It is possible to make comparisons upon one other item—age—by converting the form in which the data were obtained into a single base. On no other characteristics—for example, income, social class, educational background, ownership of household goods, type of housing, sex, marital status—could all six surveys be compared (Table 1).

But the lack of comparability does not appear simply in the types of data that are sought; it arises also in the ways in which they are sought. All of the six surveys above sought information about the respondent's occupation. But there are different data that can be obtained about occupation; for example:

1. Whether or not the respondent is employed.
2. Which firm employs him.
3. The type of firm.
4. The job he actually does.
5. Any specific qualifications he has for this job.
6. The length of his official working week.
7. Opportunities for paid overtime.
8. Whether paid weekly or monthly.

It may not be necessary, of course, for the investigator to seek information about all of these items, but there ought to be general agreement about which are the basic ones to seek in order to obtain an adequate profile of occupation. The *Pilot National Recreation Survey* [6] asked about five of the eight items; the British Broadcasting Corporation's Study [1] asked about two items; the *Survey of Major County Cricket* [35] asked about three, as did the Greater London Council in its study [25]; the *Leisure and Planning Inquiry* [109] and the survey of *Village Life in Hampshire* [27] each asked about two items. Similar patterns have emerged from a comparison of these six studies on other profile data; for example, on *marital status*, both the *Pilot National Recreation Survey* and the *Leisure and Planning Inquiry* have three possible groups. Each has 'married' and 'single,' but while the former has a third group 'widowed or divorced,' the latter has 'widowed, divorced or separated'. There is no indication whether respondents to the former study who described themselves as separated have been included in the category married (since this is still their legal status), whether they have been included with widowed and divorced respondents, or whether they are regarded as single.

44

The two major problems that have arisen in interview surveys of recreation demands are, therefore, obtaining a sample which is adequate for a meaningful analysis to be made of minority activities, and ensuring comparability between surveys, particularly in the profile data of respondents. Potential solutions to these problems were examined in the experimental research which is described in later chapters of this book.

Self-Administered Surveys

Self-administered surveys are ones in which questionnaires are completed by respondents themselves: there is no interviewer. The most usual form of such surveys is the postal survey, but there have been cases where the questionnaires have been delivered to respondents in other ways. The major limitation of the self-administered survey lies in the difficulties of obtaining a high response rate and, hence, the possibilities of creating bias in the findings. There are two elements of concern here: firstly, to examine methods of increasing response rates; and secondly, to investigate methods of detecting and measuring the significance of the bias arising from non-response. Experience has suggested that a response rate of between 30 and 50 per cent is usual for this type of survey, and that a response rate of more than 50 per cent must be considered very good, in operational terms. But, in analytical terms, the chances of there being a statistically significant bias in the findings of a study with such a relatively poor response rate are very high. Many suggestions have been made in recent years for tackling this problem. They range from technical suggestions concerning the design and operation of the questionnaire to the offer of financial inducements to respondents. A discussion of many of them is to be found in a report from the Centre for Urban and Regional Studies at the University of Birmingham, to which the reader is directed for further details.*

One other disadvantage of self-administered surveys merits brief consideration here. This is their bias in favour of the literate. There is clear evidence that respondents to self-administered questionnaires are often more literate than non-respondents. While this is a greater problem in educationally backward countries than in advanced countries, a recent report has suggested that, even in Britain, perhaps one in ten of school leavers is unable to read [94]. Any survey utilizing

---

* T. L. Burton and G. E. Cherry, *Social Research Techniques for Planners*, George Allen & Unwin, 1970.

self-administered questionnaires, especially those sent by post, would automatically exclude this section of the population.

Considerable use has been made of self-administered surveys in recent recreation research. Indeed, it has become established as the primary method for securing data about recreation supplies. The *Initial Appraisals* of facilities for sport and recreation made by ten of the Regional Sports Councils in 1967–8 [49–62] were all carried out by means of postal surveys of local authorities. In each case, a questionnaire was sent to every local authority in the region (of rural district, urban district, borough and county status) requesting data about the numbers and types of facilities available within their areas for six major recreation activity-groups; thus, the survey covered swimming pools and baths, indoor sports halls, sports and athletic stadia, golf courses, water recreation areas, and general leisure areas. The surveys had one major advantage over most other postal and self-administered surveys: the fact that the sponsors of the surveys were local and central government-backed organizations, while the respondents were local government authorities. As a result of this, the response rates were very high indeed, ranging from about 90 to 100 per cent. There was some variability, however, in the coverage of each of the surveys. Some were carried out in great detail while others appeared to have been rather superficial. Certainly there is a significant lack of comparability between the studies. This is because there were no instructions about which facilities were to be included (and which excluded) that were common to all of the studies. This arose because the studies were not conceived, and were never thought of, as parts of a complete national study. They were conceived solely as initial appraisals of the broad levels of provision in each region. (Indeed, more detailed and co-ordinated regional studies—as distinct from initial appraisals—are currently being carried out.) The emphasis was upon regional provisions. Nevertheless, the lack of a common definition does make interregional comparisons difficult. Thus, the Southern region is shown to have only two sports halls, while the County of Lancashire in the North-West region has 247! Clearly, there has been a radical difference between the two regions in the definition of a sports hall. The Lancashire survey includes many community halls which are used only occasionally for sports activities.

The question of comparability between responses is particularly crucial in self-administered surveys. Since there is (usually) no third person to act as intermediary between the investigator and the respondent it is essential that there should be as little ambiguity as possible in the meaning of questions in the survey. The possibilities for the respondent to misinterpret questions must be minimal. This often requires that precise definitions must be used in seeking data about such things as the numbers and types of facilities available in an area or the kinds of activities that a person has taken part in during a given period of time. It is vital that respondents are quite clear in their own minds as to which items should be included in, say the activity *driving for pleasure*; and, furthermore, that these items should be identical for all respondents.

Several recent self-administered recreation studies have been able to avoid, at least in part, the difficulties arising from ambiguities in question-wording by establishing direct consultation between the investigator and the respondents. This can be done wherever it is possible to use a 'captive audience' as respondents. Thus, the study of the leisure activities of post-school adolescents by Griffiths [101] has been able to use this approach. The objective of the study is to examine the factors which affect the role which physical recreation activities play in the lives of post-school adolescents. For this purpose data were obtained from teenagers during their final year at school, and further data will be sought from the same respondents two years after they have left school. The first series of data were obtained by the use of self-administered questionnaires completed by final-year schoolchildren during school hours in fifty-three Lancashire schools. The survey was administered at each school by a member of the Department of Physical Education of the University of Manchester, in which the study was being undertaken. These staff explained the purpose of the research to the children, made personal guarantees of anonymity in the responses, answered queries as they arose, and generally supervised the conduct of the survey. The availability of a 'captive' set of respondents undoubtedly increased the rate of response. Although a few children declined to take part, the vast majority were very keen to participate. But perhaps more important is the fact that the presence of the supervisory staff enabled the respondents to clarify, to their own satisfaction, the meanings of questions which might have been open to ambiguous interpretation. As a result, there were only five completed questionnaires which were subsequently unusable out of a total return of 2,690.

Another study which sought data from a captive group of respondents was the Newcastle-upon-Tyne *Evening Leisure Survey* [110]. This study was in two parts: the first consisted of a traditional postal survey of a sample of households in the city; the second consisted of a self-administered survey at selected theatres in the city, undertaken during the intervals of theatre performances. The response rate for the postal survey was about 70 per cent, which compares favourably with the rate of between 30 and 50 per cent which is commonly obtained from postal surveys. The response to the Theatre Survey was, however, even higher —about 89 per cent. This was due, in part, to the fact that data were sought from a 'captive audience' and, in part, to the fact that persons who completed questionnaires were entered for a draw in which the prizes were vouchers for free tickets to future theatre productions. There is no indication as to which of these two factors was the most significant in helping to secure such a high rate of response. What is clear, however, is that the use of a self-administered survey appears to be, statistically, quite satisfactory in situations in which the investigator may use a 'captive audience' as respondents.

This problem of obtaining an adequate response is crucial to the validity of the findings of any self-administered survey which attempts to secure a sample of the general population. In these cases, several of the methods that have been used in social surveys generally can be employed for recreation studies: for example, the use of stamps on return envelopes rather than reply-paid envelopes, the use of follow-up letters, the offer of opportunities to win a prize, and so on. But, even after several of these techniques have been applied, experience has shown that response rates can still be relatively low as compared with the rates that are generally obtained in interview surveys. This is not so, however in the case of studies which refer to special groups of persons within the general population, as long as significant numbers of these groups can be contacted. This was the method employed in both the *Theatre Survey* in Newcastle and the study of the *Leisure Activities of Post-School Adolescents* in Lancashire. In these circumstances, response rates can be kept high while other advantages—of cost, elimination of ambiguity in question-interpretation, removal of delay in the timing of returns, and so on—can be obtained.

Observation

Observation can be defined as the purposeful and selective watching and counting of phenomena as they take place. As a systematic method of research it should satisfy three main conditions: it should be suitable for investigating the problems in which the researcher is interested; it should be appropriate to the populations and samples that he wishes to study; and it should be reliable and objective.

Moser [73] has suggested that the method has significant weaknesses on all three counts. He argues that it is usually suitable only for a small fraction of the subjects that the investigator wants to study since it is confined in time and place (in the sense that it can be carried out no more rapidly than the event itself and only in the place where the event happens). It is often not easily combined with sampling procedures. And it usually gives too much scope to the subjective influences of the individual investigator.

Sampling problems are, indeed, particularly difficult: if the characteristics of a population are to be inferred from those of a sample, then that sample should (usually) be randomly selected. This is virtually impossible when observation alone is the research method employed. Subjectivity is also a difficult problem. Observation tends to give too much scope to the subjective influence of the individual investigator. Thus, the observer may have to observe something of which he is himself a part. Observation is necessarily partial and selective; and even though trained and experienced observers may attempt to separate observation from interpretation, it is likely that their own particular biases and feelings may cause them to observe selectively. This can be termed *the myth of objectivity*. It should perhaps be recognized that observation untinged with inference and interpretation is virtually impossible; so that work should be directed towards a system of measuring and controlling the degree to which inference and interpretation are present rather than towards trying to eliminate them altogether.

Despite these objections, observation can be a useful research method. It may be valuable, for example, in situations where subjects are unable or unwilling to provide information to the researcher by other methods. Moreover, even though the subjective influence of the investigator may affect the research findings, it does at least reduce the possibilities of falsifying the data through the conscious or unconscious desires of subjects to present inaccurate pictures of themselves, or to distort information.

Observation can be particularly useful as a complementary technique to interview surveys. It can be applied, for example, to indicate the respondent's style of life, his non-verbal responses in relation to his verbal ones and to check actual behaviour against the respondent's report of his behaviour. The method is particularly valuable for studying small communities and institutions in action and for assessing how people live and how they behave in given situations. It has been used with considerable success in a number of studies of small communities and 'closed' groups within society [72].

A number of different observational methods have been identified by various research workers—participant and non-participant, controlled and uncontrolled, simple and systematic. These descriptions are, however, merely slight variations of similar concepts. Despite the wealth of terms, we can identify only two basic and distinct groups of methods: *participant-simple-uncontrolled* methods; *non-participant-systematic-controlled* methods. The former refers to situations which the observer has witnessed or in which he has taken part on an entirely random basis. The investigator's observations are not checked by other observers or against a set of specific items to be noted down; and the observations do not form part of a detailed outline of experiments. The latter refers to situations in which the role of the investigator is not detectable and, therefore, the naturalness of the situation is not disturbed. In practice, however, it is rarely possible to obtain a true non-participant observation; it usually means, in fact, quasi-participation.

Very little use has been made of observation in recent recreation research. The major study is by Hole [28] and covers children's play on new housing estates. The difficulties of attempting to interview very young children are formidable, so that observation is, prima facie, an attractive alternative. The only other major recreation study in recent years to employ observation as a basic research method was Wager's study of the public use of the National Trust property at Ashridge [46], which he undertook as part of a wider study of *Outdoor Recreation on Common Land* [47]. Difficulties arose in this study, however, as a result of the physical nature of the recreation site. It was unfenced so that 'for the purposes of this study it was assumed that those people recorded twice will be cancelled out by those missed altogether'. No reasonable explanation was given for this assumption, which appears dubious.

It is, however, worth examining Hole's study in greater detail:

'A layout plan of each estate was divided into a series of observation areas. Each area was one which an observer could conveniently view from a single spot and note any children who might be there at the time of the visit. Each child's activity and where he was playing was noted as at the moment of observation; subsequent changes which occurred while the observer was still at a particular observation point were ignored. If the same child appeared later in another observation area or was still in the same observation area when the observer returned for a second visit, he was noted again. Each observation area was visited in strict rotation during a walk-round which covered a whole estate. These walk-rounds were repeated at intervals throughout the day.' [28].

In creating these observation areas Hole's objective was to reduce the effects of extraneous random factors in the data that were obtained through the observations. The intention was to create a systematic observational situation: and, to some extent, this was achieved through the establishment of the walk-round routine. But Hole gives no indication that the observations themselves were systematic. It is not clear whether each observer was instructed to carry out observations and note activities against a predetermined check-list of items and activities to be observed; or whether the activities undertaken by the children were to be described by the observers in their own words. The former procedure has the disadvantage, of course, that certain activities may be ignored because they have not been included on the predetermined check-list which each observer has; but the latter approach has the equally significant disadvantage that the activities noted by the observers are subject to the preferences and prejudices of the observers themselves—inference and inter-pretation could be present to a significant extent in the findings of the study.

Observation is, potentially, a useful method of social research. Its chief value lies in the field of small-community and small-group studies. It could be particularly useful for assessing how people behave in given situations. Through observation, the investigator avoids bias arising from exaggeration, status-consciousness, a failure of memory, and so on, which the interview survey cannot wholly avoid. Observation is limited, however, for studies of larger groups, or for those which require strict sampling, or for those in which personal characteristics of random groups—that is, profile data—are required in great detail. That the method has received so little attention from those engaged in recreation research is unfortunate; certainly, it is a research method which has significant potential and one which requires further investigation and testing.

Documents

Documentary sources are of two main kinds: continuous records of the community or sections of the community; and discontinuous records of one kind and another. There is a wide variety of documentary sources which can be used for social research, including records of births, marriages and deaths, city and town directories and development plans, electricity consumption records and so on. There are, however, two inherent sources of bias in documents—*selective deposit* and *selective survival*. The further back in time the investigator goes in his search for documents, the greater these sources of bias are likely to become. The major characteristic of documents is, of course, that they have been produced by someone other than the investigator, for someone other than him, and usually for some purpose other than his. This is true of both continuous and discontinuous records.

Continuous records offer a large mass of pertinent data for many areas of social research. They are relatively cheap to obtain and easy to sample. Furthermore, 'population' restrictions associated with them are often known and therefore capable of control. They range in kind from the Census data to sales records, club membership lists, ticket sales and so on. Their major advantage is that they create opportunities for study over time—although, often, the time scales are dictated by the availability of the records rather than by the choice of the investigator. Their major disadvantages are, of course, the twin problems of selective deposit and selective survival. Data may vary selectively over time and across different geographical areas.

A particular difficulty with continuous records is to assess the effects of extraneous factors, such as administrative and definitional changes. Records of expenditures upon entertainment, for example, may be non-comparable over time; that is, they may be affected by changes in the methods of recording data, or by alterations in official definitions of entertainment.

Surprisingly, there has not been much use of continuous records in recreation research. The study of the *Norfolk Holiday Industry* [37] in 1961 utilized records of bread sales in the county as a method of measuring the seasonal flow of holidaymakers. Some small local studies have utilized the records of the membership of clubs to assess the demands for particular recreation facilities [33]; but, these apart, there does not appear to have been any other major recreation demand study which has made direct use of continuous records. There has, of course, been considerable use of such records in supply studies; and also some substantial indirect use of them in demand studies. Many interview surveys, for example, have used Census and other records to supplement the profile data obtained from respondents; and electoral lists have long been established as sampling frames. There is, however, a need for further investigations of the potential use of continuous records as direct sources of data about recreation demands.

Discontinuous records are of two main kinds—*institutional records* and *personal documents*. The former consist of data collected from time to time concerning public and private institutions, each set of data usually referring to the single point in time at which it was collected; for example, the data collected from member-firms by The Industrial Society about the length of paid holidays given to employees [30]. Personal documents consist of autobiographies, diaries and letters. These are either existing documents which the investigator is able to utilize, or elicited documents which are produced by the subject at the instigation of the investigator. Discontinuous records are often more difficult and costly to acquire than continuous records, but they usually provide a greater specificity of content.

Particular emphasis has been given in recent years to the use of personal documents in social research. These provide a richness of detail which cannot be obtained from sales records, institutional records, continuous and discontinuous public records, observation and survey methods. They are, however, of no value for predictive purposes—except in very unusual cases; and it is usually extremely difficult to get an adequate sample of them. Comparability, too, presents obvious difficulties.

There is, however, one kind of personal document—half-way between the diary and the self-administered questionnaire—which has proved to have some use, especially in recreation studies. This is the *time budget diary*. Respondents are supplied with a blank diary-form corresponding to the period for which data are required, but never for less than one full day. In most cases, each day is divided up into convenient time periods—say, one-hour intervals—and the respondent is asked to record all activities undertaken during each time period. In addition, he is often asked to supply other information relating to each activity, such as the persons with whom it was undertaken, the times at which it was begun and ended, the place at which it was undertaken, and so on. The object is to secure a comprehensive record of the way in which a complete day (or longer period) is used; that is, a total breakdown of all daily activities, including leisure and recreation, but also household tasks, work, education, religious activities, and so on. Thus, it aims at collecting a comprehensive picture of how respondents allocate their time among different activities—hence, the use of the term time budget diary. It is not, however, concerned with the budgeted allocation of time in the generally accepted meaning of the word 'budget', since empirical evidence has suggested that the use of time tends to be budgeted for only the most essential and obligatory forms of activity. In fact, a prime characteristic of activities undertaken during a

53

person's leisure time is that they often appear to be totally opposed to the concept of a budget; there is often an unplanned, even impulse, use of free time. Perhaps a better description of the time budget diary would be a time use diary, but the former title has now become generally established.

There are many problems inherent in the use of time budget diaries in social research. Perhaps the most difficult is to secure a satisfactory sample of data. There are two possible sources of bias: the first arises from rates of response, the second from the periods of time covered by responses. The two are, to some extent, related; for, the longer is the period of time for which the diary is to be kept, the greater is the likelihood of respondents dropping out and failing to complete the diary. Thus, for example, we would expect the response rate to be lower for a study which required diaries to be kept for a week than for one which required them to be kept for only a day. But non-response is not only a function of the length of time for which the study is operative. Response rates are generally lower, anyway, for time budget studies than for comparable interview and self-administered surveys. This is not, in itself, a disastrous problem—as long as the level of non-response does not significantly bias the findings of time budget studies (as yet, there is little precise information about the biasing effects of non-response).

Another major problem arises with the grouping and coding of activities undertaken by respondents. The description and wording of activities is in the hands of the respondents themselves. While this means that significant activities are unlikely to be omitted (which could be the case with precoded interview surveys) and that ambiguities in the definition of groups of activities can be avoided, it does make the study more complex and difficult to carry out. All time budget studies invariably involve complicated and laborious coding exercises before a full analysis can be undertaken.

There have been several time budget studies in recent years which have thrown considerable light upon recreation activities. Perhaps the most important, methodologically, is the *Cross-National Time-Budget Study* [82] which was co-ordinated by Szalai at the European Centre for Research and Documentation in the Social Sciences. The objectives of this study were threefold:

(i) to study and compare in different countries, in a concrete and systematic manner, changes taking place in the nature and temporal distribution of daily activities of populations subjected in varying degrees to the influences and consequences of

54

urbanization and industrialization in industrial agglomerations and their more or less immediate surroundings;

(ii) to develop methods of collecting data and evaluating time budgets which, apart from their theoretical interest, are of considerable importance for the organization of working life and for the creation of satisfactory conditions for the use of leisure;

(iii) to promote co-operation, standardization of research techniques and the exchange of quantitative data at an international level between research workers in this field endeavouring to collect comparable results with a view to their common evaluation.

The study included research teams in ten countries—but not the United Kingdom—for whom guidelines were drawn up in Vienna concerning methods of data-collection, coding, recording, and the presentation of findings. The American part of the study was undertaken by Robinson and Converse at the Survey Research Center, University of Michigan, and has recently become generally available. [44]. The diary was set out in one-hour intervals and sought data about primary and secondary activities undertaken during each hour, the times at which activities were begun and ended, where activities took place, and with whom, and any general comments and remarks of the diarists. The use of one-hour intervals may be thought, perhaps, to be rather long, but there are several obvious difficulties that would arise in increasing the amount of data obtained by reducing the time intervals; and, anyway, the importance of the formal one-hour structure was reduced significantly by asking also for the times at which activities were begun and ended. In addition, the use of smaller time-intervals would, apparently, have complicated the task of co-ordinating the study over ten countries.

As may be expected, the most difficult problem in the analysis of the data from this study was the grouping and coding of activities undertaken by respondents. All the activities on the diary day were eventually coded into ninety-six basic activity-groups, all of which fell into one or other of two main categories—obligatory or non-leisure activities, and leisure or spare-time activities. This coding was a particularly difficult and laborious exercise, but was by no means impossible. At the completion of the analysis, it was shown that the study had produced an average figure of about twenty-three activities per person per day—covering sleeping, eating, travel, work, personal hygiene, shopping, and a wide variety of spare-time activities.

One of the expected difficulties in undertaking time budget studies —that of low response—did not, however, materialize in this study. The overall response rate was 72·5 per cent which is not very significantly lower than in most normal interview surveys; and, indeed, is significantly higher than is generally obtained from self-administered and postal surveys. This unexpectedly high rate of response was the result, at least in part, of two factors: firstly, the diary had to be completed for one full day only by each respondent rather than, say, for several days or a week; secondly, in those cases where respondents had not made any entries at all in their diaries by the time the interviewers returned to collect them, diaries filled out in retrospect with the aid of the interviewer were accepted. The validity of this latter practice is doubtful, and it would be valuable to know the extent to which the rate of response was increased by this form of completed diary. Prima facie, it would seem likely that entries completed with the aid of interviewers will differ from those completed independently by respondents; although, whether or not such a difference would be statistically significant is not known. Converse and Robinson made no attempt, however—at least in their initial report—to examine this relationship. Seen in this light, therefore, the high rate of response is rather illusory.

A second recent American time budget study was the *Household Activity Systems Study* [17] by Chapin and Hightower at the Center for Urban and Regional Studies, University of North Carolina. This study was an attempt to obtain information about the activity patterns of households comparable to the type of data obtained for trip patterns in origin-and-destination transport studies. The Pilot Investigation was of an exploratory nature, concerned with the development of a typology of household activities and with experimentation with different techniques of identifying activities that could be used in later, more comprehensive, studies. The diaries used in the pilot and main studies were not set out in the form of specified time-intervals. Instead, respondents were asked only to begin recording at midnight one day and to cease recording at midnight on the next day, listing all activities in sequence and giving for each the time at which it was begun and ended, the place at which it was undertaken, and the persons with whom it was undertaken.

Unlike Converse and Robinson, Chapin and Hightower found that response rates for the diaries were very low: about 25 per cent, compared with the 72·5 per cent obtained by Converse and Robinson. It must be remembered however, that the latter study included in its responses diaries which were completed retrospectively with the aid of the interviewers. This probably increased the rate of response considerably. Furthermore, the Converse and Robinson study used trained and experienced interviewers, while Chapin and Hightower used students from the University of North Carolina to carry out their fieldwork.

The most difficult problem encountered by Chapin and Hightower was, however, identical to that encountered by Converse and Robinson. This was the grouping and coding of the activities of respondents, who had, of course, described these in their own words. In particular, they faced the problem of defining an 'activity': when does some particular act qualify to be called an activity? Several criteria for this were discussed and rejected until, finally, it was determined on an *ad hoc* basis; in effect, an act qualified to become an activity if sufficient numbers of respondents clearly conceived it as such. This led to the establishment of nine major categories of activities:

(i) Income-producing and related activities.
(ii) Child-raising and family activities.
(iii) Education and intellectual development.
(iv) Religious and human welfare activities.
(v) Social activities.
(vi) Recreation and relaxation.
(vii) Participation in club activities.
(viii) Participation in community service and political activities.
(ix) Activities associated with food, shelter, medical and similar needs.

These nine major groupings were, in turn, divided into sixty-two sub-groupings, some of which were further subdivided. This compares with ninety-six activity groups used by Converse and Robinson.

In addition to the two American studies, there has been one recent time diary study in Britain, by the British Broadcasting Corporation's Audience Research Department, the report of which was published in 1965 [1]. In many ways, this is a disappointing report. It gives virtually no information about the methodology of the study—a serious lapse when the basic methodology (the time budget diary) is very much an experimental one. The report devotes only two pages to a discussion of methods as compared with 204 pages of tables and charts. This made it particularly difficult to examine the techniques of the study and to compare these with those used in the two American studies. The report is clear, however, on two points: the length of time for which respondents were asked to complete the diary, and the rate of response. The diaries were kept for a full week, as compared with a single day in each of the two American studies. Yet, despite this major difference, the response rate was significantly higher than for the Chapin and Hightower study, although lower than that obtained by Converse and Robinson. Of an initial sample of 4,026 names and addresses issued to interviewers, 2,363 provided an unambiguous record of activities for the full seven days: a response rate of about 58·5 per cent. With no further methodological information, however, we cannot assess what techniques (if any) were used to increase the level of the initial response: or whether, indeed, this figure represents the level of the initial response itself.

These recent time diary studies have all been, in a sense, experimental. The technique is relatively new and, as yet, little is known about its merits and limitations. In outline, however, it appears to offer an interesting and valuable method of obtaining data, in depth, about recreation habits. The major difficulties seem to be fourfold: first, how to secure significant and adequate rates of response; second, related in part to this, how to determine the time-periods for which diaries should be kept; third, how to decide the time-intervals into which the diary itself should be divided; and fourth, how to undertake the coding and grouping of activities. Further experimental studies should consider one or more of these problems in greater detail.

Other kinds of discontinuous records have received relatively scant attention in recent recreation studies. Hemmens [103] at the University of North Carolina's Department of City and Regional Planning is currently working with data derived from origin-and-destination travel surveys in an attempt to identify from these the spatial demands of persons in urban areas, including their demands for recreation facilities. We could find no major recreation demand study in Britain which had derived any significant part of its data from such discontinuous records.

Some use has, nevertheless, been made of discontinuous records in studies of recreation supplies. Burton [10] used a record of holiday caravan sites in Britain to draw up a picture of the location, regional distribution and density of sites throughout the country. He obtained his data from a commercial directory (*Caravan Sites, 1965*) which had, in turn, obtained data from each licensing authority in the country. This directory simply listed each site, together with its address, the name of its operator, and its caravan capacity. The investigator then used these data to build up a picture of the regional distribution of sites, their concentration into coastal areas, their different sizes and densities—thereby showing the impact that the growing practice of taking caravan holidays had had upon the use of land in Britain. The scope of this study was restricted, but it provides an illustration of the way in which discontinuous records may be utilized.

A further possible use of discontinuous records is to be found in the secondary analysis of data obtained from previous recreation studies, particularly those which were conducted by means of interview and self-administered surveys. This is not the same thing as a 'bringing together' of information and findings from several recreation studies; but involves the 're-working' of the data obtained from other studies—to test a different hypothesis, perhaps, or to examine correlations which the primary analysis had ignored. Again, there is little evidence of such secondary analysis having been undertaken in British studies of recreation demands. Another study by Burton [9] does, however, provide an example of this approach. He used data obtained by the British Travel Association in its *Home Holiday Survey of 1960* [2] to draw up a picture of the regional distribution of holidaymakers throughout Britain. In particular, he produced a statement of the holidaymaking 'balance of trade' between regions, thus illustrating the net importance of the holiday industry to such regions as the South-West and Wales; for, although the British Travel Association's primary analysis of the data from the survey had shown the *gross* importance of holidaymaking in these regions, it had not considered its *net* significance. Burton's analysis showed that, although the North-West region was the second most important holiday region in the country in gross terms (receiving 15 per cent of all holidaymakers), the importance of holidaymaking to the region in net terms was relatively small—since the proportion of holidaymakers going to the region only just exceeded the proportion coming from it (15 per cent to 14 per cent). Again, this study was restricted in its scope; but, like the previous one, it provides an illustration of the way in which documentary sources can be utilized by research workers.

Physical Evidence

Physical evidence refers to data about physical traces surviving from past behaviour and events. These data have, usually, not been collected specifically for research purposes; but they are available to be exploited by the research investigator. Webb *et al.* [84] distinguish two main kinds of physical evidence: *erosion*, where the degree of wear and tear on a given material serves as a measure; and *accretion*, where the evidence relates to a deposit of material. They give as an example of an erosion measure the experience of the Chicago Museum of Science and Industry. Officials noted, from maintenance records, that the vinyl tiles around an exhibit containing live hatching chicks needed replacing about every six weeks, while in the remainder of the museum they often did not need replacing over periods of several years. It was suggested that this provided a crude measure of the popularity of this exhibit as compared with others. Indeed, it could be hypothesized that the rates of tile replacement around the various exhibits throughout the museum provided a crude index of the relative popularity of all of them. This hypothesis was in fact tested and partially confirmed by direct observation. Thus, the measure of popularity was the degree of physical erosion, although the source of the data was maintenance records supplemented by direct observation.

Webb *et al.* also cite an example of a physical accretion measure in their description of Sawyer's study [76] of the sales of alcoholic drinks in Wellesley, Massachusetts. Because of particular local difficulties the usual methods of observation, survey and study of sales records were not available to the investigator. Instead, he examined garbage which had been collected from different parts of the town and counted the numbers of empty bottles. The resulting data, while incomplete and subject to unknown variables—for example, he had no knowledge of bottles which had been broken or of those which had been retained in households for some other use—none the less, gave a partial measure of the incidence of alcohol consumption in the town.

Data derived from physical evidence are valuable for securing measures of incidence, frequency, levels of attendance, and the like. The major advantage is that physical evidence is entirely objective in character (although the investigator's interpretation of the evidence may introduce a subjective element). The data are produced without the subject's knowledge of the use that will be made of them. This avoids the problems that arise from the bias of respondents in the more usual survey methods. On the other hand, there is the major disadvantage that the quality of physical evidence may vary haphazardly over time and space. Some materials, for example, will endure for much longer periods of time than others—a problem which has been apparent in archaeological research for many years. Again, the coverage of physical evidence also tends to vary haphazardly. There is usually no possibility of systematic sampling of physical evidence; and there is therefore no clear indication of how representative the data are.

There have been few attempts to apply physical evidence measures to recreation research. The study at the Chicago Museum of Science and Industry above is a rare example. Occasionally, for publicity purposes, attempts have been made to gauge the attraction of major festivals and events by noting the volume of litter that was collected afterwards. No attempt seems to have been made, however, to use such data for anything other than publicity purposes. Coppock hopes to use erosion measures, derived from aerial photographs, in his *Pilot Survey of Tourism in Part of the Borders* [100]. Such photographs may be particularly valuable for before-and-after studies, since they usually show very clearly former states of vegetation for almost any type of area.

The chief value of physical evidence measures appears to be, therefore, as complementary or supplementary information to data obtained by alternative methods of investigation; for example, by sample survey and observation. If physical evidence measures are used in conjunction with such methods, it will often be possible to control the problems arising from haphazard variations in the quality and coverage of data, while allowing some check on the degree of error in the other methods arising from such factors as respondent bias. There appears to be only limited value, however, in the use of physical evidence as a means of measuring recreation demands. As long as the concern is simply to obtain a measure of levels and intensities of use of given recreation areas, then physical evidence is potentially quite useful as a measure. But as soon as further details are required about the characteristics of users, then its value is severely limited.*

Mechanical and Electronic Devices

Mechanical and electronic devices may be used simply as means of recording data, or as supplements to other methods of research, or, indeed, as alternatives to other methods. As simple recording devices, they are most valuable in providing measures of incidence, attendance and the like. The adaptation of devices used for measuring the numbers of cars passing over a given stretch of road so as to record, say, the number of footsteps passing over a stile has been employed in a number of studies. The survey of visitors to the Wye and Crundale National Nature Reserve [21] utilized such a device. One of the two

---

* J. Greaves has suggested, however, in private correspondence, that physical evidence (and, indeed, mechanical and electronic devices) are potentially valuable tools of *management* for use in countryside recreation areas.

stiles used by the majority of visitors was modified so that pressure on the lowest bar of the stile activated an electro-mechanical counter. Thus a count was obtained of the total numbers of visitors entering the Reserve at that point.*

In their present state of development however, these devices are of relatively limited use—mainly as counters to provide overall totals for the number of persons carrying out some particular act. They can tell us very little more about these persons. When used as supplements to other research methods, however, they are of greater value. Hidden cameras and microphones have been used, both as supplements and alternatives to observation, in many studies in the United States [84]. They have been particularly useful in child psychology. Weir [86] made audiotape recordings of a 2½-year-old child falling asleep, thereby obtaining an insight into language learning processes which it would have been impossible to obtain by simple observation.

One of the major problems encountered in the use of mechanical and electronic devices is the difficulty of securing a satisfactory sample of data. If the recording device is located in a single place, such as a camera or counter at a picnic site, then the investigator is forced to accept the data obtained from the persons who pass this spot. If, on the other hand, the recording device is mobile, such as a microphone hidden in a hearing aid, then he can exercise greater choice in his search for respondents; and is able, if he wishes, to make an attempt to obtain a meaningful sample of respondents.

Insufficient is yet known about the use of mechanical and electronic devices on a large scale in social research. They are, clearly, very valuable as counters, for establishing 'populations' and totals of various kinds. But their use for more analytical research has been confined largely to the field of psychological investigation where the problems of sampling present few difficulties. They have not been applied systematically to social research. This situation is likely to remain for some time, although Coppock's proposed use of aerial photography, mechanical counters and similar devices in his study of the Borders may provide some evidence of their potential for use in large-scale studies.

* Coppock (100) intends to use similar devices in his forthcoming study of tourism in the Borders.

Chapter 2
Analysis of Recreation Data

One of the major needs in recreation research in Britain at the present time is for the analysis of data to be undertaken in such a way that prediction of future trends becomes possible. Predictions about the processes of change in habits and tastes are extremely difficult and hazardous to make. They can be justified only on two basic assumptions: firstly, that certain key variables influence—and will continue to influence—the formation of tastes and habits; and secondly, that they do so in a consistent fashion and over a long enough period to make the attempt at prediction worth while. If these assumptions are valid, then the need is to discover a means whereby to identify and distinguish between groups of people whose patterns of recreation differ significantly from each other. Up to the present time in this country, the data which might have been used for such a process of identification and grouping have been collected and analysed only in a relatively superficial manner. That is to say, we now know from the findings of a number of studies that income, occupation, age, sex, education and so on all play an important role in determining the amount of time and money that an individual or family (or other group) will spend on recreation. Thus, it is possible to make crude estimates of, say, the growth of incomes in Britain and, hence, to state that a given recreation pursuit in which participation is strongly influenced by income levels will become more popular. It is impossible, however, on this basis, to predict how given individuals or groups of individuals will react to, say a rise of 20 per cent in real incomes over the next five years. Whether it will ever be possible to do this in an entirely accurate way may justifiably be doubted; but an attempt should at least be made to narrow the range of possible reactions and to increase the predictive value of statements by a useful amount. This can only be done, however, if the analysis of research data is carried out in a way which allows the interaction of independent (and dependent) recreation-related variables upon each other to be measured.

The analyses of most recent recreation studies in Britain have been largely descriptive and have concentrated upon comparisons of the recreation patterns of different socio-economic groupings within the general population. Thus, respondents to recreation surveys have usually been divided into five social classes (or seventeen socio-economic status groups), five marital status groups, six age-groups, and so on. Moreover, as was pointed out in the previous chapter, even these groupings have not been standardized: some investigators, for example, make use of only four social classes and two marital status groups. This practice not only obstructs comparability between studies, but also complicates, unnecessarily, the task of prediction: for there is no doubt that predictive models can only be built upon the systematic analysis of data which have been assembled into meaningful groups. Since one survey alone can rarely obtain a sufficient range of data, it would be valuable if this could be supplemented with data from other surveys. But this can only be done, of course, if the findings of the separate surveys are comparable, in the sense that the background variables are similar and have been analysed in a similar fashion.

A discussion of the analysis of any research data may be conducted at two quite distinct levels. At one level the concern is with the machinery of analysis—coding, punched cards, sorters, tabulators, collators and computers. This can be best described as the *operational* level. At the other level the discussion focuses upon methods of analysis—the use of chi-square tests, latin squares, variance analysis, factor analysis, and so on. This can be defined as the *interpretive* level. Both levels have been considered in some detail in recent texts and its is not intended to repeat these here.* Instead, the present discussion will be confined to a critical review of the analyses, mainly interpretive, that have been undertaken as part of a few recent major recreation studies in this country. Three studies have been selected for review:

1. British Travel Association/University of Keele, *Pilot National Recreation Survey—Report No. 1*, British Travel Association, 1967.
2. British Broadcasting Corporation, Audience Research Department, *The People's Activities*, British Broadcasting Corporation, 1965.
3. Greater London Council, *Surveys of the Use of Open Spaces—Volume 1*, Greater London Council Research Paper No. 2, 1968.

* For a discussion of the operational level see T. L. Burton and G. E. Cherry, *Social Research Techniques for Planners*, George Allen & Unwin, 1970. For a discussion of the interpretive level see K. A. Yeomans, *Introducing Statistics*, Penguin Education Books, 1968; also, W. J. Reichmann, *Use and Abuse of Statistics*, Pelican Books, 1964.

These three studies have been chosen not because they employed original or revolutionary methods of analysis. Indeed, as was mentioned earlier, the analysis of recent recreation studies in Britain has been almost exclusively descriptive. They have been chosen, rather, because they represent, at the time of writing, the most wide-ranging recreation studies that have yet been carried out in this country.* The first two studies consisted of national household surveys; the third included both household and site surveys within the administrative area of the Greater London Council.

Pilot National Recreation Survey—Report No. 1 [6]

The report of the Pilot National Recreation Survey is based upon the findings of interviews held with 3,167 persons—2,839 adults aged 17 years and over, and 328 children aged from 12 to 16 years. These formed a random sample representative of the total population aged 12 years and over, both urban and rural, and spread across the Standard Regions of Britain. The concern was with those (largely outdoor) recreation pursuits which generate substantial demands for land and, thereby, become involved directly in the planning process. The purpose was to discover, for the benefit of those persons concerned with planning, how the patterns of demand for recreation facilities have changed in the immediate past and are likely to change in the immediate future:

> 'Are old-established forms of recreation, like golf and tennis, becoming more or less popular? Are new activities like skin-diving and water-skiing still the preserve of a small minority? Do they have a potentially broader appeal; and, if so, to which age and income ranges? How do people use their cars for recreation? Is driving itself seen as a recreation, or is the car merely a means of transport?'

These are the kinds of questions which the survey set out to answer. The hope was that the results would be useful to local, regional and national authorities, and commercial and voluntary organizations, who are concerned with and responsible for the allocation of land for recreation purposes. The interviews were carried out in September 1965.

* Two other major studies had been undertaken but were not yet published at the time of writing. They were (i) The Government Social Survey's *Leisure and Planning Inquiry* and (ii) National Opinion Polls' *Outdoor Leisure Activities in the Northern Region.*

C

The intention was to produce three reports from the analysis of the survey. The first was to be essentially descriptive, consisting of a general commentary on the national tabulations. This was to be followed by a second report, also essentially descriptive, which would examine regional contrasts, using a breakdown of the data by standard regions, and which would also analyse contrasts in recreational patterns between different types of urban environments. The third report was to be more rigorously analytical, involving a detailed statistical examination of the many conclusions and hypotheses advanced in the previous reports. The first report, which is considered here, was published in 1967. The remaining two reports were not yet published at the time of the writing of this review.

No attempt was made in the first report to carry out any sophisticated statistical analysis of the survey data. The purpose was simply to present the major tabulations with an explanatory commentary. The author was, however, aware of 'the risks that attach to quoting speciously precise values derived from a small national sample'. To avoid such risks, the data were presented, in some tabulations, in the form of rank numbers rather than frequency values—the argument being that a distribution expressed in terms of rank-order is less liable to sampling error than one expressed in terms of frequency values. In addition to this occasional ranking, a considerable volume of chi-square testing was undertaken to establish whether or not contrasts between classes of respondents (for example, between those who have had some higher education and those who have not) were meaningful and not simply the result of sampling error. In general, differences between classes were only considered to be meaningful if they were found to be significant at the 5 per cent probability level; and, in fact, most of the data on which the commentary was based were found to be significant at the 1 per cent probability level.

Apart from the use of rank-orders and chi square tests, the only statistical analysis carried out for the first report was to test the validity of the sample of respondents. The author was fully aware that 'for a national survey a sample of rather more than 3,000 may seem relatively small'.* In these circumstances, it was important to establish some measure of the validity of the sample. This was done by a series of sample data against known national data. The results are shown in Table 2. It can be seen that for only two characteristics —percentage unemployed and household size distribution—do the

* Though it should be pointed out that other surveys of a similar kind—for example the *1960 National Recreation Survey* in the United States of America— used samples of broadly equivalent (or smaller) size.

national and sample values differ substantially. In the former case the sample value is exactly twice that of the national figure—although it should be noted that the sample value includes a small number of persons who were simply 'non-employed', and not in any official sense unemployed. It is acknowledged, however, that the proportionate difference is none the less significant, and all that can be argued is 'that the sample gets a correct *order of value* which seems to lie closer to the national mean than the regional extremes'. In the

Table 2. *Checks of Sample Validity for the 'Pilot National Recreation Survey'*

	NATIONAL VALUE	SAMPLE VALUE
1. Percentage unemployed	1·4%	2·8%
2. Length of official working week (men)	41 hours	41 hours
3. Hours actually worked per week (men)	47 hours	46 hours*
4. Average overtime worked	c. 3 hours	c. 3 hours
5. No. of cars per 100 households	53†	51
6. Household size distribution:‡		
One person	13·4%	6%
Two persons	29·5%	33%
Three persons	22·9%	24%
Four persons	18·3%	21%
Five persons	8·9%	9%
Six persons	3·8%	4%
Seven (and more) persons	2·9%	2%

Notes:

　* Refers to hours worked *last week* in the sample.

　† Includes cars not distributed to households (e.g. hire cars, 'pool' cars, dealers' registered cars, etc.).

　‡ Figures for the sample refer to the distribution of household sizes for the adult sample only (i.e. those aged 17 years and over).

case of the household size distribution, the sample is clearly biased—although not seriously so, except for one-person households which are heavily under-represented and four-person households which are heavily over-represented.

None of these checks prove, of course, that the sample is either valid or biased in respect of recreation values. The checks show, for example, that the sample value for the average length of the official working week corresponded almost exactly to the national value; but this does not necessarily imply that the sample therefore measures the incidence of participation in any particular recreation pursuit accurately. All that can be argued is that 'the greater the number of item validations that can be made, the greater the general sense of confidence that we can allow ourselves to feel in the sample'. It would be unwise to go beyond this and to invest the data with a specious precision.

The chi-square tests and sample checks permit a certain degree of confidence to be placed in the findings of the survey. They are clearly adequate to permit the kind of descriptive conclusions drawn in the report. They strongly support, for example, the conclusion that age, income, education and occupation are the key factors influencing participation in recreation pursuits. They even support the view that, for some pursuits, income is the most important influence, while for others it is education. But to go beyond this, sharper analytical tools are required. Any attempt to measure quantitatively the independent effects of each of these four variables, for example, requires some kind of multivariate analysis which allows the segregation of those income effects which really derive from occupation and those which truly derive from income, and so on. This kind of analysis could well be undertaken, at least for the national sample, as part of the more sophisticated statistical analysis that is promised for the third report of the survey.

The People's Activities [1]

The report of *The People's Activities* is based upon data obtained from a sample survey of the total population of Britain aged 15 years and over. The original sample consisted of 4,026 persons selected at random from the Electoral Register, and drawn in two stages. The first stage was the selection of 105 administrative areas, so arranged that the three largest B.B.C. regions (London, North and Midland) were included in proportion to their total populations, while the three smallest regions (West, Wales and Scotland) were sampled twice as heavily as their populations warranted. The second stage of the sample was the selection of wards within the 105 administrative areas, from which the respondents were drawn. The selection of wards was made with probability proportional to the number of electors and the wards were stratified by juror index. Successful interviews were held with 3,116 adults, plus a further 345 persons between the ages of 15 and 20 years who were contacted at the same addresses as the adult respondents. All persons who were successfully interviewed and who owned or had the use of a radio or television set were then asked to keep a diary for the complete week following the interview. The request to keep the diary was made of 3,384 persons, of whom 2,363 provided 'an unambiguous record of their behaviour for the whole seven days'. The survey was carried out in April 1961.

The main concern of the survey was with listening and viewing habits, but the use of time budget diaries enabled a picture to be obtained of the whole range of activities, recreational and non-recreational, undertaken by the population over a period of one week. The purpose was to obtain data which would act 'as a source of reference for programme planners, whose business it is to try to reconcile the many conflicting needs and wishes of listeners and viewers'. The report of the survey is in four parts. The first two parts consist of charts designed to enable the 'day' to be seen as a whole.* The first part outlines what the population and various groups within it were doing throughout each day. The second part concentrates on listening and viewing, showing, from each half hour to the next, how many people were listening to the radio and how many watching television. Part three outlines in greater detail what the population as a whole was doing *at each half hour* of the day. Finally, in part four, this same analysis of each half hour is undertaken for various groups within the total population—for example, different social classes, different age-groups and different educational groups.

In view of the great volume of data obtained from the survey and the wealth of detail which it represents, the analysis made in the report is disappointing. The only formal statistical exercise which is clearly known to have been carried out is the regional reweighting of the sample data. Otherwise, the analysis is entirely descriptive. It is true that in the introduction to the report a cautionary note is made about the risks of drawing unwarranted conclusions from the data; but even this is drawn in general terms: 'The data presented are inevitably subject to limitations, including those inherent in any social survey. If only because the survey is based upon sampling, small differences between one figure and another, and figures which are small in themselves, need to be treated with caution.' With this elementary proviso, the report goes on to provide 204 pages of charts and tables, each of which has a short descriptive commentary accompanying it. No attempt has been made in the commentary to indicate whether differences between figures are meaningful, or whether, in fact, they can simply be ascribed to sampling error. Thus, for example, the commentary on the data in part four relating to the period from 3 p.m. to 3.30 p.m. states that:

* The week was divided into three 'days'—Saturdays, Sundays and Weekdays.

'Relatively few men and only about 40 per cent of women are at home at this time on weekdays, but on Saturdays over 40 per cent of men and of women are at home, and on, Sundays over 60 per cent of men and 70 per cent of women.'

In view of the similarity between the figures for men and women at home on Saturdays, it would be interesting to know how significant is the difference of 10 per cent between the proportions of each who are at home on Sundays. This kind of simple need arises many times throughout the report. At no point is there any indication of the statistical significance of differences between classes of data. And yet, all that would be required is a short statement somewhere in the report to the effect that, say, 'differences between classes were only considered to be meaningful if they were found to be significant at the 5 per cent probability level'.

In a similar way, there has been no attempt to check the validity of the sample, in the manner, for example, that was used for the *Pilot National Recreation Survey*. The introduction to the report includes a table outlining the composition and size of the sample on which the analysis in the report is based. This is reproduced here in Table 3. It gives an interesting and useful breakdown of the characteristics of the sample but, of course, provides no indication of how representative this is of the total population.

The lack of information about statistical tests and sample checks throws considerable doubt upon the value of the findings of the survey. The organization of the survey and the resulting volume of data obtained are evidence of a serious attempt to provide a comprehensive picture of the daily activities of the population throughout a complete week. But the rather elementary analysis of the data, and particularly the failure to apply basic statistical tests, severely restricts the value of the survey and limits the certainty with which conclusions can be drawn. There is obviously much more that could be done with the data, both in the form of standard statistical tests, such as chi-squares, and more sophisticated kinds of analysis.

Surveys of the Use of Open Spaces—Volume 1 [25]

The Greater London Council's study of the use of open spaces consisted of three quite separate but complementary surveys. The first was a household interview survey conducted by means of a stratified random cluster sample in the then County of London. Wards formed the primary sampling units and were stratified according to a

70

fivefold classification based upon the degree of open space deficiency. Wards in the strata which were most well provided with open space were given a higher probability of selection in order that a greater

Table 3. *Composition of the Sample for 'The People's Activities'*

	NUMBERS	PER CENT
TOTAL	2,363	100
SEX		
Male	1,135	48
Female	1,228	52
AGE-GROUPS		
15–24	358	15
25–44	926	39
45–64	827	35
65 and over	252	11
SOCIAL CLASS		
Upper middle class	129	6
Lower middle class	691	29
Working class	1,520	64
(Not classified)	(23)	(1)
EDUCATIONAL GROUPS		
Full-time education to 17 or over	310	13
Full-time education to 15 or 16	801	34
Full-time education to 14 or less	1,246	53
(Not classified)	(6)	(—)
OCCUPATIONAL GROUPS		
Professional, Managerial, Highly skilled	465	20
Moderately skilled, Clerical	1,126	47
Semi-skilled, Unskilled	654	28
(Not classified)	(118)	(5)

number of persons visiting open spaces would be contacted. Within each stratum wards were arranged geographically and a systematic sample chosen with probability of selection proportional to the size of population. In this way, thirty-three wards were selected for second-stage sampling. The latter was then carried out by a systematic sample, from random starts, from the Electoral Register.* A total of 2,015 completed interviews were held. The interviewing took place during June 1964.

The second survey was conducted by means of interviews with visitors to thirteen open spaces in the London County Council area. These open spaces were not selected at random, but were chosen because of their particular interest to the London County Council. A total of 2,164 persons were interviewed in the thirteen parks. The method of selecting visitors for interview has already been described on page 25 in the previous chapter. The interviewing took place over a period of four days (Tuesday, Thursday, Saturday and Sunday) in July 1964.

The third survey was carried out among schoolchildren aged between 11 and 16 years in London schools. The sample was stratified by type of school (that is, comprehensive, grammar, secondary modern, other and independent), by distance of the school from Central London, and by its distance from open spaces. Within these strata, seventy-six schools were selected at random. Within each school the sampling unit was to be a class, and Heads were asked to select a class within the predetermined age range for the school and from the middle of the ability range. A total of 3,013 self-administered questionnaires were completed and, after editing, 2,655 were used in the analysis. The survey took place in September and October 1964.

The purposes of each survey were quite distinct but complementary. The object of the household interviews was to establish overall patterns of use of open spaces and to discover general attitudes towards open space. The interviews in open spaces were intended to provide a picture of the different ways in which parks of varying sizes and with varying functions were used; and, in particular, to establish the aerial extent of the influence of parks.† The survey among schoolchildren was intended to place the use made of open spaces within the context of overall leisure patterns for an age-group not included in either of the two previous surveys.

In many ways the analysis of the data obtained from these three surveys is the most interesting and useful of any recent recreation study in Britain. In addition to the straightforward description and statistical testing of the major characteristics of respondents to the surveys, the analysis attempted to test the validity of two major hypotheses. The first was the proposition that 'careful analyses of the

* Some non-electors were also sampled.
† The term *park* is here taken to be synonymous with *open space*.

recreational habits of a representative sample of the population would reveal groups of individuals whose patterns of recreational usage (of open spaces) would show sufficient similarity in volume and emphasis for them to be treated as distinctive units, or demand groups, for planning purposes'. The assumption was that the division of each group's activities between: (i) urban open space, (ii) urban entertainment and indoor sport, (iii) home-based activities and (iv) countryside recreation would allow a greater flexibility to be incorporated into planning for recreational needs. The second hypothesis was that 'usage of open space could be expressed as a supply and demand relationship, in terms of size and function of open space in relation to distances travelled to them, and the way that choice is exercised by the user'. Such a relationship, if established, would be valuable for demonstrating the degree of effectiveness of each size-range of open space at different distances from the users' homes. Before examining the analyses carried out to test these hypotheses, however, it is worth considering briefly the descriptive analysis of the characteristics of respondents.

The main body of the report of these surveys consists of the presentation of major tabulations with an explanatory commentary. In a similar manner to the *Pilot National Recreation Survey*, the data were subjected to basic statistical tests to establish reliability and significance. In particular, since the selection of respondents in the household survey had been biased towards areas well provided with open space, the data were weighted to restore the correct population proportions. After weighting, the characteristics of respondents were compared with those of the total population of the then County of London as a means of checking the validity of the sample (Table 4). Unfortunately, unlike the *Pilot National Recreation Survey*, these checks were made for only two characteristics—age and sex. For both characteristics, however, the sample compared well with the total population; although there was a clear over-representation of persons between the ages of 15 and 19 years, and an under-representation of those between the ages of 20 and 34 years and those aged 65 years and over. The same kind of check was made in respect of the respondents to the survey of schoolchildren (Table 5). Again, the characteristics of the sample compared quite well with those of the total population. The only significant age differences were an over-representation in the sample of girls aged 13 years and an under-representation of boys aged 14 years. In terms of sex there was a total over-representation of girls and an under-representation of boys.

The most interesting part of the analysis of these surveys lies, however, in the attempts to establish specific demand groups for open space and to construct demand schedules based upon open space opportunities. The establishment of demand groups was only possible in a limited way; limited because only two characteristics of the

Table 4. *Checks of Sample Validity for the Household Survey in the 'Surveys of the Use of Open Spaces'*

AGE AND SEX		ADULT POPULATION OF COUNTY OF LONDON (1961) (per cent)	SAMPLE (per cent)
1. 15–19 years	Male	4·0	5·9
	Female	4·2	6·1
2. 20–34 years	Male	13·9	13·1
	Female	13·8	11·4
3. 35–44 years	Male	8·5	7·1
	Female	8·6	10·0
4. 45–64 years	Male	15·3	15·2
	Female	17·1	17·8
5. 65 years and over	Male	5·3	4·6
	Female	9·4	8·2

Table 5. *Checks of Sample Validity for the Survey of Schoolchildren in the 'Surveys of the Use of Open Spaces'*

AGE	BOYS		GIRLS	
	Children at L.C.C. Secondary Schools (per cent)	*Sample* (per cent)	*Children at L.C.C. Secondary Schools* (per cent)	*Sample* (per cent)
11	10	11	10	9
12	10	11	10	11
13	10	8	10	13
14	11	8	10	11
15–16	9	9	9	9
Total	50·7	48·0	49·3	52

population were used (age and sex), and because it referred to only a single facet of an individual's recreation experience (use of open spaces). The analysis itself is disappointing, since it is not made clear what techniques were used to establish the groups. It appears that they were established by the same kinds of statistical tests used in the main body of the report, these being applied to the detailed data pertaining to age and sex sub-groups. What is unclear is the extent to which predetermined age-groups were modified as a result of the findings about demand. The report is vague on this point: 'In the light of preliminary tabulations the grouping by age was revised to clarify the variations in interest in sport, activities with children and other activities. The groupings for adults used in this analysis were 15–19, 20–34, 35–44, 45–64, and 65 and over.' Since the analysis was done only for age and sex, and since sex is divided into two groups only, it is important to know why and on what basis age was divided into these five groups. All that the report does is give a detailed descriptive analysis of the differences and similarities between the various age-groups and the sexes within them.

The report provides a much greater amount of methodological information in respect of the attempt to construct demand schedules for open space. The concern here is with what was defined in the Prologue to this book as *economic demand*—that is, a relationship between quantities and prices. In this case, however, price is expressed not in terms of money but in terms of *distance travelled* to open spaces. Similarly, quantity is expressed not simply as the numbers of visits made to open spaces, but as *the numbers of visits as a percentage of the total numbers of opportunities available to visitors*. The basic assumption behind this approach, which is a variation upon methods proposed by Clawson, Trice and Wood, and others, is that travel is a cost which adequately reflects the benefits derived from the use of open space [13]. This assumption has been strongly contested in respect of recreational trips from urban areas into the countryside, the argument being that travel is itself a recreation activity in such circumstances. In the case of visits to open spaces within urban areas, however, there are much stronger prima facie grounds for believing that the assumption is a valid one.

The application of the method is not itself a difficult exercise. For each visit to an open space listed by respondents to the household survey, data were collected about, firstly, the size of the open space visited and its distance from the respondent's home and, secondly, the number of other open spaces which could have been visited by the respondent, grouped according to size and distance from the home. These latter data were then defined as *opportunities*. For conceptual reasons, not all possible opportunities were noted. In particular, opportunities to visit open spaces of the same size group within the same catchment zone were ignored. Otherwise, it was argued, to have included all of these duplicates would have meant that a relatively few visits in areas well supplied with a large number of open spaces of

Table 6. *Visits and Opportunities for Open Spaces of 50–75 Acres*

DISTANCE TRAVELLED (Miles)	NUMBER OF VISITS	OPPORTUNITIES NOT UTILIZED	TOTAL OPPORTUNITIES	VISITS AS A PERCENTAGE OF TOTAL OPPORTUNITIES (per cent)
0–¼	3	9	12	25
¼–1½	2	10	12	17
1½–2¾	1	11	12	8

a particular size group would have distorted the general picture. With the data thus collected demand curves were constructed for each size group of open space, with distance travelled measured on the vertical axis (price) and numbers of visits as a percentage of total opportunities measured on the horizontal axis (quantity). An example, for open space in the size group 50–75 acres, is shown in Table 6 and Figure 3. The first column in the table represents price, while the last column represents quantity. These values have been transferred to the vertical and horizontal axes respectively in Figure 3. Thus, at a

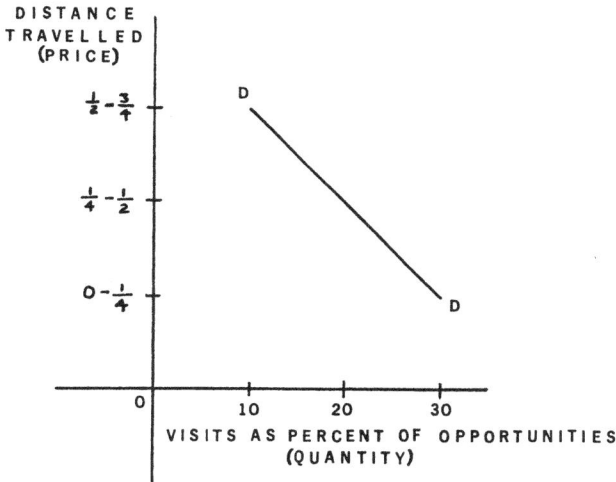

Figure 3. Demand for open spaces of 50–75 acres

distance of $0-\frac{1}{4}$ miles the quantity demanded is 25 per cent, at $\frac{1}{4}-\frac{1}{2}$ miles it is 17 per cent, and at $\frac{1}{2}-\frac{3}{4}$ it is 8 per cent. If these three points are then joined in the normal way, we have a demand curve, DD, for open space of between 50 and 75 acres. This represents an individual's demand, total demand being the aggregate of the demands of individuals. The report includes a detailed analysis of the demand curves for different size groups of parks, based upon the data obtained from the household interviews.

This kind of analysis represents an attempt to improve upon the simple process of defining the characteristics and behaviour of people at recreation so as 'to provide a basis for planning'. It constitutes a more meaningful basis for the planning and provision of specific kinds and amounts of recreation facilities. No doubt there are improvements that can be made to the mechanics of the method—for example, attention needs to be given to the period of time to which the data pertaining to visits and opportunities relate. (Should these be per week, month, quarter or year, and how are they to be brought to a common base?) Again, the method needs further application, to test its validity and usefulness in other environments, such as small and medium-sized towns. But clearly, it is an advance on the kind of descriptive analysis which, until now, has been the chief contribution of recreation research to the specific problems encountered in planning and providing for the recreational needs and demands of the population of this country.

The Proctor Study

In addition to the three major British studies that have been discussed here, it is worth making a brief examination of one recent American study which offers a particularly interesting analytical approach. This is the study by Proctor—*Dependence of Recreation Participation on Background Characteristics of Sample Persons in the September 1960 National Recreation Survey* [43]—which utilized a factor analysis. There have, of course, been many recent recreation studies in the United States which have included analyses of a more sophisticated kind than have yet been applied in this country. In particular, there has been considerable use of multivariate analysis. Several of these studies have been examined in the course of this review, but it was not felt necessary to outline them all here. The study by Proctor is perhaps the most interesting and innovative in recent research, in that it experiments with the application of factor analysis to recreation data. For this reason, it has been briefly outlined below.

For his study, Proctor planned a factor analysis, and hypothesized that it would show four basic 'leisure types', people whose leisure activities could be grouped together on the basis of statistically significant relationships in rates of participation. That is, he argued that people were more likely to take part in several activities within a given group of activities than to take part in activities which fell into different groups. The hypothesized groups were:

Backwoods Recreation. Such as camping, hiking, hunting and mountain climbing. The characteristic features of this type of recreation were thought to be escape from the formality of inter-personal relations and the observance of rules for gaining approval

78

which are mutually exclusive with those used in ordinary day-to-day situations.

Boat Culture. Such as boating activities and water skiing. The characteristic features of this kind of recreation were thought to be speed, showmanship and an element of risk or danger.

Country Club and Picnic Area Recreation. The essential characteristics of this include a large public participation and extensive generally-accepted standards of behaviour. It covers activities such as sailing, swimming, bicycling, horseback riding, outdoor games and sports, and picnicking.

Passive Outdoor Recreation. Including driving for pleasure, sightseeing, attending outdoor events, and attending sports events.

The purpose of this hypothesized grouping was to identify a particular method for determining similarities between individuals in their recreation patterns. Thus, if one person goes camping while another undertakes nature studies, they are similar from the point of view which contrasts backwood recreation with, say, an urban recreation setting. The object of the factor analysis was to test the validity of the four hypothesized groups.

Proctor's analysis was carried out, in great detail, for eight subgroups of the population and for fifteen separate activities which could be classified, with varying degrees of strength, into the four main groupings outlined above. The data that were used were taken from the *National Recreation Survey.* The fifteen activities were:

Camping	Games and sports
Fishing	Hiking
Bicycling	Nature walks
Horseback riding	Picnics
Driving for pleasure	Walking for pleasure
Boating	Sightseeing
Swimming	Attending outdoor events
Water skiing	

A 'score' was calculated for each respondent reflecting levels of participation in each activity. An attempt was then made to 'predict' this score, by identification and analysis of thirty background variables, which statistically 'explained' a significant part of the variance in 'activity scores'. Thus, the data gave an index of the extent to which participation in any one activity was related to participation in the others and to the possession, in varying degrees, of the thirty background variables (Table 7). The fifteen activities

Table 7. *The Proctor Study: Construction of Independent Variables in Recreation Regression Computations*

VARIABLE	POSSIBLE VALUES	DEFINITION
X_1—Linear age	12 to 99	Age of sample person (S.P.)
X_2—Quadratic age	144 to 9,801	Square of age of S.P.
X_3—Cubic age	1,728 to 970,299	Cube of age of S.P.
X_4—Rurality	0, 1	Rural farm ($= 0$), others ($= 1$).
X_5—SMA city	0, 1	Not in SMA ($= 0$), in SMA ($= 1$).
X_6—Urbanization	1 to 8	Reproduces col. 15, card 1. From: Urbanized area 3 million or more ($= 1$) to rural ($= 8$).
X_7—Married	0, 1	S.P. is married ($= 0$), unmarried ($= 1$).
X_8—Child impedance	0 to 3	No children in family ($= 0$). Youngest (child or sibling) is 12 or over ($= 1$). Youngest is 5 to 11 ($= 2$). Youngest is under 5 ($= 3$).
X_9—Meaningfulness of response on employment status of S.P.	0, 1	S.P. at work or looking ($= 0$), other ($= 1$).
X_{10}—S.P.'s occupation (status, prestige)	1 to 6	Codes: 00 to 05 ($= 1$). 06 to 09 ($= 2$). 10 to 13 ($= 3$). 14 to 27 ($= 4$). 28 to 36 ($= 5$). 37 up ($= 6$).
X_{11}—S.P.'s occupation (middle classness)	0, 1	Codes 06 to 27 ($= 1$), others ($= 0$).

X_{12}—Meaningfulness of response on employment status of head	0, 1	See X_9.
X_{13}—Head's occupation	1 to 6	See X_{10}.
X_{14}—S.P.'s completion of high school	0, 1	High school incomplete (= 0), others (= 1).
X_{15}—S.P.'s education	11 to 56	From never attended (11) through elementary (31–38), high school (41–44) and college (51–56).
X_{16}—Previous farm residence	0, 1	Yes (= 0), no (= 1).
X_{17}—Response on health	0, 1	Response (= 0), no response or don't know (= 1).
X_{18}—Health of S.P.	1 to 4	Excellent (= 1) through poor (= 4).
X_{19}—Physical impairments of S.P.	0 to 2	None (= 0), some (= 1) to limits recreation activity (= 2).
X_{20}—*Per capita* income in S.P. family linear	1 to 9	Col. 61 divided by col. 37.
X_{21}—Quadratic *per capita* income		Square of X_{20}.
X_{22}—Cubic *per capita* income		Cube of X_{20}.
X_{23}—Family income		Col. 61.
X_{24}—Square family income		X^2_{23}.
X_{25}—Cubic family income		X^3_{23}.
X_{26}—Marital status non-response	0, 1	No response (1), some (= 0), zero st. dev.
X_{27}—Education non-response	0, 1	No response (= 0), some (= 1).
X_{28}—Income non-response	0, 1	Some (= 0), none (= 1).
X_{29}—Previous farm residence non-response	0, 1	Some (= 0), none (= 1).
X_{30}—Colour	0, 1	White (= 0), non-white (= 1).

Source: C. Proctor, 'Dependence of Recreation Participation on Background Characteristics of Sample Persons in the September 1960 National Recreation Survey', Appendix A to O.R.R.R.C. Study Report No. 19, 1962.

were, in fact, grouped by means of rates of participation, and correlation: that is, the number of days (annually) of participation per person was given, for each activity, as an index of relative popularity. Then, correlation coefficients were calculated between each activity and the remaining fourteen activities, providing an index of the extent to which each activity was associated with the others and, hence, showing which activities generally 'go together'.

The analysis also indicated which of the thirty background variables were most significant for 'explaining' levels of participation in each activity, and, hence, each activity grouping. This analysis would permit at least a measure of prediction, based upon the activity patterns that had been identified and their relationship to each of the thirty background variables. Proctor, however, did not attempt to make any such predictions, but contented himself with making some general forecasts. Thus, for example, he was able to say, on the basis of the findings of the factor analysis, that 'in future it may be reasonable to expect that the level of participation in such activities as are closely dependent upon demographic variables, place of residence, and health conditions will not change. Those activities which are more closely associated with occupation, education and income might be more unstable.' This general analysis was then related by Proctor to each of the four activity groups: so that, for example, 'the level of passive pursuits may be expected to rise'.

Although this kind of forecasting represents no significant improvement upon recent work in this country, and elsewhere,* Proctor's study has advanced our thinking about the analysis of recreation data in two main ways. Through his factor analysis, he has directed thinking towards the concept of 'leisure types' based upon the grouping of activities that 'go together'. All previous groupings of recreation activities have arisen from the classification of recreation facilities: this one arises from an analysis of demands. At the same time, he has advanced the identification of the background variables affecting levels of participation in recreation activities. Whereas we knew before only that, in broad terms, levels of income and standards of education affect participation in recreation activities in certain broad ways, we can now classify, for example, the effects of income more precisely, in terms of (i) *per capita* income and (ii) family income. Proctor's important contribution was to identify and to test the validity of some of the micro-components of the known recreation-related variables, such as income, occupation and education.

* See below, Chapter 3.

Chapter 3

Forecasting

The essential characteristic of planning is its concern with the future, whether in the short or the long term. Thus, a necessary prerequisite of any rational policy in respect of the planning and provision of recreation facilities is some forecast of the demands for these facilities. Those people who are responsible for making decisions about the future, whether in government, industry or commerce, are concerned to obtain the best possible information that they can about likely changes in the social and economic parameters over which they exercise little or no direct control. They will want to discover, for example, whether they should provide more football pitches in a given area or more tennis courts; whether recreational spending will increase most rapidly for consumer durables, such as record players and television sets, or for entertainment services, such as concerts, plays and films; ·whether more free time will be spent in making visits to the countryside or whether the cities and towns will prove to be more attractive; and so on. The argument has been put particularly well by Clawson and Knetsch [18]:

'Investments in facilities and improvements must rest upon some idea of the nature of future demand patterns, especially in the immediate years ahead. The level of management operations, even season by season, is dependent upon future use. If we are to behave at all rationally in planning the provision of outdoor recreation, then some insight into the future becomes a necessity. Provision of public areas requires public decisions, primarily by political processes, and facts and estimates of the future can be very helpful to such decisions. The practical question is thus not whether to make projections but how to make them.'

It is pertinent at this point to distinguish between several different concepts of forecasting which are often loosely assumed to be identical—such terms as *estimate, extrapolation, projection, prediction* and *prospective*. There has been considerable confusion, from time to time, in the use of such terms. Even Clawson and Knetsch, in the passage quoted above, appear to consider the terms *estimate* and *projection* as more or less synonymous. Similarly, the studies of the Outdoor Recreation Resources Review Commission include a report on the *Prospective Demand for Outdoor Recreation* [41] which really consists of projections. Moreover, a concern with the meanings of these terms is not merely playing at semantics. The use of one term to describe the processes of another could easily invest the resulting forecast with a specious degree of precision. To speak of an estimate of the future level of participation in water sports as a projection is to suggest that it is the product of a fairly sophisticated statistical process when, in reality, it is probably the result of an (informed) guess.* In the remainder of this chapter, four basic concepts will be identified: *estimate, extrapolation, projection or prediction* and *prospective*. Most examples of their use will be drawn from American experience, since there has been little recreation forecasting attempted at all in this country up to the present time.

Estimate

An *estimate* implies the use of judgement. It represents a subjective 'hunch' on the part of the person who makes it. Such an estimate may be based upon a great deal of detailed information and experience; or, alternatively it could derive from one single but powerful experience on the part of the forecaster. Generally, estimates are more credible when made by persons with experience of the subject for which a forecast is required. In the case of future demands for recreation facilities, such persons might be officials of sports clubs, community organizations and social groups of one kind and another, managers of swimming pools and sports centres, librarians, curators of museums and art galleries, managers of commercial facilities, academics, and so on.

Most recreation forecasting to date in this country has consisted of such estimates, often based upon a subjective assessment of the effects of projections of recreation-related variables, such as population increases, changes in available leisure time and increases in real *per capita* incomes. Projections have been made of these and other recreation-related variables, which have then been considered subjectively to produce estimates of future developments. This was the approach adopted by both Burton and Wibberley [15] and Dower [23]. The value of such estimates is directly related to the experience and knowledge of the person making them. The factor

---

* This is not to imply that a projection will necessarily be more accurate or more useful than an estimate, but rather that they have been derived from different processes which inevitably have given different emphasis to a range of causal factors.

which makes them more credible than the guesses of the 'layman' is the amount of knowledge that the forecaster has about current and past trends in recreation patterns. This is an *informed judgement* rather than a simple guess. But the credibility of such estimates is still relatively low.

Extrapolation

Extrapolation consists of the extension of past trends into the future. Its chief advantage is, of course, its simplicity of operation. Its major disadvantage is its assumption that past trends will continue into the future: that is, that causal factors will continue to operate in the future *in the same ways and to the same extent* that they have operated in the recent past. Its value is, therefore, greatest for short-term forecasting. The longer is the period for which forecasts are required, the greater is the possibility for error in those based upon extrapolation.

The extrapolation of past trends in recreation activity as a means of forecasting is an exercise which has not been carried out in Britain, although it has been used, with varying success, in the United States of America. Wherever past trends have been relatively stable, it can prove to be quite useful—at least for short term forecasting. The justification for extrapolation is quite simple. It is that 'some forces must be operative to produce a marked or regular trend, especially if it has been long continued. Even if these forces are not fully known, yet they must exist and presumably will continue to be effective' [18].

It is, of course, this final assumption which is at the heart of the difficulties encountered in the use of extrapolation as a tool for forecasting. The assumption that the past is a total reflection of the likely future is the chief disadvantage of extrapolation. It is rarely true that causal factors continue to operate in one decade in precisely the same ways and to precisely the same extent as they did in the previous decade. Yet this is what the extrapolation of past trends must assume. It follows, therefore, that extrapolation is likely to be most useful for relatively short term forecasts. Clawson and Knetsch [18] provide several excellent illustrations of this point, which are shown here in Table 8. This shows trends in the use of several different kinds of outdoor recreation areas in the United States for three different periods—1910/11, 1946/60 and 1953/60. Each of these trends has been extrapolated to 1980 and 2000. The results are highly revealing. In the case of the National Park System, the extension of the trend for 1910/11 (making full allowance for the period of the

Table 8. *Forecasts of Recreation Activity by Extrapolation, U.S.A., 1980 and 2000*

	MILLION VISITS			PER CAPITA VISITS		
	1960	1980	2000	1960	1980*	2000†
1. National Park System	72·3			0·40		
(i) 1910–11 trend		3,000	50,000		12·50	153·50
(ii) 1946–60 trend		425	2,300		1·77	7·07
(iii) 1953–60 trend		175	485		0·73	1·49
2. National Forests	92·6			0·51		
(i) 1934–41 trend		190	800		0·79	2·46
(ii) 1946–60 trend		750	6,600		3·12	20·30
(iii) 1953–60 trend		1,700	24,000		7·08	73·70
3. State Parks	259·0			1·43		
(i) 1942–60 trend‡		1,200	5,200		5·00	16·00
4. Corps of Engineers Reservoirs	109·0			0·60		
(i) 1950–60 trend		11,500	800,000		45·70	2,455·00
(ii) 1954–60 trend		2,000	32,000		8·32	98.30
5. T.V.A. Reservoirs	52·7			0·29		
(i) 1947–60 trend		700	7,400		2·91	22·70
(ii) 1953–60 trend		360			1·50	7·07

Notes:
* Assuming 240 million total population.
† Assuming 325 million total population.
‡ Omitting the war years.

Source:
M. Clawson and J. L. Knetsch (18).

Second World War) results in 'virtually astronomical figures for 1980 and 2000. In the latter year the average citizen would have to visit some unit of the national park system 150 times or more if this estimate were to be realized.' The contrast between this forecast and the one based upon the trend for 1953/60 is truly staggering. Differences of a similar kind of magnitude emerge from the extrapolation of the trends for different years in the use of other outdoor recreation areas—for example, the national forests, state parks, Corps of Engineers reservoirs and the Tennessee Valley Authority reservoirs.

This discussion of extrapolation has, so far, been concerned simply with the extension of trends in recreation activity itself. But forecasts can also be made by the extrapolation of a major causal variable determining levels of recreation activity, such as income levels or available leisure time. The argument here is that levels of recreation activity have been in the past—or are *a priori*—dependent upon another variable which can be more easily or more accurately forecast. Thus, for example, it may be said that levels of recreation have, in the immediate past, been growing twice as fast as the growth in levels of real income; and, since income levels are expected to double during the next two decades, then levels of recreation activity can be expected to quadruple.

The strongest argument against the extrapolation of levels of recreation activity itself is that it assumes that causal factors will continue to operate in the future in the same ways and to the same extent that they have operated in the past. Yet, as the figures in Table 8 have shown, this assumption is, at best, dubious and, at worst, highly dangerous. Attempts to forecast levels of recreation activity by relating them to a major causal factor determining activity are a recognition of this and constitute an attempt to understand the forces underlying changes in levels of recreation activity. The assumption is still made that past trends will continue into the future; but, in this case, the past trends relate to a major causal variable of the factor which is being forecast, rather than to the factor itself.

The operation of the method is quite straightforward. Past trends in a causal variable are related to past trends in, say, visits to national parks to establish a correlation between them. Extrapolations are then made for the causal factor, and the derived forecast value for it, at the desired future date, is multiplied by the correlation value determined at the base date to give a forecast of levels of recreation activity at the desired future date. Thus, for example, if the correlation value for income is shown to be 1·5 (that is, that the level of recreation activity rises 1·5 per cent for every 1 per cent rise in income), then the extrapolated level of income for, say, the year 2000 is multiplied by 1·5 to give a forecast of the level of recreation activity in that year.

There are, however, two assumptions inherent in this approach which can be seriously challenged. They are, firstly, that a major causal factor is known or can be identified; and, secondly, that the correlation between it and the measure of recreation activity being considered (for example, visits to national parks) will remain constant throughout the period for which forecasts are to be made. Neither assumption is wholly satisfactory; but, while the latter is necessary if any kind of forecast is to be at all possible by this method, the former is much more questionable. Experience has suggested that a number of different factors are closely correlated with changes in levels of recreation activity—for example, population increase, levels of *per capita* disposable income, and levels of motor car ownership and use.* But there are other factors, such as family composition and life cycle, about the effects of which we are less sure. And, more important, there is little direct evidence to indicate the relative importance of each assumed causal factor. In other words, there is no indication of which variable is the major one. As for the assumption of a constant correlation coefficient, it is known that this is not valid over long periods; but it is hoped that it is sufficiently valid over short periods to make short term forecasts worth while.

It is clear from the discussion above that extrapolation—either of recreation activity directly or of a major causal factor—is a method which simply cannot be relied upon for long term forecasts. For shorter periods, however—say, up to about five years—it may be quite useful. In the absence of violent and unexpected fluctuations in causal factors, it would probably yield more accurate estimates than any other method. The major difficulty that would arise in an attempt to apply extrapolation in Britain stems from the lack of any satisfactory data about past recreation trends in this country. Such data as are available have two major weaknesses. Firstly, they are fragmentary, giving only a partial picture of trends. Secondly, they usually go back only a very short distance in time—perhaps, even, only two or three years. Effectively, this means that we must often attempt to forecast for a period in the future which is longer than the period in the past for which we have trend data. Yet, ideally, it

* Of course, a high degree of correlation does not necessarily imply causation; but it is generally assumed that these factors are, indeed, causal.

88

should be the other way round. In principle, though, the method could be applied for short term forecasting in this country.

Projection and Prediction

Projection and prediction are, essentially, two different terms used to describe the same process—the forecasting of trends based upon the extrapolation of more than one variable. The forecasting of population levels, for instance, can be carried out by either the simple extrapolation of past trends in population levels themselves, or by the forecasting of past trends in the component determinants of population change—birth rates, mortality rates and migration. The forecasts of these component variables are then related to each other, in various ways, to provide forecasts of future population levels. The advantage of this approach is that it recognizes that there is rarely one single and 'correct' interpretation of the cause of any event. A steady increase in total population over a period of, say, ten years could be the result of a high birth rate or, equally, of a high level of inward migration. An extrapolation of the one rather than the other would give a quite different figure for the level of the total population, say, ten years ahead.

What distinguishes this approach from the extrapolation of a major causal variable described in the previous section is of course its concern with more than one causal variable; and, hence, the need to utilize a technique or techniques whereby these variables can be related to each other. It follows from this that it is impossible to make predictions without a model of some kind which combines the causal variables in such a way that the population can be divided into meaningful groups. The purpose is to seek an understanding, in quantitative terms, of the interrelationships between two or more variables: in recreation, for example, to establish not only the extent to which such factors as population increase, rising incomes, increasing standards of education and longer periods of paid holiday each influence levels of participation in recreation pursuits, but also the extent to which they operate *through each other*. It constitutes an attempt to discover the relative significance of each of the causal factors in recreation.

There have been no attempts to date to construct predictive models for forecasting levels of recreation activity in Britain.* A few studies

* Two studies which are currently in progress in Britain are National Opinion Polls' *Outdoor Leisure Activities in the Northern Region* and the Polytechnic Planning Research Group's study of *Indoor Sports Centres*.

in the United States have, however, employed this kind of approach, the most comprehensive being the Outdoor Recreation Resources Review Commission [O.R.R.R.C.] study [38]. This consisted of a summary report, with recommendations, and twenty-seven study reports covering such matters as levels of participation in outdoor recreation generally, the availability of outdoor recreation facilities, policy issues, economic considerations, and so on. Several of the study reports briefly consider likely developments in recreation demands: but two, in particular, carry out analyses which are relevant to forecasting. Study Report No. 26 [41] constitutes an attempt to predict levels of participation in sixteen recreation activities, while Study Report No. 23 [42] makes detailed projections of some major causal factors in recreation. It is worth considering the first of these in some detail.

In brief, the method of approach was to estimate the gross effects from 1960 to target dates (1976 and 2000) on participation rates, of each of five socio-economic factors, the estimates being calculated by reweighting the 1960 rates according to projected distributions of the population by each of the five factors—family income, education, occupation, place of residence and age–sex. The *gross* effects were reduced to a *net* basis by adjustments developed through multi-variate analysis. For two additional factors, leisure time and per capita opportunity to participate, net effects were estimated independently. The composite effect of all seven factors acting together was then estimated from these net effects to secure projected rates of participation for each activity for application to the projected size of the population. The multivariate analysis that was employed to calculate the adjustments necessary to reduce gross effects to a net level for each of the five socio-economic variables was adopted from the Survey Research Center's O.R.R.R.C. Study [40]. It is worthwhile discussing this method in some detail. The simplest way to do this is to trace the steps by which a projected value was obtained for one of the sixteen activities. This is done below for swimming.

The *National Recreation Survey* had provided data about rates of participation in swimming related to levels of family income.* Rates of participation were measured as 'the numbers of separate days on which persons of 12 years and over participated in swimming during the months of June, July and August 1960, for each such

* Data were, of course, obtained about rates of participation related to the other four variables (education, occupation, place of residence and age–sex) but income is here used to describe techniques which were applied to all of the variables.

person in the subclass of the population'. These rates of participation were then reweighted to give estimates of the *gross* effects on these rates that could be expected from changes to 1976 in incomes. The weights were equal to the family income distribution of the population in 1960 and the projected distribution for 1976, given as proportions rather than percentages (Table 9). Multiplying weights and participation rates within classes and summing the products yields weighted averages of 5·214 for 1960 and 6·861 for 1976. The gross effects upon participation rates to be expected from changes in the income distribution are defined as the percentage change in weighted rates: for swimming, an increase of 31·6 per cent in rates of participation between 1960 and 1976 ([6·861/5·214] × 100). This relatively

Table 9. *Gross Effects of Income Level upon Participation Rates in Swimming, O.R.R.R.C. Model.*

FAMILY INCOME PER ANNUM	PARTICIPATION RATE IN 1960	WEIGHTS = PROPORTIONATE DISTRIBUTION OF THE POPULATION	
		1960 (Actual)	1976 (Projected)
Less than 1·5	1·20	0·102	0·056
1·5 to 2·9	2·21	0·133	0·065
3·0 to 4·4	4·47	0·175	0·089
4·5 to 5·9	5·02	0·211	0·124
6·0 to 7·9	6·67	0·166	0·166
8·0 to 9·9	7·55	0·093	0·153
10·0 to 14·9	9·49	0·087	0·232
15·0 or more	10·05	0·032	0·116

simple method for estimating the effects of changes in income distribution also accounts for all other factors which affect levels of participation in swimming *in so far as these factors are reflected by income*. But, if similar calculations are made for estimating the effects of changes in other factors, such as education, then there will be an element of duplication in projected values—in so far as changes in income are reflected in changes in education, and vice versa. In order to avoid this type of duplication, it becomes necessary to estimate the effects of each factor on a net basis: that is, the separate effect of each factor while all other factors are held constant. This can be done by a multivariate analysis. Unfortunately, such an analysis was not carried out using the data from the National Recreation Survey. One had been devised, however, for use with the data obtained from the recreation survey carried out by the Survey

Research Center and analysed in *Participation in Outdoor Recreation* [40]. The findings of this analysis were, therefore, taken by the forecasters and adapted to fit the data from the *National Recreation Survey*.

The Survey Research Center's analysis estimated the separate effects, while holding all other factors constant, upon 'activity scores' of income, education, occupation, paid vacation, place of residence, region, age–sex, life cycle and race. An activity score was calculated for each respondent to the survey by assigning values to (i) whether participation in selected activities was mentioned spontaneously by respondents or only after prompting; (ii) the number of activities undertaken during the previous year; and (iii) whether such participation occurred 'a few times' only or 'often'. Scores had a possible range from 0 to 26, and were a means of combining participation in particular activities into a single overall measure of particiation. The device was not regarded as highly accurate, but was thought to be a satisfactory means of ranking the population according to the degree of its participation in outdoor recreation activities. The report of the study concluded that, while the analysis could not 'separate the individual explanatory value of several intercorrelated variables with complete accuracy', it could yield 'estimates of the net relation between the dependent variable and each of a set of intercorrelated independent variables which may be regarded as fairly good approximations'.

The results of the analysis were given separately for men and women for selected groupings of each of the recreation-related factors (for example, income groupings of (i) less than $1,500 per annum, (ii) $1,500 to $3,000 per annum, and so on) in terms of 'deviations from their respective grand means'. The deviation from the grand mean represents the *gross* effect within the grouping of classifying sample persons by only one particular factor. The 'adjusted deviation from the grand mean' represents the *net* effect within the grouping of this factor alone, while all other factors are held constant. For projection purposes, the sexes were combined, and both the net and gross deviations calculated from the combined grand mean. Thus, for swimming in relation to income, the values were as shown in Table 10.

It can be seen that the adjusted and unadjusted deviations are of the same sign within each income grouping, so that the ratios of net-to-gross effects are all positive. The largest difference among the ratios was found to be in the income group from $3,000 up to $5,000 per annum, where both adjusted and unadjusted deviations

92

were near to zero. Instability can be expected in a situation of this kind, so it was ignored when a constant adjustment was calculated for all groups by averaging the values within all groups. This produced a 'net-to-gross effect' ratio of 0·44.

A similar analysis was undertaken for the other four recreation-related variables. The values of the constant adjustments that were

Table 10. *Net Effects of Income Level upon Participation Rates in Swimming, O.R.R.R.C. Model*

FAMILY INCOME PER ANNUM ($000)	DEVIATION FROM AVERAGE		NET EFFECT÷ GROSS EFFECT
	GROSS EFFECT (unadjusted)	NET EFFECT (adjusted)	
Less than 3·0	−2·49	−1·06	0·43
3·0 to 4·9	−0·12	−0·11	0·92
5·0 to 7·4	+1·19	+0·41	0·35
7·5 to 9·9	+1·79	+1·24	0·69
10·0 or more	+1·44	+0·46	0·32

Table 11. *Calculation of Net Effects of Five Socio-Economic Characteristics upon Participation Rates in Swimming, O.R.R.R.C. Model*

FACTOR	ESTIMATED CONSTANT NET-TO-GROSS EFFECT RATIO	PROPORTION OF PERSONS 12 YEARS AND OVER IN NATIONAL RECREATION SURVEY	ADJUSTMENT TO BE APPLIED TO GROSS EFFECTS OF FACTOR
Family income	0·44	1·00	0·44
Education	0·50	0·71	0·36
Occupation	0·35	0·58	0·20
Place of residence	0·75	1·00	0·75
Age–sex	0·67	1·00	0·67

thereby obtained then had to be further modified, in the case of the education and occupation variables, because the *National Recreation Survey* had collected data about these two factors only for persons over the age of 25 years (for education) and for persons in the labour force (for occupation) whereas the Survey Research Center's data referred to all respondents over the age of 12 years. The resulting final adjustment values to be applied to the gross effects of each factor are shown in the final column of Table 11.

It was shown earlier that the gross effects of expected changes in family income upon rates of participation in swimming were expected to raise the rate of participation by 31·6 per cent between 1960 and 1976. Applying the 0·44 adjustment calculated below as being necessary for the income factor yields a net expected increase of 14 per cent in this period as a result of changes in family income. Similar adjustments made for the other recreation-related factors yield the increases shown in Table 12. The separate effects of these five factors, together with two others, the effects of which were calculated independently, were then compounded by multiplication, in their ratio forms, to secure the composite effect upon rates of participation.

Table 12. *Net Effects of Five Socio-Economic Characteristics upon Participation Rates in Swimming, O.R.R.R.C. Model*

FACTOR	NET EFFECTS OF CHANGES IN FACTORS 1960–76 (percentage change in participation rate)
Family income	14·0
Education	6·2
Occupation	0·7
Place of residence	0·8
Age–sex	0·8

The two additional factors were changes in available leisure time and changes in *per capita* opportunities to participate (in terms of the availability of facilities). The former was calculated by analysing the relationship between each activity and three measures of leisure time—hours worked, number of holidays, and length of paid vacation—as they were at the time of the *National Recreation Survey* in 1960. Projections were then taken for each of these three measures of leisure time and the net effect upon participation rates for each activity projected on the assumption that the correlation coefficient between participation in each activity and each measure would remain at its 1960 level.

Changes in *per capita* opportunities to participate were calculated in a similar fashion. Days per person rates of participation were plotted against average opportunity scores across regions, the latter being derived from a study of recreational opportunities in sixty-six areas of the country [38]. 'Judgement was employed in drawing a line describing the apparent net relationship through the 1960 averages of these charts.' It was then assumed that changes would result in movement of the *average* along this line towards the *best*.

It was admitted that the values derived for these two factors, particularly the latter, were likely to be less objective and would involve greater value-judgement than those obtained for the other five factors, but it was thought worthwhile to include them, as their effects were (relatively) much greater than all but the income factor.

The expected increases to 1976 in rates of participation in swimming as a result of these two factors were 7·9 per cent arising from changes in leisure time, and 8·3 per cent from changes in opportunity. The composite effect of all seven factors on rates of participation in

Table 13. *Combined Net Effects of Seven Recreation-Related Variables upon Participation Rates in Swimming, O.R.R.R.C. Model*

×	1·140	(Income)
×	1·062	(Education)
×	1·007	(Occupation)
×	1·008	(Place of residence)
×	1·008	(Age–sex)
×	1·079	(Leisure time)
×	1·083	(Opportunities to participate)
=	1·448	(All factors)

i.e. 44·8 per cent increase in rate of participation

swimming could now be calculated by multiplication, in their ratio forms (Table 13). The composite effect was multiplied by the rate of participation in 1960, as shown by the data from the *National Recreation Survey*, to give an estimate of the number of days participation per person for 1976. This latter figure was then multiplied by the projected population of 12 years and over for 1976, to give the number of swimming occasions for that year—or, more correctly, for the months of June, July and August of that year, since the projection exercise was carried out for each quarter of the year separately.

The O.R.R.C. predictions were based upon a rather complex procedure which made use of data from at least two surveys and which projected variables by more than one method. The essential difficulty was that the forecasters were unable to apply multivariate analysis to their own data and were, therefore, compelled to adapt the findings of the multivariate analysis used in the Survey Research

Center's study and apply them to their own data. It was for this reason that they found it necessary to calculate 'net-to-gross effect' ratios for the five recreation-related variables being considered. There have, however, been simpler prediction exercises carried out in the United States, since the O.R.R.R.C. study, based upon more direct multivariate techniques. One particularly interesting study was the *Michigan Outdoor Recreation Demand Study* [34] which utilized a simple multivariate model. Like the O.R.R.R.C. model, this made allowance for interaction effects among the independent variables. The advantage of the O.R.R.R.C. model was that it attempted to include the effects of two variables—available leisure time and opportunity to participate—which are known to be particularly significant factors in determining levels of recreation activity but which are usually difficult to assess quantitatively. The Michigan model did not include these. This attempt was not wholly successful, but it did represent an advance over previous work. The advantage of the Michigan approach was that it applied a multivariate technique directly to the data which it had obtained and, hence, was much simpler to operate.

There were some weaknesses of a relatively minor nature in the O.R.R.R.C. predictions. In particular, the method of calculating the effects on participation of changes in leisure time and opportunities to participate are too subjective, especially since these two factors have such relatively significant effects when compared with the others. Again, the basis of the multivariate analysis is the 'activity scores' obtained from the Survey Research Center's study: and yet there is some doubt as to the validity of this device as a means of measuring participation. Further, the statistical rigour of the method was reduced by such devices as combining the Survey Research Center's data about the two sexes into a single set of data and calculating net and gross deviations from the combined grand mean. All of these are, however, problems which derived from the inadequacy of the data that were available for computation, rather than from the inadequacy of the method itself. They constitute difficulties which can be eliminated—or, at least, reduced—by the collection of more precise and direct data, such as was done for the Michigan study. There is, however, one major methodological problem which is not of this kind and which cannot be so easily solved.

The method assumes that the correlations between activities and the five recreation-related factors that were calculated from the *National Recreation Survey* data would remain constant in the future: 'The N.R.S. study report contains detailed analyses which strongly suggest the existence of stable associations between socio-economic characteristics of the current population and the rates at which the population currently engages in outdoor activities. *These observed associations were assumed to continue into the future.*' Thus, it is assumed that the correlation coefficients between each socio-economic factor and each activity will remain unchanged for the period to which the projections relate. Thus, each variable can be projected forward and the level of participation in each activity forecast by multiplying the projected value of the variable by the correlation coefficient that existed at the base date.

It may be reasonable to assume that correlation coefficients will remain constant; it may even be necessary to assume this if any predictions are to be at all possible: but no attempt has yet been made to test whether or not such an assumption is valid. Clawson [98] has suggested that it might be tested by making 'reverse projections': that is, a projection backwards to discover what levels of participation in certain activities would have been, say, ten years ago on the basis of the current values of the correlation coefficients, and then to compare these with actual levels of participation at that time. This might possibly be done with American data, but there are few available data in Britain to indicate what were actual levels of participation in recreation activities as far back in the past as this. Furthermore, it is unlikely that this procedure will go far towards explaining the *causes* of changes in correlation coefficients. One such cause, we know in general terms, is changing technology. Another is fashion. Both were key factors in promoting the sudden growth of participation in tenpin bowling in Britain in the early years of the present decade. Yet, such is the effect of fashion that the level of participation in this activity rose and fell dramatically in a space of three years: from 10,000 regular participants (measured in terms of the membership of clubs) in 1963, to 25,000 in 1964, and 15,000 in 1965.

This need to assume constant correlation coefficients in making predictions of recreation activity certainly constitutes a weakness in forecasting techniques, but it is one which simply has to be made if any kind of forecast is to be at all possible on the basis of any approach other than judgement. Moreover, there is no firm evidence that this assumption is catastrophic. It reflects, in fact, the major characteristic of all forecasting techniques—namely, the need to assume that the future is in some way reflected by the past. All forecasting techniques utilize this assumption in varying degrees. Extrapolation is unique in assuming that the variable under consideration will continue to act in exactly the same way in the future as it has done in the past. Other techniques utilize less rigid interpretations of this principle; but all assume that the future is, to some degree or other, reflected in the past. Moreover, the assumption of constant correlation coefficients utilized in the O.R.R.R.C. model is not a problem which is unique to the forecasting of recreation and recreation-related variables. It also applies to, for example, transportation models. It is known that the assumption is not valid over long periods; it is hoped, however, that it is sufficiently valid over short periods (say, a maximum of five years) for attempts at prediction to be worth while. There is really, at present, no alternative to using such an assumption. There is scope, however, for some empirical observation and measurement of changes in these coefficients, as is taking place in other fields.

Simulation Models

No discussion of analytical models would be complete without some reference to simulation models. These attempt to take account of the fact that the phenomenon being studied may be the result of the interaction of several interdependent systems. Thus, an economic model designed to produce forecasts of national income may subdivide the economy into interdependent components so that, for example, the output of the steel industry is partly determined by the demands of the car industry which is itself determined by consumer demand which arises partly from incomes generated by the steel and car industries. In this sort of model, instead of one equation there are several, with the dependent variables from some forming independent variables of others.

An example of a relatively simple model of this type in the field of recreation is given in Chapter 6 of the *Michigan Outdoor Recreation Demand Study* [34]. The model was designed to simulate the flow of campers to state parks in Michigan and is similar in many respects to the familiar land-use–transportation model. The system was divided into three sets of components. The first of these was the *origins*, or the areas of the state from which campers came. No complex equation was formulated to explain the generation of campers, but experimental forecasts with the completed model assumed that the number of campers would increase—in proportion to the populations of each origin area. The second component was the *hignway system*. The flow of camper-trips along each highway was related to the costs of travelling along the highway (including tolls) and to the time taken. The third component was the *destinations*, or the state parks, where the number of campers attracted to each park was related to the attractiveness (as measured by an index) of each. A computer programme produced the flows along the highway links from data on origins and destinations of campers, travel time, and costs associated with each length of highway. When the model had been perfected using available 1964 data it was possible to conduct experiments in forecasting and policy changes. Four main experiments were conducted with the model, and in each case it gave the expected distribution of campers between parks as a result of the particular situation being examined. The four experiments were to examine the effects of (i) the removal of tolls on a major bridge; (ii) an increase in camping resulting from expected population increases to 1980; (iii) the expected increase in highway capacity to 1980; and, (iv) the addition of new parks.

Though the concepts used in this type of model are fairly simple, the amount of computation that they entail is enormous and necessitates the use of electronic computers. The computation for the model described above 'would take a mathematician with a desk calculator about one million hours or approximately 200 working years . . .' to complete. The computer took six minutes.

The value of this type of model, both for forecasting and as an aid to more detailed planning decision-making, is amply illustrated by the nature of the experiments conducted with the particular model described above.

Prospective

A prospective is not really a forecasting technique at all, but rather, a planning tool. It is mentioned here, however, because there has sometimes been confusion as to its precise nature and its relationship to forecasts generally. Essentially, a prospective is deterministic. It embodies a definite—and often quite specific—purpose. Boudeville [121] has described it particularly well: 'It aims at establishing an objective . . . and at determining the ways and means necessary to reach this objective. . . .' Most recent economic forecasts, for example—such as *The National Plan* of 1965—have really been prospectives. They have established desirable objectives and have then considered the instruments and policies that will be necessary to achieve them. Thus, although a prospective is concerned with the future and is, in a sense, a forecast, it is fundamentally different from the other four techniques of forecasting which have been described above.

Conclusion

The above survey of forecasting techniques has in no way attempted to cover the whole range of studies that have been undertaken, particularly in the United States, in recent years. It has concentrated, rather, upon the identification of the main *types* of forecasting techniques, illustrating these by reference to particular studies. What has emerged is, essentially, a threefold division of techniques. The first, and least objective, approach is the *estimate*, based upon judgement. The second is *extrapolation*, whether of some measure of recreation activity itself or of a major explanatory variable, such as income levels. The third, entitled *projection*, or *prediction*, involves the consideration of more than one variable and, hence, the construction of some kind of model. This model may vary from a simple multivariate kind to a complex simulation system.

One final point is worth noting here. Prediction models require that forecasts can be made of the causal variables determining levels of recreation activity—such as the size of the total population, its age–sex structure and its geographical distribution, levels of real disposable *per capita* incomes, and changes in the volume of available leisure time. The *National Recreation Survey* in the United States and the study by the Survey Research Center both related participation rates in recreation activities to such background variables. Indeed, virtually all recreation surveys have done so—although, as was shown in an earlier chapter, not necessarily in any comparable way. Data about background variables are essential to the proper analysis of recreation data, and are a first requirement for any predictive model. Some of these variables, however, are not capable of projection: we cannot, for example, make projections of changes in technology or in fashion.* Many, on the other hand, can be projected, at least in a relatively simple way: for example, the size of the total population, its age and sex structure, and its urban–rural distribution. All predictive models will require, at some stage, projections of some or all of these background variables. Fortunately, many of these variables have already received attention for other reasons. Thus, for example, projections of the size and age–sex of the future population are needed for assessing a wide range of social wants, such as housing requirements, school and hospital places, water, gas and electricity needs, and so on. Much work has therefore already been done on alternative methods of projecting these variables. Five, in

* But even in this field advances are being made. See, for example, H. Kahn and A. J. Wiener (95).

particular, are known to be closely linked to recreation patterns: the size of the total population and, more important, its age–sex structure; standards of education; levels of motor car ownership and use; income levels; and working hours and holidays. Some alternative methods of projecting each of these five variables have been examined during the course of this study, and a general discussion of them is to be found in Appendix 1 to the Interim Report of the research, published in 1969 [14]. A list of sources can also be found in the Bibliography to this volume, pages 360–362.

Chapter 4
The Experimental Studies

The brief review of recent recreation research suggested that there were three broad groups of problems to which attention should be directed in the experimental studies which were to form the second part of the project. The first has to do with the classification and analysis of recreation data in such a way that prediction of future trends becomes possible. The second, related to this, concerns the kinds of profile data that are needed about the subjects of recreation studies, so as to secure greater comparability between studies. The third involves an examination of alternative methods of securing data, especially the potential value of such procedures as the secondary analysis of previous studies and the use of time budget diaries. These are not of course wholly independent groups of problems. On the contrary, they overlap at many points; for example, it will be necessary to classify and group profile data so as to make these useful for projection purposes. In general terms, however, the three groups of problems are sufficiently distinct for them to be considered separately.

The problems of classification and analysis are, perhaps, the key ones to be tackled in the experimental studies. The object of such classification and analysis should be to identify distinct 'recreation types': that is, groups of people whose recreation patterns fall into similar categories. A start has been made towards this by the traditional analyses which relate patterns of recreation activity to the possession of different kinds of profile characteristics: the *Pilot National Recreation Survey* [6] showed for example, that golf, gliding, sailing, camping and water-skiing are, broadly, high income and high education status pursuits. Proctor took the concept further by hypothesizing, and then confirming (with modifications), that certain pursuits 'go together' into groups such as 'backwoods recreation' and 'country club and picnic area recreation'. The final objective should be to assess whether there is any predictable relationship between different pursuits, and between pursuits and socio-economic characteristics. If, for example, a person with a university education and a civil service occupation plays golf regularly, can we predict, in fairly precise statistical terms, the relative chances of his also taking up, say, sailing? Proctor's study was a first attempt to identify and define such relationships: but it related to a very few recreation activities of a relatively restricted kind. They were all outdoor activities, most of which take place in rural settings. The concept can, however, be widened, at least in theory, to cover a greater range of leisure pursuits, including activities that take place in the home and in urban settings.

There are three main ways in which an analysis of recreation types could be carried out. The first approach would be to undertake a time budget study which would give an overall picture of daily—or, perhaps, weekly—activity patterns. These time diaries could then be analysed to ascertain whether or not there are any systematic relationships between different activities. Studies by Chapin and Hightower [17] have suggested, for example, that there are several systematic activity relationships among non-leisure pursuits: many housewives, for instance, will always combine shopping expeditions with trips to collect their children from school, so that the two activities have become closely linked. Are there any similar patterns to be found among recreation pursuits? A time budget study would also have the secondary objective of testing the potential of diaries as an alternative to, say, interview surveys as a means of measuring recreation demand.

The second approach would be to carry out a large-scale interview survey in which data would be collected about levels and frequency of participation in a wide range of recreation pursuits. These data would then be subjected to a factor analysis of the kind employed by Proctor [43] in an effort to establish recreation types. The survey could be designed to include both indoor and outdoor pursuits and to cover social and cultural activities as well as sports. Thus, it would be wider and more comprehensive than Proctor's study.

The third approach could be linked to this. It would consist of a secondary analysis of the data obtained from one or more previous recreation studies, such as the *Pilot National Recreation Survey*. This study has already related participation in each selected recreation activity to a range of different socio-economic characteristics. The new analysis would attempt to identify relationships between activities, and so establish whether or not the existence of well-defined recreation types can be confirmed. This approach would also have the subsidiary objective of showing how recreation data can be re-analysed to test different hypotheses or to examine correlations that were not considered in the primary analysis.

One of the objectives of exploring the validity of hypothesized

103

recreation types would be, of course, to examine whether such types could then be used in a predictive model of some kind. At present, there are two major problems encountered in attempts to build predictive models. The first is how to incorporate within such a model data about aspirations, since these are very likely to influence future recreation patterns. The problem is not only one of how to incorporate such data within the model, however; there is, also, the prior difficulty of how to collect such data in a way that will ensure a clear distinction between aspirations which have a reasonable chance of fulfilment, and those which are merely 'pipe dreams'. Here, it might be possible to utilize a similar method to the 'game' developed by Chapin and Hightower [97, 104] in their household activity studies. The major problem is clearly how to build reasonable time and income restraints into enquiries designed to identify aspirations and intentions. It is worthwhile investigating this further, since a knowledge of aspirations might indicate likely future movements between different recreation types or groups.

A second difficulty in attempting to predict future patterns of recreation activity has to do with the problem of allowing for changes in the statistical relationships between levels of participation in pursuits and predictor variables. All of the O.R.R.R.C.'s projections assumed that the 'observed stable associations between socio-economic characteristics of the current population and the rates at which the population currently engages in outdoor activities would remain constant throughout the period for which projections were made' [41]. Each socio-economic characteristic was then projected forward and the future level of participation in each activity forecast by multiplying the projected value of each characteristic by the correlation coefficient that existed between it and the activity at the base date. As was suggested in Chapter 3, there has been little empirical evidence to indicate the extent to which this assumption is valid. Moreover, we can suggest no way in which it might be tested, at this point in time, for recreation patterns in Britain. A possible method would be to carry out other national recreation surveys, similar to the *Pilot National Recreation Survey*, in, say, 1970 and 1975, and then to compare the established coefficients found in each of these three surveys. Fortunately, there have been two large-scale national recreation surveys in the United States, in 1960 [38] and 1965 [7], which might be used for a crude analysis of this kind. Certainly it should be possible to establish whether or not there have been any significant changes in these correlations over this short time period. It is unlikely, however, that the time interval between the two surveys is sufficiently long for any systematic pattern of change to be identified.

The second outstanding group of problems that emerged from the review of recent studies was the need to establish some comparability between studies. The paramount need here was for the identification of the types and quantity of profile data that should be obtained about respondents in recreation studies. As was indicated earlier, the review of six recent recreation studies in this country showed that they were directly comparable on only four socio-economic characteristics. Clearly, one of the primary objectives of the field studies should be to establish which characteristics are most significant in determining recreation activity, the ways in which these should be collected, and the groups into which they should be divided for analysis. Particular attention would have to be paid to age and income groupings, and to the kinds of data that should be sought about education and occupation. The best way to tackle this problem would be to carry out an interview survey in which information would be sought about a range of different characteristics in a number of different ways. For education, for example, information would be sought about six different items: the type of school attended; the operator of the school; whether it was co-educational or single sex; the age of leaving school; the amount of further or higher education received (if any); and the educational qualifications obtained. It might then be possible to determine which of these data are significant in shaping patterns of recreation and to what extent; and hence, which should be sought in future national, regional and local studies. The same approach would be adopted in respect of occupation, income, age, marital status and other socio-economic characteristics.

The third group of problems that was identified related to the evaluation of different methods of collecting data about patterns of recreation. Six basic methods were identified during the review: interview surveys, self-administered and postal surveys, observation, documentary sources, the use of physical evidence, and mechanical and electronic devices. Broadly, there seemed little doubt that the interview survey is the most comprehensive and useful method of collecting data. A vast amount of research has been carried out into the many methodological problems to which it gives rise; for example, response bias, over-rapport, questionnaire design, and so on. There is unlikely to be much that could usefully be added to this in the experimental studies that were proposed. There is, however, another level at which a useful contribution could be made. An investigation could be made of the kinds of situations and circumstances in which other methods of collecting data could be used, either as alternatives or supplements to the use of interview surveys. In addition, an attempt could be made to identify situations in which interview surveys at recreation sites would be preferable to household surveys. The former problem could be examined by demonstrating, for example, how previous studies may be subjected to secondary analysis, and by employing self-administered questionnaires in some of the experimental studies. The latter problem could be examined by seeking data about some selected activities both from surveys at recreation sites and in household surveys.

Broadly, then, there were three kinds of methodology with which this project was to be concerned: methods of collecting data, methods of grouping and analysing data, and methods of prediction. Within these three groups, there were three broad problems which it was thought should be investigated in the experimental studies: how to classify and analyse data in such a way that prediction of future trends becomes possible; what profile data should be collected about respondents, how should they be collected, and how should they be grouped for analysis; and in what situations could alternatives to interview surveys be used as methods of collecting recreation data. To investigate these problems four experimental studies were carried out. The remainder of this chapter is taken up with a brief description of the objectives of these. Their operation and results are outlined in later chapters.

II

(i) The Household and Activities Survey

The first and most comprehensive experimental study consisted of a large-scale household interview survey in selected areas of the City of Birmingham. Use was made in this survey of both interview schedules and time budget diaries. The survey was carried out in two areas of the city which had broadly similar socio-economic characteristics, but which contrasted significantly with each other in the volume and types of recreation facilities available to their populations. A sample of 500 households was drawn from each area and interviews sought with the head of household or housewife in each. These interviews covered two distinct subjects: first, the respondent was asked to supply information about the household—its composition, ownership of various household goods, type of housing, and so on; then, he (or she) was asked to provide data about his own recreation activities. In addition, all other persons in the household aged 12 years and over were asked to complete questionnaires relating to their own recreation activities, or, alternatively, to complete time budget diaries for a 24-hour period. These questionnaires and diaries were left at the household by the interviewer and later collected by her on a second visit. Thus the survey incorporated three methods of collecting data—interview schedules, self-administered questionnaires and time budget diaries.

The objectives of the survey were fivefold. Firstly, it was intended to test the potential value of a mixed (interview and self-administered questionnaire) survey as a means of securing data about recreation activities on a greater scale than is possible, with given resources, by the use of an interview survey alone. As was pointed out in Chapter 2, there is a large number of recreation pursuits in which only 1 per cent or less of the population takes part: 'Thus, unless the sample is relatively large, a household interview survey on recreation habits generally is unlikely to pick up sufficient numbers of persons who take part in minority pursuits to make statistical analysis worthwhile and meaningful.' It was noted in the *Pilot National Recreation Survey* that for only ten of the thirty activities listed was the proportion of respondents who had participated even only once during the whole of 1965 greater than 1 per cent. It was suggested in the report that a tenfold increase in the size of the sample—from 3,167 respondents to, say, 30,000—would have been necessary to pick up sufficient numbers of participants in minority activities to make possible a meaningful analysis of their characteristics. But to do this, of course, would have meant a very large increase in costs and in resources needed (not by a similar proportion, but perhaps as much as an eightfold increase). The purpose in carrying out the household and activities survey by the use of both interviews and self-administered questionnaires was to discover whether a significant increase above the norm could be achieved in the numbers of respondents without a correspondingly significant increase in costs and a decrease in the quality of data obtained.

The second objective of the survey was to examine the usefulness of time budget diaries as a method of securing data about patterns of recreation. The studies by Chapin and Hightower [17] and Robinson and Converse [44] suggested that time budget diary studies have significant potential as sources of comprehensive recreation data. They appear to be particularly useful for providing a picture of the relationship between recreation and other activities, especially as regards the length of time spent on recreation pursuits and their distribution throughout a day or longer period. At the same time, both studies drew attention to the difficulties encountered in attempting to analyse diary data mechanically: in particular, the problem of systematizing codes for open-ended responses so that they could be transferred to punched cards. The numbers of diaries that were requested in the survey were relatively small, but they provided a useful pilot study on the basis of which a full-scale time budget study could be undertaken.

Another objective of the survey was to test the validity of the concept of recreation types hypothesized and tested by Proctor [43]. Respondents to the questionnaire about recreation activities—both those who were interviewed and those who completed the questionnaire themselves—were asked to indicate how many of more than sixty activities they had taken part in during 1968. These data were then subjected to cluster and factor analyses to establish whether or not respondents could be grouped into types according to those activities in which they had participated. In a sense, this repeats Proctor's work and, thereby, provides a useful check upon it; but it is also wider and more comprehensive, covering both indoor and outdoor activities and including social and cultural pursuits as well as physical recreation activities.

The fourth objective of the survey was to seek to provide guidelines relating to the collection of profile data in recreation studies. The review of previous research clearly indicated the need for general guidance as to those profile characteristics which are most closely correlated with participation in recreation activities; and, perhaps more important, the need for guidance as to which aspects of these characteristics are most significant. Respondents to the survey were asked, therefore, to provide information in great detail about such characteristics as age, occupation, income and education. The data thereby obtained were then subjected to statistical tests to determine which were most closely related to recreation activity.

The final objective of the survey was to investigate the impact of recreation supplies upon demands. By carrying out the survey in two contrasted areas (in terms of available facilities), it was hoped to obtain some indication of the significance of supply in creating or stimulating demand. It was obviously impossible to 'pair' the two areas in such a way that the only major contrast between the two was a lack of facilities in one area and an abundance of them in the other. But, by matching the two areas on the basis of selected and (presumed) important socio-economic characteristics, it was hoped to neutralize, to some extent, the effects of these characteristics in shaping patterns of demand and, thereby, to throw into sharper relief the effects of differences in the availability of facilities.

(ii) The Measurement of Supply

The second of the experimental studies was concerned with the measurement of supply. The physical restriction of the demand surveys within two selected areas of the city and the proposal to investigate the interaction of demand and supply within these two areas both necessitated a clear and detailed measurement of the availability of facilities within and immediately surrounding these areas. This study considered various alternative ways in which an inventory of supplies could be compiled. It examined the relative value of maps and photographs, documentary sources, self-administered postal surveys and observation. In particular, it investigated the possibility of using demand surveys as a means of determining available supplies, by requiring respondents to record all facilities used by them. The study also examined difficulties of definition and comparability in compiling inventories of available facilities and drew up a classification of supply.

(iii) Forecasting

The third experimental study was concerned with forecasting techniques. In view of the lack of satisfactory data for this country relating to forecasts of the major causal factors in recreation activity, and the lack of resources to produce independent forecasts, no attempt was made to predict levels of participation in selected recreation activities in a similar manner to the O.R.R.R.C. predictions for the United States [41] and those in the *Michigan Outdoor Recreation Demand Study* [34]. Instead, attention was directed toward the problems associated with the need to assume constant correlation coefficients between participation in recreation activities and each causal factor, or predictor variable, when constructing prediction models. A brief comparative analysis was made of the two national recreation surveys carried out in the United States in 1960 [38] and 1965 [7] to examine the kinds and extent of changes in these coefficients between the two dates. This, it was hoped, would give an indication of the validity of the basic assumption of constant coefficients. In addition, some of the major problems of forecasting, identified in the review of previous research, were further discussed. These included the difficulties encountered in forecasting causal variables, the effects of policy decisions upon forecasts, and the fundamental question of whether or not forecasts can, or should, be attempted for periods of more than a few years at a time.

This study was rather different in kind to the others. It was, for example, much more discursive, concerned less with tests of techniques and more with considerations of objective. Yet it provides a fitting conclusion to the two previous studies. For the techniques of forecasting are not, prima facie, matters to which much may be added by the present research. Given the necessary data, it would not be difficult to make extrapolations and predictions of recreation activity for this country; and, within the technical constraints of the models, these would be quite satisfactory. It is not so much in the technical operation of prediction that advances are sought, but rather in the data which are the raw materials of these technical processes. The relevant questions are to identify the assumptions that are made in forecasting models and to probe their validity; and, perhaps most important of all, to consider whether the factors that we are attempting to predict are indeed the ones with which we should be concerned.

(iv) A Strategy for the Provision of Recreation Facilities

The final experimental study consisted of interview surveys at two recreation sites within the areas in which the household survey took place. The purpose was, first, to further investigate the impact of the supply of facilities upon the demand for them; second, to examine the effectiveness of surveys at recreation sites as opposed to household surveys as a means of collecting data about recreation activity; and third, to consider various methods of establishing criteria upon the basis of which public authorities could decide whether or not to provide additional recreation facilities in urban areas and, if so, where to provide them. The study is essentially different from the others in that it sets out a theory for the provision of recreation facilities which the site surveys were then designed to test.

The theory, or series of models, is applicable to a wide range of recreation facilities, but for a number of organizational reasons the experiments had to be restricted to only one kind of facility—public libraries. The major problem was the lack of financial resources. In particular, this meant that it would not be possible to use professional interviewers for the survey. Instead, it was proposed to use students from Bordesley College of Education, reinforced where necessary by members of the staff of the Centre for Urban and Regional

Studies. These students were only available, however, on weekdays during the daytime. This meant that, if the study was to be fully effective, it should relate to those kinds of recreation facility which are heavily used by the general public on weekdays during the daytime. The majority of recreation facilities are characterized, however, by a diametrically opposite profile of use: they are used most intensively at weekends and during weekday evenings—for example, swimming pools, sports stadia and community centres. The only major weekday daytime use of such facilities is by school groups. In fact, the only kind of publicly-provided recreation facility which fits at all satisfactorily into the required character is public libraries. It was decided, therefore, that a survey of the use of public libraries would provide the most effective test of the model. It should be stressed, however, that the theory is applicable to many other kinds of recreation facilities and that, given the required numbers of field staff available at the necessary times of the day and week, the survey could, and would, have been concerned with other kinds of facilities as well as libraries.

Part Two

The Household and Activities Survey

Chapter 5

Structure and Organization of the Survey

The household and activities survey, as outlined in Chapter 4, had five main objectives: first, to discover whether, by the joint use of interviews and self-administered questionnaires, a significant increase over the norm could be obtained in the numbers of respondents to a survey without a correspondingly significant increase in costs and a decrease in the quality of data obtained; second, to examine the usefulness of time budget diaries as a method of collecting data about patterns of recreation; third, to test the validity and to assess the potential use of the concept of 'recreation types' hypothesized and tested on a relatively small scale by Proctor [43]; fourth, to seek to provide guidelines for future studies relating to the collection and analysis of profile data; and fifth, to investigate, in a general manner, the interrelationships between recreation supply and demand. Such widely varying objectives required that the structure and organization of the survey should be very different from a normal sample survey. The present chapter will outline the structure and organization that was finally adopted. It will be followed by four chapters, each dealing with one of the first four experimental problems outlined above. The fifth problem—the interrelationships between supply and demand—will be examined in Chapter 11, after the inventory of supply has been outlined and discussed.

It is worthwhile, before describing the structure and organization of the present survey, to consider the general rules guiding the preparation and conduct of a research study. These can be best illustrated by examining the various stages—nine in all—of a research study. The first stage consists of a statement of the problem, of the circumstances producing it, and of the nature and amount of uncertainty involved in it. This should be followed by a statement of the objectives of the study, where these are clear, and of the hypotheses that are to be tested. Following this should be a review of previous research and knowledge of the problem. It is at this stage that the investigator should make certain, as far as this can be done, that the answers to the problem are not already known or being examined by another investigator.* The fourth stage involves the

* This is not to suggest that one should give up doing a study simply because another person is investigating the same problem. But one should try to be aware

determination of the nature and volume of data needed to achieve the objectives of the study and to test the hypotheses. This should be followed by the determination of the method or methods that will be used to obtain the required data. This involves a consideration of the availability of resources—of time, money and manpower. It also requires an assessment of the possible agencies through whom the data may be obtained, as well as a consideration of methods themselves. The sixth stage requires the determination of the procedures that are to be followed in the collection and analysis of data. It should

Table 14. *Stages in the Preparation and Conduct of a Research Study*

STAGE	WORK TO BE DONE
1	Statement of the problem, the circumstances producing it and the nature and amount of uncertainty involved in it.
2	Statement of the objectives of the study.
3	Review of previous research on the problem.
4	Determination of the nature and volume of data needed to achieve the objectives of the study.
5	Determination of the method or methods that will be used to obtain the required data. It involves a consideration of the availability of money and other resources and of possible agencies through which the data might be obtained.
6	Determination of procedures to be followed in the collection and analysis of data.
7	First consideration of possible methods of presentation of findings.
8	Collection and analysis of data.
9	Writing of the report, including final consideration of methods of presentation and suggestions for further research, if any.

be followed by a consideration, in general terms, of alternative methods of presentation of the findings of the study and, in particular, of the type of audience to whom they are to be addressed. Following this should be the actual collection and analysis of data; and, as the final stage of the study, the writing of the report, an appraisal of the findings, conclusions and comments, and suggestions for further research (if any). This ideal scheme of operation is laid out in full in Table 14. It should be emphasized here, however, first, that the nine stages are not necessarily consecutive—some stages may take place concurrently—and, second, that it is not necessary for them to take place in the precise order in which they are shown.

of other people who are investigating the same problem, perhaps with a view to some degree of co-operation.

This scheme of operation was laid down at the commencement of the present study and, with minor modifications, has been followed throughout. The first two stages—a statement of the problem and of the objectives of the study—were outlined in the terms of reference for the study and in the Prologue to this book. The review of previous research has been described, in considerable detail, in Chapters 1 to 4. The present chapters will outline the fourth, fifth and sixth stages, specifically as they relate to the household and activities survey. Alternative methods of presentation of the findings of the study were considered, first, at the time that it was commissioned and, again, before this report was drafted. Finally, the last two stages— the collection and analysis of data and the appraisal of findings—will be described and discussed in the chapters which follow this one.

The present chapter—a description of the structure and organization of the household and activities survey—is in six parts: the choice of survey areas; the selection of the sample; the design of the survey; a discussion of the survey documents; the organization and findings of the pilot survey; and the arrangements for the fieldwork. These will now be considered in turn.

Choice of Survey Areas

The major factor determining the choice of survey areas was the proposal to investigate the interrelationships between recreation supply and demand: in particular, to examine the extent to which demand is determined by supply. There were, essentially, two possible methods of approach. The first was to select an area (or areas) in which a major new recreation facility was in process of development. A survey could then be carried out before the development was complete and again after it was in full operation. It would then be possible to identify changes in recreation patterns resulting from the provision of the new facility.* The major difficulty with such an approach is that it can only be carried out over a relatively long period of time. The shortest period in which two such surveys could be carried out, allowing also some time for the new development to come fully into use, is probably about five years. *Before-and-after* surveys of this kind may well be the most effective way of investigating the impact of supply upon demand, but they do require considerable resources over periods of five years or more. Neither the

---

* Always assuming, of course, that there are no major changes in the other variables, such as income levels, which significantly affect patterns of recreation activity.

resources nor the time were available to adopt this approach in the current study. Instead, it was decided to tackle the problem by means of simultaneous surveys in areas with significant contrasts in available recreation facilities. This approach was based upon the assumption that certain major variables determine patterns of recreation, including socio-economic status, race, type of living environment, and availability of recreation facilities. The object was to select areas in which all of these variables had, as nearly as possible, equal values, except in the availability of facilities: in the latter respect the areas would show great contrasts. In other words, it was hypothesized that, by matching areas on the basis of certain significant recreation-related variables but differentiating them on the basis of available recreation facilities, it would be possible to neutralize, to some extent, the effects of these other variables in shaping patterns of recreation and, thereby, to gain an insight into the effects of differences in the availability of facilities.

This kind of approach, based upon the matching of areas in terms of mutual social and economic characteristics, has largely been impossible before in this country. This is because social and economic data have usually been available only for administrative areas, which 'are frequently artificial in social and economic terms ... (and) tend to be too large for meaningful social analysis: the differences *within* them can be of greater significance than differences *between* them' [89]. Data are now more easily available, however, for Census Enumeration Districts. These are very much smaller areas than Wards—the smallest administrative districts—and can be used as building blocks to compile socially meaningful areas based upon concentrations of particular socio-economic variables.* Indeed, the availability of this kind of data has made it possible for typologies of social areas to be developed. Perhaps the most well known of these is the Shevky–Bell typology [78]. This has recently been applied to data for the City of Birmingham and a complete typology worked out for the whole city.† This social areas classification was adopted as the first criterion for the choice of areas in which to carry out the household and activities survey.

The Shevky–Bell typology is a product of two variables: *social*

* The relative sizes of the two kinds of area can be best illustrated by an example: the City of Birmingham, with a total population of approximately 1·1 millions, has 39 wards and 472 Enumeration Districts. Ward populations range from about 16,000 to 37,000. Each Enumeration District, on the other hand, contains approximately 2,500 persons.

† B. N. Downie, *The Social Areas of Birmingham*, Centre for Urban and Regional Studies, Occasional Paper (forthcoming).

rank and *family status*. Areas are classified, first, according to their position on a social rank dimension. This is based upon a consideration of socio-economic groups within the area, and is measured on an index with a range from 1 to 4: an area with the lowest social rank is given a value of 1, while an area with the highest social rank is given a value of 4. Each area is then classified again according to its position on a family status dimension. This is based upon fertility ratios and the numbers of adult women not in paid employment. It, too, is measured on an index, with a classification from A to D: an area which is high in family status is classified as A, while one which

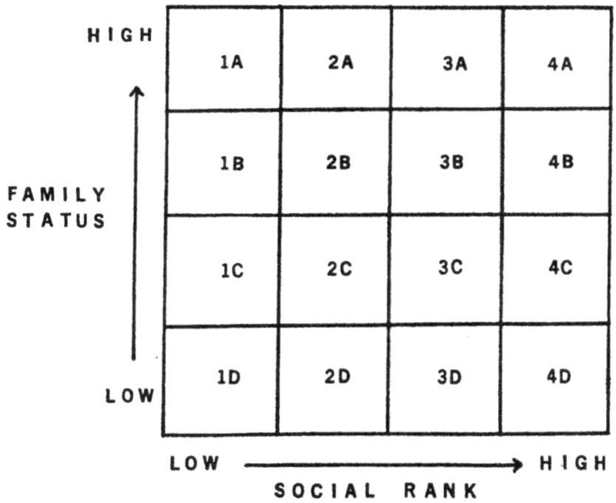

Figure 4. The Shevky–Bell typology of social areas

is low in family status is classified as D. This results in a typology of the kind shown in Figure 4. Each Enumeration District in the City of Birmingham was classified within this typology, so that it was possible to group them into socially homogeneous areas which could then be matched for research purposes.

In addition to this social areas typology, five other social indicators were used as criteria upon which to construct and match two areas in which to carry out the household and activities survey. The first of these was a measure of population density—the number of persons per room—expressed in quintiles, the first quintile, or figure 1, showing the lowest density and the fifth quintile, or figure 5, showing the highest density. The second was a measure of the stability of

119

population in the area, showing the proportion of the total population that had moved into the area in the five years up to 1966. This, too, was expressed in quintiles, the figure 1 showing the most stable population and the figure 5 the least stable. The third criterion was a measure of the ratio of households to dwellings, showing the proportion of households sharing a dwelling. This was expressed in quartiles, the figure 1 denoting the lowest level of multi-occupation and the figure 4 showing the highest level. The fourth criterion was, essentially, an indicator of race, showing the proportion of the total population of an area born in the Commonwealth and colonies (excluding Australia, Canada and New Zealand). This was expressed in quintiles related to the average figure for the city as a whole (4·6 per cent). The first quintile represents a value equal to or less than the city average, while the fifth quintile represents a value of more than four times the city average. The final criterion was a crude measure of housing standards, showing the proportion of households having the exclusive use of four basic amenities: hot water, fixed bath, w.c., and cooking stove. It was expressed in quartiles, the lowest quartile showing a proportion of less than 20 per cent, the highest showing a proportion of more than 80 per cent.

The other major criterion upon which the choice of survey areas was based was the availability of recreation facilities. In this case, however, the search was for areas which contrasted widely rather than for areas which were closely matched. It proved impossible to base this choice upon figures of the total range of recreation facilities within any particular area, since data were not readily available for all kinds of facilities. Indeed, one of the objectives of the household and activities survey was to try to assess the value of demand surveys as a means of measuring the supply of such facilities as private sports and social clubs and commercial facilities.* Instead, the basis for choice was taken to be the volume of public open space, sports fields and allotments to be found in each area. A crude estimate of the availability of these kinds of facilities could be drawn up very rapidly on the basis of Ordnance Survey Maps, and later refined by reference to local authority documents.

The final decision that had to be taken before the actual selection of the survey areas concerned their size. Given the knowledge that an overwhelming majority of recreation activities are undertaken by a very small minority of the total population—a fact which became readily apparent during the review of previous research—it was essential that the final sample should include a sufficiently large

* See Chapter 10, pages 243–260.

120

absolute number of respondents so that a meaningful statistical analysis could be made of at least some minority activities. At the same time, the proposal to investigate the interrelationships between demand and supply required that the physical area should be sufficiently large for demand and supply to be capable of some degree of interaction. Resources were available for a total sample of 1,000 households, 500 in each area. This, it was felt, would provide a sufficient absolute sample.* A check, on Ordnance Survey Maps, of the approximate area taken up by each Enumeration District suggested that each study area ought to consist of at least four of these Districts—and, preferably, five—in order to give a total area which would be sufficiently large for a meaningful analysis to be made of interrelationships between demand and supply.

What was finally being sought, then, were two areas, each consisting of four or five Enumeration Districts, which could be matched as nearly as possible on the basis of the six social and economic criteria, but which contrasted significantly in the volume of available recreation facilities. The first stage in the selection was to compare areas on the basis of the six social and economic criteria. The best pair to emerge from this process were groups of Enumeration Districts in Billesley and Duddeston Wards. These compared almost perfectly on five of the six criteria, the odd one out being housing standards. Unfortunately, however, most of Duddeston Ward was situated within several of the city's Comprehensive Development Areas. As a result, there had been a large volume of redevelopment in the area between 1966, the year to which the social data related, and 1968, the year in which the survey was to be carried out. It was likely, therefore, that the people living in Duddeston in the latter year, and the type of housing there, would no longer correspond to the figures available for the former year.

The second best pair of areas consisted of groups of Enumeration Districts in Billesley and All Saints Wards. These compared favourably on five of the six criteria, though not as well as the Billesley and Duddeston pair. Again, the criterion on which they did not match at all well was housing standards, The two areas compared almost perfectly on the important criterion of the sharing of dwellings (Table 15, Criterion 4). They also compared very well on the two criteria of population mobility (Criterion 3) and proportion of immigrants (Criterion 5). They compared less well, though still quite satisfactorily, on the criteria of social rank and family status (Criterion 1) and population density (Criterion 2). But on the

* But see Chapter 11.

121

criterion of housing standards (Criterion 6) they did not match at all. The All Saints area included four Enumeration Districts which had less than 20 per cent of households with exclusive use of the four required basic amenities; the Billesley area included four with between 40 and 80 per cent of households having exclusive use of these.

In comparing the availability of public open space and sports fields, it seemed reasonable to begin by comparing areas on the edge of the Green Belt with others in the heart of the Conurbation, since it

Table 15. *Selection of the Survey Areas*

BILLESLEY Enumeration Districts					CRITERIA [see notes]	ALL SAINTS Enumeration Districts				
13	14	16	17	20		2	5	6	7	10
3A	1D	2D	3A	2A	1	2D	2A	1A	1D	2D
3	4	5	3	4	2	1	4	4	5	3
1	1	1	1	1	3	2	1	1	1	1
1	1	1	1	1	4	1	1	1	1	1
1	1	1	1	1	5	2	1	1	2	1
3	4	3	3	3	6	3	1	1	1	1

Notes:
  (i) *Criterion 1.* Index of Family Status and Social Rank (see text).
  (ii) *Criterion 2.* Persons per room. 1 = lowest density, 5 = highest density.
  (iii) *Criterion 3.* Shows percentage of population that has moved into the area in the five years up to 1966. 1 = 0–4 per cent; 2 = 5–9 per cent; 3 = 10–14 per cent; 4 = 15–19 per cent; 5 = 20 per cent and over.
  (iv) *Criterion 4.* Shows percentage of households sharing a dwelling. 1 = 0–9 per cent; 2 = 10–19 per cent; 3 = 20–29 per cent; 4 = 30 per cent and over.
  (v) *Criterion 5.* Shows percentage of population born in the Commonwealth and Colonies. City Average 4·7 per cent. 1 = up to city average; 2 = more than city average up to twice city average; 3 = 2 to 3 times city average; 4 = 3 to 4 times city average; 5 = more than 4 times city average.
  (vi) *Criterion 6.* Shows percentage of households with exclusive use of four basic amenities. 1 = 0–19 per cent; 2 = 20–39 per cent; 3 = 40–79 per cent; 4 = 80 per cent and over.

could reasonably be assumed that the supply of facilities would be much greater in the former type of area than in the latter type. It happened that the Billesley and All Saints areas provided examples of each kind. Billesley is on the southern border of the city (Figure 5) with about 220 acres of public open space and sports fields, consisting of soccer, rugby and cricket pitches, putting and bowling greens, tennis courts, children's playgrounds and fishing and boating lakes, located within or immediately surrounding the survey area. In addition, there are ten allotment gardens and two golf courses—one municipal, the other private—also within or immediately surrounding the area. To the south is the Green Belt, including farmland and another golf course. The All Saints area presents a major contrast to this. Although it, too, is close to the boundaries of the city, there

Figure 5. The survey areas

is no Green Belt land just beyond. It borders on the Warley—West Bromwich part of the Conurbation, which consists of built-up industrial and residential areas. There is very little public open space available. Within the survey area itself there are no public open spaces at all. To the south there is Summerfield Park, to the north Handsworth Park—a total of about 100 acres, but at a distance of almost

123

a mile from the survey area. In addition, there are six small recreation grounds also within about a mile of the area.

The chosen survey areas would therefore appear to satisfy the selection criteria reasonably well. They compare favourably on five of the six social and economic criteria for matching. They do not compare at all well on the sixth criterion, housing standards, but it can be argued that to expect this is to be very optimistic. In a sense, housing standards and the availability of recreation facilities are both a function of physical environment, deriving from historical growth. By requiring that the two survey areas should contrast significantly in their provision of open space, we were virtually ensuring that one area would be considerably older than the other and, hence, that housing standards would differ significantly between the two areas. Certainly, there is no doubt that the two areas do contrast significantly on the basis of available public open space and sports fields. Billesley is chiefly residential, is on the edge of the Green Belt, and is well provided with allotments, open spaces and recreation grounds. All Saints, on the other hand, is much closer to the City Centre—though still close, also to its borders—is a mixed residential and industrial area, and is located well within the conurbation. While it is obviously not totally isolated from public open space, since there are two large parks to the north and south, it is considerably less well endowed than Billesley.

Selection of the Sample

Households to be contacted by the interviewers were selected from a list of addresses compiled from the Electoral Register. This, of course, will only give addresses at which at least one elector lives, so that it is unlikely to be fully comprehensive—although the numbers of addresses in any area at which no elector lives will probably be very small. With a total of about 4,000 households in each area and with a known overall multi-occupation rate of less than 1 per cent in each area, the predetermined absolute size of the sample (500 households) required that about 1 in 8 addresses should be selected. These were selected, essentially, on the basis of a systematic sample, whereby the first address is usually chosen by taking a random number between 1 and 8 inclusive, and then every eighth address thereafter. There was, however, a slight modification of this procedure. Since the survey would attempt, among other objectives, to investigate interrelationships between demand and supply, it was thought that the sample should be representative of the whole area, in spatial terms. For this reason it was required that at least one address in every street within the area should appear in the sample. A straightforward systematic sample of 1-in-8 addresses would mean that very small streets, with only three or four addresses, could be omitted. To avoid this, each street was taken, effectively, as a separate sampling frame. If there were eight or more addresses in the street, then the sample was selected by taking a random number between 1 and 8 inclusive for the first address, and every eighth address thereafter. If there were less than eight addresses in the street, then one address only was selected, by taking a random number between 1 and the figure corresponding to the number of addresses in the street. Thus, if there were only six addresses, then one was selected by the use of a random number between 1 and 6 inclusive. In this way it was ensured that at least one address in every street in the area was included in the sample. It also meant, however, that the overall sample would not necessarily be exactly 1-in-8, but might be slightly more or slightly less.

Design of the Survey
The design of the survey was largely the product of two of the major objectives of the study: first, the attempt to discover whether, by the joint use of interviews and self-administered questionnaires, a significant increase above the norm could be obtained in the numbers of respondents to a survey without a correspondingly significant increase in costs and a decrease in the quality of data obtained; and second, the attempt to assess the utility of time budget diaries as a method of collecting data about patterns of recreation. To meet these objectives, the survey was designed with three main components: an interview with the head of household or housewife seeking, first, information about the composition of the household and, second, information about his or her own recreation activities; a self-administered questionnaire, to be completed, in two out of every three households, by all other members of the household aged 12 years and over (that is, excluding the interviewed person), and seeking information about each person's own recreation activities; and a time budget diary, to be completed, in the third household in every three, by all other members of the household aged 12 years and over, and seeking a record of the ways in which these persons used their time throughout a 24-hour period. The age of 12 years was chosen largely because of the belief that an independent pattern of recreation activity begins to emerge at about this age; but, also, because it was felt that, on average, people below this age would probably not have

125

been able to cope adequately with the self-administered question-naires and diaries.

The purpose in seeking information from the interview about the composition of the household was threefold: first, to obtain a profile of the household and, hence, to discover obvious constraints on patterns of recreation activity, such as the presence in the household of a very young child; second, to provide a frame of reference for the interviewer so that she would know how many self-administered questionnaires or diaries were to be left and, later, collected; and third, to provide at least some profile information about those members of the household who refused to complete a self-adminis-tered questionnaire or diary. It is always valuable, in self-administered surveys, which tend usually to have relatively low response rates, to have some information about the characteristics of non-respondents.

The Survey Documents

Three documents were employed in the survey: a household question-naire, an activities questionnaire, and a time budget diary. A copy of each of these is reproduced in *Research Memorandum No. 3*, obtain-able from the centre for Urban and Regional Studies at the University of Birmingham, which also includes some specific comments about each document. Comments in the present chapter are of a more general kind, giving the broad outline of each document and indicat-ing some of the more important peculiarities of each.

The household questionnaire was completed by means of an interview held with the head of household or housewife. Its object was to secure information about the age, sex, marital status and relationship to the head of household of all members of the house-hold, and about certain other characteristics of the household itself—such as length of occupancy of the dwelling, type of tenure, kinds of recreation goods in the household and so on. It was very short, con-sisting of only nine questions, and could be completed, on average, in about five minutes. With the exception of Question 2—which consisted of a Standardized Household Composition Chart aimed at securing data about age, sex and marital status—all of the questions had precoded responses. The only unusual element in the document was a chart at the end which was used for recording the response by each member of the household to the self-administered questionnaire or diary. This chart showed, at a glance, whether the latter document had been obtained or refused.

The activities questionnaire was a much longer and more detailed document than the household questionnaire. It had two unusual characteristics. In the first place, it was designed for use by two quite different groups of people: by interviewers when data were sought by means of an interview with the head of household or housewife; and by respondents themselves when data were sought by the self-completion of the questionnaire. This had a considerable influence upon its design. For example, several previous methodological studies have suggested that the most effective way of recording responses to precoded questions in self-administered surveys is to get the respondent to place a tick or cross in the box which corresponds to his reply. Interviewers, on the other hand, have usually been trained to place a circle around the actual code corresponding to the respondent's answer. In this document, therefore, both methods were catered for: interviewers were enabled to encircle the code, self-completing respondents to place a tick in the box. Self-completing respondents were deterred from marking codes in any way by the use of the heading *Office Use Only*.

The other unusual characteristic of the activities questionnaire was the volume of space given over to questions about the profile characteristics of respondents. Since a particular objective of the survey was to examine the relative importance of different socio-economic characteristics in determining levels of recreation activity, there were many more questions about the socio-economic characteristics of respondents than would normally be included in a survey of this kind, while the number of questions relating to recreation itself was less than might have been thought desirable. In fact, half of the questions were directly concerned with the profile characteristics of respondents.

While, on average, the household questionnaire took less than five minutes to complete, the activities questionnaire sometimes took as little as ten minutes and sometimes as much as forty minutes to complete. The length of time taken depended upon, firstly, whether it was being answered by interview or by self-completion; secondly, the number of recreation activities in which the respondent had participated during 1968, since a potential sixty activities were listed; and thirdly, whether or not he was employed, since the section on employment was a very long one consisting of twelve questions.

The third document employed in the survey was the time budget diary. This was made up of twenty-four one-hour blocks in which the respondent could record all activities undertaken during each hour of the day. There were also columns for indicating the time at which each activity was begun and ended, the place at which it was undertaken, and the persons with whom it was undertaken. A final column was provided in which respondents could make any remarks that they wished, either of a specific kind relating to a particular activity or time, or of a more general character. Each diary also included a list of the kinds of activities that might be done during the day, from preparing meals to visiting night-clubs, together with an example of how a completed page of the diary might look. Instructions on the completion of the diary were kept to a bare minimum, in order to leave respondents as free as possible in their forms and modes of expression. The only significant point was the suggestion that respondents should fill in the diary at convenient moments during the day, and not leave it to the end of the day, as 'it is so easy to forget things.'

The only major problem that arose in the design of the time budget diary concerned the length of time-intervals into which it should be divided. The review of previous studies showed that there was no clear precedent about this: the study by the British Broadcasting Corporation [1] used half-hour intervals, the one by Robinson and Converse [44] used one-hour intervals, while the Chapin and Hightower study [17] did not use time intervals at all, but simply required respondents to begin recording at midnight on one day and to finish recording at midnight on the next day, having listed all activities undertaken during this period. Both of the latter studies did, however, seek information about the times at which each activity was begun and ended. Clearly, this was the most useful way of obtaining unambiguous data about the length of time for which each activity was undertaken. But, on the other hand, there also appeared to be strong arguments, on grounds of giving respondents an adequate frame of reference, for dividing the diary into time blocks. The pilot survey was too small to test this proposition, or to test whether one-hour or half-hour blocks would be the most useful; but a second examination of the three previous studies, particularly in terms of their response rates and the design of their diaries, suggested that some time-blocks would be more useful than none, and that one-hour blocks would probably be more helpful than half-hour ones. But together with this, it was decided to request respondents also to indicate the times at which each activity was begun and ended.

The Pilot Survey

The primary objective of the pilot survey was to test the usefulness, design and wording of the survey documents, It was carried out in a part of the City outside the two survey areas, but one which has some similar characteristics to these. It included a total of forty-one respondents, all of whom were interviewed, these interviews being carried out by research and technical staff attached to the research project. In addition to the forty-one interviews, there were fifteen refusals and four non-contacts. There were only two survey documents, as compared with the three used in the main survey: the first was an interview schedule which included questions about both the composition of the household and the recreation activities of the respondent; the second was a time budget diary which was to be completed by the same person who had been interviewed. It would be impossible to outline here, in detail, all of the ways in which the pilot survey influenced the structure and organization of the main survey; for example, how the responses to several questions in the pilot survey enabled these to be precoded in the main survey. It has been decided, therefore, to focus attention upon the major changes that were made to the proposals for the main survey as a result of the findings of the pilot survey.

Perhaps the most important point to emerge from the pilot survey was the confusion engendered among respondents by the use of the term 'leisure': 'People tend to be a little confused about what constitutes a leisure activity, so that, at a later stage of the study, the question of passive leisure versus specific recreation activities could give trouble and cause some kind of bias in statements about what things people actually do.'* Moreover, some of the activities were linked in various ways with considerations of moral value. Thus, depending upon his social class and background a respondent might admit to undertaking some activities and not others: 'the intellectual within my sample required considerable prompting from his wife, and considerable apologies for honesty, before he admitted to watching television on most nights of the week'. What all this indicated was the need for a frame of reference for respondents—a list of activities which would serve both to illustrate the kinds and range of activities with which the survey was concerned and to indicate that the survey carried no hints of approval or disapproval of particular kinds of recreation activity. This led directly to the inclusion of a question on the activities questionnaire in the main survey which listed more than sixty activities, including such pursuits as 'bingo' and 'visits to the pub', both of which have, at one time or another,

* Unless otherwise indicated, all quotations in this section are from the reports prepared by interviewers upon the completion of the field work for the pilot survey. All of the interviewers were members of the research team.

E

received statements of approval or disapproval from public figures.

Since the major concern of this study was to be with research techniques that might be useful to planning, it was intended originally that the survey should distinguish between home-based pursuits and those undertaken outside the home and between those undertaken in summer and those in winter. The distinction between home-based activities and those undertaken outside the home was catered for by making the latter the primary concern of the questionnaire and by seeking to cover the former in the time budget diaries. The distinction between winter and summer activities was built into the pilot questionnaire. This, however, created several problems. In the first place, for only about 25 per cent of respondents was the distinction between winter and summer activities wholly appropriate. These were mainly people who took part in traditional team sports out of doors—soccer or rugby in the winter and cricket (or, sometimes, tennis) in the summer. Some pursuits, such as gardening, become virtually impossible to do for a short period of about two months during the winter, but as long as there was only an (undefined) twofold division between summer and winter, most respondents felt that they undertook such pursuits at some time during both seasons. The second problem arising from this division was technical. Several questions, relating to such issues as frequency of participation and cost, were asked separately about each summertime and wintertime pursuit mentioned by the respondent. This required that the interviewer should make continual references back to responses made to earlier questions in the questionnaire, which no amount of re-ordering of questions could eliminate. There was also considerable repetition in cases where the wintertime and summertime pursuits were the same. The result was confusion, irritation on the part of both interviewer and respondent, and a loss of rapport: 'Considerable confusion arose for both the interviewer and interviewee over the repetition and jumping back and forth. Respondents tended to forget which activity they were discussing. The whole section seemed long drawn out, monotonous, rather artificial and extremely irritating.' This provides a very good example of a design for a survey which appeared to be wellnigh perfect from the investigator's point of view—one which would provide a wealth of data about each kind of activity—but which proved impossible to operate in the field. The problem was solved in the main survey by the complete elimination of the distinction between summer and winter. Instead, a new question was introduced into the activities questionnaire, which sought data about participation in a very wide range of activities, with no distinction between winter and summer, and which was followed by further questions concerning those activities undertaken most often.

This leads on to consideration of another problem which emerged from the pilot survey. Each respondent was asked to indicate his favourite way of spending his leisure time. This created problems of interpretation. For some people, the word *favourite* implied that they could mention any activity at all, whether or not they had actually ever taken part in it. Thus, they gave responses which indicated, more correctly, the ways in which they would most *like* to spend their leisure time. For others, the word *favourite* was simply taken to mean the activity in which they took part *most often*. So, there was further confusion: 'One impression that I received very strongly was that some people were confused as to what was meant by *your favourite way of spending your leisure time*. The confusion between *favourite* and *most common* was prevalent, though seldom explicitly.' This situation required that a much stricter assessment be made of the precise objectives of the survey and of this particular question. As a result, questions were asked in the main survey about both those activities undertaken *most often* and the activity which the respondent would most *like* to do in his spare time.

There were other differences between the questionnaire used in the pilot survey and those used in the main survey, but only one of these constituted a major change. This was in the actual number of questionnaires. There was only one questionnaire used in the pilot survey. It was asked of the head of household or the housewife and included questions about the composition of the household as well as those about recreation. A major new proposal was advanced, however, for the main survey. This was the proposal to test the utility of the joint use of interviews and self-administered questionnaires as a means of obtaining a greater volume of data than could be obtained from a normal interview survey, without a significant decrease in the quality of data obtained. If this was to be fully effective, however, it was necessary to separate the questions about household composition from those about recreation activity, so that the former were asked only of the head of household or the housewife. The most effective way of doing this seemed to be to have two quite separate questionnaires.

The pilot survey provided no significant data upon the basis of which a judgement could be made about the time budget diaries. The practice of dividing the diary into twenty-four one-hour blocks worked satisfactorily, while the column which had been provided for respondents' remarks proved to be a useful vehicle for securing their participation. Many of the remarks in this column were flippant; but some were more serious, pointing out, for example, that a certain activity was unusual for that particular day or time of the day. In any event, the column helped to retain an interest which, in many cases, had been roused by the novelty of the diary method: 'Reception of the diaries was neutral, with initial reluctance being disguised as puzzlement. People found it hard work filling them in, but were, on the whole, amused at the idea.' Certainly there seemed no reason, on the basis of the pilot survey, to change the design and format of the diary. Some slight changes were made, however, in the covering letter.

In view of its very small size, the pilot survey was a major success. It helped to identify some quite serious practical flaws in the design of the activities questionnaire, as a result of which several questions were removed altogether from the main survey. It certainly helped with the construction of precoded responses to some of the questions which were retained in the main survey. It also showed how a conceptually sound scheme for distinguishing levels of participation in leisure activities between different times of the year was, in practice, too complicated for use. And, of course, it helped to improve the wording and layout of the questionnaires that were used in the main survey. It undoubtedly represented a good return for the resources invested in it.

Arrangements for the Fieldwork

The final exercise to be undertaken before carrying out the main survey was to make arrangements for the fieldwork. The Centre for Urban and Regional Studies has no interviewing staff of its own and must, therefore, sub-contract its fieldwork to market research organizations. In these circumstances, the degree of control which the investigator has over the conduct of the fieldwork is likely to be much less than if he had interviewing staff of his own. Much will then hinge, of course, upon his choice of sub-contractor. At the least, no choice should be made until the investigator has visited the market research organization's field control centre and seen something of its administrative structure and capabilities.

For the present study, estimates for carrying out the fieldwork were invited from six market research firms. These estimates were requested before the pilot survey had been carried out and, in consequence, were for a straightforward household interview survey with no self-administered questionnaires and diaries. The specification for the work was as follows:

> '2,000 interviews to be held with the Head of Household or the Housewife, to be completed in a period of about four weeks beginning at the end of November 1968. The questionnaires would be prepared in the Centre for Urban and Regional Studies which would also be responsible for drawing the sample and for later office work, punching, and so on. Each interview can be expected to last between 20 and 40 minutes.'

One of the six firms stated that previous commitments made it impossible for it to consider undertaking the work. Estimates were received from the remaining five firms, and ranged from a low figure of £2,800 to a high one of £6,500. Two of these firms were then visited and, after further discussions, invited to submit estimates for a revised specification, as follows:

> 'Interviews to be sought with the Head of Household or the Housewife at 1,000 addresses in two areas of the City of Birmingham. In addition, self-administered questionnaires or diaries are to be left at each household for completion by every other member of the household aged twelve years and over, the interviewer to return within a few days to collect these. The questionnaires and diaries would be prepared in the Centre for Urban and Regional Studies which would also be responsible for drawing the sample and for later office work, punching, and so on. Each interview can be expected to last between 20 and 40 minutes. The briefing would be given by you to your interviewers, but would be held at the Centre so that we will be available for consultations.'

The two estimates for this revised specification were £1,200 and £2,100. After further discussions, the lower estimate was finally accepted. The reason for this was not simply the lower cost involved. Indeed, in terms of the services offered at each price, there was little to choose between the two estimates. The higher figure included the provision of some services which were not included in the lower estimate. But what was available with the latter was a much higher degree of control over the field staff for the investigator. In fact, in the final instance, the briefing of interviewers was carried out by the investigator at the Centre and not by representatives of the research firm. Furthermore, interviewers were instructed to address all queries and problems of a technical nature directly to the research team and not to the Area Supervisor or the Head Office in London.

133

The latter were to be contacted only in respect of problems of an administrative or professional kind. In this way, the investigator achieved a degree of control over the conduct of the fieldwork which is rarely possible when this is sub-contracted.

There is little more that need be said about the arrangements for the fieldwork. As indicated, the briefing of interviewers was held at the Centre and conducted by members of the research team. A set of instructions for interviewers was compiled in the Centre. The interviewing commenced on November 20, 1968, and was completed in a period of about six weeks.

Chapter 6

Response to the Survey

A major problem which emerged from the review of recent recreation studies concerned the need to secure a sufficient volume of data about minority recreation pursuits, mainly sports, to make possible a meaningful statistical analysis of the characteristics of participants. The first objective of the experimental studies was to test whether this could be done by the joint use of interviews and self-administered questionnaires, without a significant increase in costs and a decrease in the quality of data obtained. It was assumed that the alternative approach would have been an interview survey alone, since the known high levels of non-response to self-administered surveys were, prima facie, a strong argument against the use of this method alone. The question to be considered was whether the advantages—in costs and volume of data—of the self-administered questionnaire could be obtained without its disadvantages—mainly, a high level of non-response—by its use in conjunction with interviews.

In the event, the experiment proved to be highly successful. It was not simply that the approach yielded a higher number of completed schedules than could have been expected from an interview survey alone. Indeed, it would have been very surprising if this had not been the case. What was significant, however, was the size of the increase in the numbers of completed schedules obtained. The overall response rate to the short household questionnaire was 68 per cent, a figure which, though satisfactory, is rather low for an interview survey (Table 16). This was due in part, however, to a particular feature of the All Saints Study Area, in which the response was only 64 per cent—as compared with 72 per cent in the Billesley Area. Some parts of All Saints have been scheduled for redevelopment in the near future. As a consequence, houses which become vacant are then kept empty ready for demolition. This fact finds expression in the figures for non-response in the two study areas. The numbers of non-respondents arising from *refusals* and *no reply* were approximately the same—21 per cent in Billesley, 23 per cent in All Saints. The level of non-response arising from other causes, however, was nearly twice as high in the All Saints area as in Billesley—13 per cent against 7 per cent. Most of this discrepancy can be attributed to the empty properties awaiting demolition in the former area, which had been occupied at the time that the sampling frame was constructed—almost exactly one year before the survey took place.

The figure of 676 household interviews completed also indicates, of course, the number of activities questionnaires that were completed by interview; and, hence, the total number that would have been completed if the survey had taken place simply by interview alone. But, by leaving copies of the activities questionnaire to be completed directly by other members of the household, the total number obtained was raised to 1,056, which represents an increase of 56 per cent. In addition, 174 time budget diaries were obtained. Taken together, the total number of activities questionnaires and diaries obtained—by interviews and self-completions—represented

Table 16. *Response to the Household Questionnaire*

	BILLESLEY STUDY AREA		ALL SAINTS STUDY AREA		BOTH AREAS	
	Total	per cent	Total	per cent	Total	per cent
Sample of households	494	100	498	100	992	100
Interviews completed	357	72	319	64	676	68
Refusals	68	14	62	12	130	13
No reply	36	7	54	11	90	9
Other	33	7	63	13	96	10

an increase of about 82 per cent over the number obtained through interviews alone.

But although considerable success attended the efforts to secure a large increase in the *absolute* numbers of schedules obtained, the *response rates* for the self-administered questionnaires and diaries were not as high as had been hoped (Table 17). It was thought that the use of interviewers to deliver and collect these questionnaires and diaries would serve to raise the normally low response to self-administered schedules up to a level comparable to that usually obtained from interview surveys. In the event, the response to both documents fell below this level; although in both cases it was considerably higher than could have been expected from a self-administered survey carried out through the post. A normal response to the latter kind of survey would be between 30 and 50 per cent. In the present survey, it was 59 per cent for both the self-administered questionnaires and the diaries. It had been hoped, however, that the use of interviewers to deliver and collect these schedules would have produced a response more nearly similar to that obtained from the

Table 17. *Response to the Activities Questionnaire and Time Budget Diary*

	BILLESLEY STUDY AREA		ALL SAINTS STUDY AREA		BOTH AREAS	
	Numbers	per cent	Numbers	per cent	Numbers	per cent
Sample population aged 12 years and over in interview households	905	100	714	100	1619	100
Interviews completed	357	39	319	45	676	42
Self-administered questionnaires and Time Budget Diaries completed	326	36	228	32	554	34
Refusals	222	25	167	23	389	24
INTERVIEWS						
Households contacted*	425	100	381	100	806	100
Completions	357	84	319	84	676	84
Refusals	68	16	62	16	130	16
SELF-ADMINISTERED QUESTIONNAIRES						
Persons contacted	395	100	249	100	644	100
Completions	230	58	150	60	380	59
Refusals	165	42	99	40	264	41
TIME BUDGET DIARIES						
Persons contacted	153	100	143	100	296	100
Completions	96	63	78	55	174	59
Refusals	57	37	65	45	122	41

* Excludes households in the sample with which contact was not made, that is, those classified in Table 16 as *No Reply* and *Other*.

137

interviews—84 per cent of all persons contacted. There is no very obvious reason for this, except, perhaps, that interviewers did not speak personally with all people from whom activities questionnaires and diaries were requested, but simply made contact with the head of household or housewife, with whom copies of these documents were left, to be completed by other members of the household. Thus, the interviewer did not have the opportunity to establish *rapport* with these persons in the way that is possible in an interview situation. But failure to obtain the hoped-for response should not detract from the very real success that was achieved. The fact remains that the total number of schedules obtained was raised by 82 per cent above the figure that would have been obtained from an interview survey alone; and that the response to both the self-administered questionnaire and the time budget diary was significantly greater than could have been expected if these documents had been delivered by post.

One other aspect of the response to the self-administered questionnaires and diaries is worth noting. This is the surprising similarity in the overall response achieved. This is surprising because it has always been generally believed that the level of non-response to time budget diaries would be considerably higher than for self-administered questionnaires. A diary is more time-consuming and requires a much greater degree of tolerance and conscientiousness on the part of the respondent than does a self-administered questionnaire. Yet the difference in the overall level of response between the two was a mere 0·2 per cent, a figure which has no statistical significance whatsoever. Interestingly though, the response rates differed sharply, and significantly, between the two study areas. In Billesley the response to the self-administered questionnaire was 58 per cent, while the figure for the diary was 63 per cent; in the All Saints Area the figures were 60 per cent and 55 per cent, respectively. The reasons for this overall similarity and the differences between the two areas are not readily apparent. It may be that the note struck in the covering letter accompanying the diary—appealing to the respondents' curiosity and making a veiled challenge to their ability—helped to bolster the rate of response to the diary up to a level comparable with that for the questionnaire.* But, whatever the cause, it is a heartening feature for future time budget studies in this field.

Costs of the Survey

The additional cost involved in the joint use of interviews, self-

* A copy of this letter is to be found in *Research Memorandum No. 3*, obtainable from the Centre for Urban and Regional Studies, University of Birmingham.

administered questionnaires and diaries rather than a straightforward interview survey was approximately £100. The market research firm which undertook the fieldwork estimated the cost of an ordinary interview survey, utilizing the household and activities question- naires but not the diaries, at about £1,100. The actual cost of the interviews and the recalls to collect the self-administered question- naires and diaries was £1,200. The estimated rise in costs was, there- fore, of the order of 9 to 10 per cent. Of course, an important factor in holding this projected increase at such a relatively low level was the structure of the survey itself. Because of the small size of each area and the rather compact nature of the residential development in each, it was possible for interviewers to call back to collect self- administered activities questionnaires and diaries without making special journeys of very great length. Indeed, this was an important factor in keeping the cost of the whole survey generally at a relatively low level. It is likely that the increase in cost would be higher for a survey undertaken in a larger geographical area—say, on a sub- regional or regional basis. But, even in these cases, it is unlikely that the cost would rise proportionately to the increase in the number of completed schedules obtained; for, with skilful organization of the fieldwork, it should be possible to arrange interviewers' quotas in such a way that recalls to collect self-administered questionnaires could be mixed in with first visits to other households, as was done in this survey.

The *absolute* differences in costs between the two systems is, however, only one element in the overall picture. A more helpful comparison would be one made between the *costs per completed schedule* for the two approaches. Assuming that the response rate to an interview survey alone woud have been identical to the number of household interviews actually obtained (Table 16), the estimated cost for the whole survey of £1,100 would have resulted in a cost per completed schedule of approximately 32 shillings. The actual cost per completed schedule for the joint interview and self-administered survey was slightly less than 20 shillings. In terms of cost efficiency, therefore, the latter method was more than 50 per cent better: that is, with given resources the multiple approach can be expected to produce half as many schedules again as the interview survey.

Quality of the Data

Perhaps the most important point to emerge from the survey was the apparent absence of any significant 'loss' of data by the use of the

139

multiple approach rather than interviews alone. Certainly, the level of non-response to particular questions on the activities questionnaire was higher in the case of self-administered ones than for interviews. But even this difference was not significant, and the overall level of non-response to individual questions was generally very low. It was highest, in respect of factual questions, for the question about income —15 per cent. This has, however, always been a sensitive subject about which to obtain data. On no other factual question was the level of non-response very high. There were, however, some higher rates of non-response for opinion questions, the highest being 20 per cent for the questions about the ways in which people would choose to use extra leisure time. Generally, though, there was no indication that the level of non-response to individual questions was vastly greater for self-administered questionnaires than for interviews.

It is impossible, however, to be quite so categorical about differerences—or the lack of them—in the quality of the data which *were* obtained from the two methods. Interviewers can, by prompting and emphasis, clarify the meaning and purpose of particular questions, and, hence, can obtain more accurate data from respondents than would be forthcoming in a self-administered survey. On the other hand, there is always the danger that the interviewer will establish *over-rapport* with the respondent and, thereby, influence his responses. The solution to this problem lies, primarily, in the design of the questionnaire. All that can be said in the present case is that the activities questionnaire was designed primarily for direct use by respondents. Particular attention was, therefore, paid to possibilities of ambiguity in the meaning of questions. In general, there was no indication that the quality of data obtained from the self-administered questionnaires was significantly worse than that obtained from the interviews. There is no way, however, of judging sins of omission rather than commission in the self-administered questionnaires; that is, for example, in recreation activities which ought to have been recorded, but which were not. Here, there was no interviewer to prompt the respondent; hence, there had to be total reliance on the respondent's memory.

Respondents and Non-respondents

It is pertinent at this point to examine briefly two other aspects of the response to the household and activities survey. The first of these relates to the characteristics of non-respondents. There is no information, of course, concerning the characteristics of persons in the households where the household questionnaire was not completed. But in those cases where the household questionnaire was completed, data are available relating to the age, sex and marital status of all members of the household. This information can be related to the response made to the request to complete the activities questionnaire, either by inteview or by self-completion. It will then be possible to discover whether there are any significant differences between respondents and non-respondents in respect of these three characteristics. The findings of this exercise are shown in Table 18.* This gives three sets of information for each sub-class of the three characteristics mentioned above: the number of persons contacted, the number responding and the number not responding. The information has also been given for each study area separately and for the two areas combined. The procedure was to compare the percentage of respondents in each sub-class with the percentage for the total sample. The test of significance in differences was given by the formula

$$\frac{a-c}{\sqrt{\dfrac{a(100-a)}{b} + \dfrac{c(100-c)}{d}}}$$

in which

$a =$ the largest percentage being compared;
$b =$ its corresponding sample size;
$c =$ the smallest percentage being compared;
$d =$ its corresponding sample size.

The figure which results from this is the ratio of the percentage difference to the standard deviations of the two percentages. The critical values of this statistic are 1·96 and 2·57 which denote 95 per cent and 99 per cent probability, respectively. That is, if the resulting figure is greater than 1·96 but less than 2·57, then the difference between the two percentages is significant at the 5 per cent probability level. If the figure is greater than 2·57 then the difference is significant at the 1 per cent probability level. But if the figure is less than 1·96 there is no significance at all in the difference between the two percentages.

What has emerged from this exercise is the general conclusion that non-response tends to be significantly higher among males, the unmarried and the young than among other groups. For the two

* A similar exercise for the time budget diaries has been conducted in Chapter 7 Table 21.

Table 18. Characteristics of Respondents and Non-respondents to the Activities Questionnaire

	BILLESLEY STUDY AREA		ALL SAINTS STUDY AREA		BOTH AREAS	
	Numbers	per cent	Numbers	per cent	Numbers	per cent
TOTAL						
Persons contacted	752	100	568	100	1320	100
Respondents	587	78	469	83	1056	80
Non-respondents	165	22	99	17	264	20
SEX						
Males Contacted	346	100	253	100	599	100
Respondents	245	71*	186	74*	431	72*
Non-respondents	101	29*	67	26*	168	28*
Females contacted	406	100	315	100	721	100
Respondents	342	84*	283	90*	625	87*
Non-respondents	64	16*	32	10*	96	13*
MARITAL STATUS						
Married persons contacted	464	100	380	100	844	100
Respondents	381	82	321	85	702	83
Non-respondents	83	18	59	15	142	17
Single persons contacted	198	100	111	100	309	100
Respondents	125	63*	77	69*	202	65*
Non-respondents	73	37*	34	31*	107	35*
Widowed, divorced and separated persons contacted	90	100	77	100	167	100
Respondents	81	90*	71	92*	152	91*
Non-respondents	9	10*	6	8*	15	9*

142

RESPONSE TO THE SURVEY

AGE

12–14 years contacted	42	100	27	100	69	100
Respondents	36	86	16	59*	52	75
Non-respondents	6	14	11	41*	17	25
15–19 years contacted	73	100	23	100	96	100
Respondents	45	62*	14	61*	59	62*
Non-respondents	28	38*	9	39*	37	38*
20–24 years contacted	67	100	63	100	129	100
Respondents	41	61*	53	85	94	73
Non-respondents	26	39*	9	15	35	27
25–29 years contacted	45	100	46	100	91	100
Respondents	41	91*	39	85	80	88*
Non-respondents	4	9*	7	15	11	12*
30–44 years contacted	156	100	123	100	279	100
Respondents	134	86*	98	80	232	83
Non-respondents	22	14*	25	20	47	17
45–59 years contacted	172	100	141	100	313	100
Respondents	136	79	120	85	256	82
Non-respondents	36	21	21	15	57	18
60–64 years contacted	50	100	52	100	102	100
Respondents	38	76	45	86	83	81
Non-respondents	12	24	7	14	19	19
65 years and over contacted	134	100	83	100	217	100
Respondents	109	81	76	92*	185	85*
Non-respondents	25	19	7	8*	32	15*

Note:
The percentages of respondents and non-respondents within each sub-class of the three characteristics have been compared with the percentages for the sample as a whole within each area. Those percentages marked with an asterisk are ones which differ significantly from the average at the 5 per cent probability level. (Many, in fact, differ significantly at the 1 per cent probability level.)

143

areas taken together, the differences by sex and marital status were significant at the 1 per cent probability level. Males were much more likely to be non-respondents than females, and single persons more so than married, widowed, divorced and separated persons. The same pattern emerged when the two study areas were examined separately.

On age, however, the pattern was not nearly so clear-cut. In the two study areas taken together, significant differences were observed for the age-groups 15–19 years, 25–29 years, and 65 years and over.* In the former case, the level of non-response was significantly higher than for the sample as a whole; in the two latter cases, it was significantly lower. There were, however, important differences between the two study areas in this respect. In Billesley, significant differences were observed for a larger number of age-groups, including the two groups 15–19 years and 20–24 years in which the level of non-response was significantly above-average, and the groups 25–29 years and 30–44 years in which it was significantly below-average. In All Saints, in contrast, the level of non-response was above-average for the two groups 12–14 years and 15–19 years. Thus, the only difference that was significant in both areas was in the age-group 15–19 years. With other groups the two areas showed varying results.

There is no very obvious reason for this discrepancy between the two study areas: the more so, since the two areas compare closely on the other characteristics and on most of the age-groups. A first thought was that these differences might reflect the abilities of the different interviewers in the two areas to persuade contacts to complete the activities questionnaires and diaries, but a glance at the overall success rates achieved by each interviewer does not support this. It is most likely, in fact, that the cause is to be found in some other characteristic—say, standard of education—for which data are not available. All that can be said with certainty, however, is that there are significant differences in levels of non-response for certain age-groups, not simply between different age-groups, but also between the same age-groups in the different areas.

What has emerged, then, is the knowledge that levels of non-response are significantly higher among males, single persons and, less assuredly, young persons than among other groups. The implications of these findings are important, both for the present study specifically and for recreation surveys generally. For the present study

* The age-groups used correspond to those employed in the 1966 *Sample Census*, except for the group 12–14 years. The latter derives from the fact that only persons aged twelve years and over were asked to complete the activities questionnaire.

it means that the data about recreation habits give too much weight to females, married persons, and those aged 25 years and over. These persons are over-represented in comparison with males, single persons, and those below the age of 25 years. This bias is only dangerous, however, in respect of general statements about the recreation activities of the total population of each area. It carries much less force when activities are related to the possession of these characteristics anyway: each characterstic is then the defining feature of what is, effectively, a separate sample.

The implications of these findings for recreation surveys generally are more immediately alarming. It is known already from previous social surveys of many kinds that young, single persons—both male and female, but especially the former—are the most difficult group of persons with whom to make contact in social surveys. These are the people most often away from home, during the daytime and in the evenings. This point was noted in the *Pilot National Recreation Survey*, and the sampling procedure adjusted in an attempt to offset the problem. But it now appears that even when these persons are contacted, they are the ones most likely to refuse to give information. In the case of recreation surveys, the problem is even more acute, since these are in fact the people who, by and large, have the largest volume of available leisure time and the most diverse recreation experiences, and who place the strongest pressures upon recreation land and facilities. The implication is, therefore, that considerable effort must be devoted to ways and means of increasing response rates among this particular group of people.

The Sample

The final purpose of the present chapter is to make a brief examination of the general characteristics of the sample population obtained in the survey and to compare these with published data. This can be done for two sets of data: the first relates to the composition of the sample households, outlined in Table 19; the second to the personal characteristics of the sample population, shown in Table 20. In each case the sample data have been compared with those obtained from the *1966 Sample Census*.

The first point to emerge from the household data was that, in both study areas, there appears to be an over-representation of households which are owner-occupied and an under-representation of those who rent their housing from the local authority. The size of the discrepancy is not very large for the Billesley Study Area, and is just

145

Table 19. Sample Checks for the Household Survey: 1. Household Data

| | BILLESLEY STUDY AREA | | ALL SAINTS STUDY AREA | |
	1966 Sample Census (per cent)	The Survey (per cent)	1966 Sample Census (per cent)	The Survey (per cent)
Households: (Numbers) per cent	(417) 100	(357) 100	(316) 100	(319) 100
TENURE				
Owner-occupied	23	29	19	23
Rented from the Council	68	65	50	36
Rented privately unfurnished	6	4	28	38
Rented privately furnished	1	0	0	2
Other tenure and No reply	3	2	3	1
PERSONS PER HOUSEHOLD				
One	11	13	14	19
Two	28	30	29	31
Three	22	19	21	19
Four	17	19	16	13
Five	9	10	9	8
Six and over	12	9	11	11

within the limits of normal sampling error. But in the All Saints Study Area the size of the discrepancy in the representation of households who rent from the local authority is much greater: 50 per cent for the Census, 36 per cent for the sample. In addition, there appears to be a large over-representation of households who rent unfurnished housing from private landlords—28 per cent for

Table 20. *Sample Checks for the Household Survey: 2. Population Data*

	BILLESLEY STUDY AREA 1966		ALL SAINTS STUDY AREA 1966	
	Sample Census (per cent)	*The Survey* (per cent)	*Sample Census* (per cent)	*The Survey* (per cent)
Sample population:				
(numbers)	(1,385)	(1,139)	(1,029)	(982)
per cent	100	100	100	100
SEX				
Males	49·5	50·4	49·0	50·2
Females	50·5	49·6	51·0	49·8
MARITAL STATUS				
Single	43	43	46	45
Married	51	49	47	47
Widowed, Divorced and Separated	7	8	8	8
AGE (in years)				
0–4	8	7	12	11
5–14	15	18	17	20
15–19	10	9	8	5
20–24	6	7	7	9
25–29	5	5	6	5
30–44	16	16	18	15
45–59	22	18	19	17
60–64	6	5	5	6
65 and over	12	14	9	9

the Census, 38 per cent for the sample. The size of the difference is, in both cases, statistically significant at the 1 per cent probability level. But, in noting this, several cautionary points should be made. In the first place, the Census figures are based upon a 10 per cent sample, giving an absolute number of households which is, in fact, in the All Saints Study Area, marginally lower than the number upon which

147

the present study is based. It would, therefore, be dangerous to consider this comparison of the two sets of data as being a check on the validity of the sample for the present study, and to conclude therefrom that this sample is significantly biased. There is no prima facie evidence to suggest that the data from the *Sample Census* are more accurate than those obtained from the present study. Indeed, there are grounds for thinking the reverse: that is, that the data from the present study are more accurate than those obtained from the *Sample Census*. For, they are more up to date. The *Sample Census* was carried out in 1966, the present survey in 1968; and, as has already been noted, this time lag could be significant for the All Saints Study Area, for it is an area which is steadily losing population in anticipation of comprehensive redevelopment.

The final point that should be made about these differences between the present survey and the *Sample Census* is, perhaps, the most important. Even if it were shown that the observed differences were, in reality, significant ones, this still does not imply that they will be significant *in considering patterns of recreation activity*. They would clearly be important for a survey of, say, housing preferences; but it can be argued that there are unlikely to be large differences in patterns of recreation activity between households whose housing is rented from different sources. The important factor, it may be argued, is that both groups rent unfurnished housing. If housing tenure does affect patterns of recreation activity at all, it is likely that the greatest differences will be between those who own their housing and those who rent it, rather than between those who rent it from one source and those who rent it from another. It must be stressed, however, that this is a hypothesis which has not been proven.

There are no other large discrepancies in the household data between the *Sample Census* and the present study. In both areas, there appears to be an over-representation of single-person and two-person households and an under-representation of three-person households. In the All Saints Study Area there is also a smaller proportion of four-person households than in the *Sample Census*, while in Billesley there is a smaller proportion of five-person households. In none of these cases, however, are the differences significant.

There are no significant differences in the population data between the survey and the *Sample Census* (Table 20). In both study areas the balance between the sexes is the opposite in the survey to that shown in the Census, but in neither case is the numerical difference significant. Apart from this, the observed differences—for marital status and age—are all of a relatively minor nature.

Conclusion

In summary, it can reasonably be claimed that the experiment with the joint use of interviews and self-administered questionnaires (and diaries) was successful. The number of completed schedules obtained, including diaries, was 82 per cent higher than could have been expected from an interview survey alone. The cost of obtaining these additional schedules was only about 10 per cent higher than for an interview survey. And, although there was some loss of data in the self-administered questionnaires (because some questions were left unanswered which would probably have been answered in an interview), there is no indication that these extra schedules were obtained at the expense of a significant reduction in the quality of data obtained.

The method is particularly suitable for local studies of the kind undertaken here. The number of interviews that can be carried out in a local survey will usually be much less than for a national survey, simply because the resources available will be less. And even though the number of interviews might be *proportionately* greater for a local survey than for a national one, there is a certain minimum *absolute* number of schedules that will be required to obtain sufficient information about minority activities for a meaningful statistical analysis to be made of them. Even the numbers of schedules obtained in the present study were inadequate for a full analysis of minority activities to be made. The present survey has not demonstrated that the characteristics of participants in minority activities can be analysed satisfactorily with a sample of the particular size obtained. What it has demonstrated, however, is a way of obtaining large numbers of completed questionnaires at an absolute cost which is not appreciably greater than for a straightforward interview survey, and at a cost per completed schedule which is considerably below this.

149

Chapter 7
The Time Budget Diaries

Four major problems arising from the use of time budget diaries for social research were identified during the review of recent recreation studies. These were, first, how to secure significant and adequate rates of response; second, related in part to this, how to determine the time periods for which diaries should be kept; third, whether or not the diary should be divided into specific time intervals, and, if so, how to determine what these shall be; and fourth, how to carry out the coding and analysis of the diary data. The purpose in employing diaries as part of the household and activities survey was to examine some of these problems in greater detail and, thereby, to provide guidelines for future large-scale studies making use of these. The numbers of diaries sought and obtained were sufficient for some definite conclusions to be formulated; but they were insufficient for comprehensive solutions to be outlined to each of these four problems. This part of the household survey should be considered, therefore, as being in the nature of a pilot investigation which has sought solutions to general problems, rather than an empirical study of the ways in which time is used by respondents in the two study areas. It constitutes an experiment upon the basis of which a full-scale time budget survey could be mounted, either within the two study areas or elsewhere.

Rate of Response

The overall response to the time budget survey has been discussed in Chapter 6, in the context of the total response to the household survey, and is outlined in full in Table 17. The latter shows that an overall response of 59 per cent was obtained for the two study areas taken together—a figure which is virtually identical with that for the level of response obtained from the self-administered questionnaires. The figures for each study area separately show that the response was greater in the Billesley Area than in All Saints—63 per cent as compared with 55 per cent—but statistically the difference is only marginally significant. The overall response compares favourably with the levels obtained in previous time budget studies. The study by Robinson and Converse [44] at the University of Michigan obtained an

150

overall response of 72·5 per cent, but this figure included an unknown number of diaries which were completed in retrospect with the aid of interviewers. In contrast, the study by Chapin and Hightower [17] at the University of North Carolina achieved an overall response of only 25 per cent. In the context of these studies, the response obtained here is encouraging.

It is not, however, the mere rate of response which is important, but rather, the extent to which the level of non-response is likely to bias the findings of the survey. As was the case with the activities questionnaire, data are available from the household interview concerning the age, sex and marital status of all persons who were asked to complete the time budget diary. These have been shown in Table 21 in relation to the response made, and the same statistical tests have been made on them as were made on the data for the activities questionnaire. The most interesting fact which emerges is the considerable difference between the diary and the questionnaire in this respect. The evidence from the questionnaire was that, generally, non-respondents were male, single and young rather than otherwise. The evidence from the diary, however, does not support this view. The figures do show that females responded more frequently than males, but the difference between the two levels of response—64 per cent for females, 56 per cent for males—is not statistically significant. On marital status, both response rates adhered closely to the average. In fact, the proportion of respondents was slightly higher for single persons than for married ones—the opposite of the situation for the activities questionnaires—but, again, the difference is not significant. As for age, the absolute figures for any particular age-group are too low for meaningful statistical tests to be performed on them. If, however, the standard age-groups are combined into only two groups —those persons below 30 years of age and those above this—then the absolute numbers are quite adequate for analysis (Table 22). Moreover, the difference in rates of non-response between the two groups then turns out to be significant—and, furthermore, to be quite contrary to the evidence of the activities questionnaire. The level of non-response was significantly below-average for young persons under the age of thirty, and significantly above-average for persons over this age.

Almost any number of reasons can be advanced for this last finding. It can be argued, for example, that young people have more free time in which to complete a diary than older people; or, perhaps, that the note of challenge evident in the letter accompanying the diary struck a more responsive chord among young persons than

151

Table 21. *Characteristics of Respondents and Non-respondents to the Time Budget Diary Survey*

	BILLESLEY STUDY AREA		ALL SAINTS STUDY AREA		BOTH AREAS	
	Numbers	per cent	Numbers	per cent	Numbers	per cent
TOTAL						
Persons contacted	153	100	143	100	296	100
Respondents	96	63	78	55	174	59
Non-respondents	57	37	65	45	122	41
SEX						
Males contacted	104	100	90	100	194	100
Respondents	65	62	44	49	109	56
Non-respondents	39	38	46	51	85	44
Females contacted	49	100	53	100	102	100
Respondents	31	63	34	64	56	64
Non-respondents	18	37	19	36	37	36
MARITAL STATUS						
Married persons contacted	90	100	84	100	174	100
Respondents	55	61	47	56	102	59
Non-respondents	35	39	37	44	72	41
Single persons contacted	56	100	57	100	113	100
Respondents	37	66	31	54	68	60
Non-respondents	19	34	26	46	45	40
AGE						
12–14 years contacted	16	+	14	+	30	100
Respondents	13	+	7	+	20	67
Non-respondents	3	+	7	+	10	33

15–19 years contacted	24	+	28	+	52	100
Respondents	19	+	15	+	34	65
Non-respondents	5	+	13	+	18	35
20–24 years contacted	11	+	27	+	38	100
Respondents	6	+	18	+	24	63
Non-respondents	5	+	9	+	14	37
25–29 years contacted	12	+	7	+	19	100
Respondents	8	+	5	+	13	68
Non-respondents	4	+	2	+	6	32
30–44 years contacted	26	+	25	+	51	100
Respondents	14	+	10	+	24	47
Non-respondents	12	+	15	+	27	53
45–59 years contacted	35	+	26	+	61	100
Respondents	21	+	11	+	32	52
Non-respondents	14	+	15	+	29	48
60–64 years contacted	6	+	8	+	14	100
Respondents	4	+	4	+	8	57
Non-respondents	2	+	4	+	6	43
65 years and over contacted	23	+	6	+	29	100
Respondents	11	+	6	+	17	59
Non-respondents	12	+	0	+	12	41

Note:

Percentage figures have not been given for the two study areas separately for age-groups because, generally, the absolute figures are too low for them to be meaningfully tested. For the same reason, data have not been included for the 9 persons contacted who were widowed, divorced or separated. Differences between sub-classes have been tested for significance in the same manner as for the Activities Questionnaire data in Table 18.

among their elders; or, even, that young people, having received a deeper and wider formal education than older people, are more able to complete forms and, therefore, more responsive when asked to do so. But, whatever may be the reason for this greater co-operation among young people, it can be of enormous benefit to those engaged in recreation research; more especially so in view of the evidence of a disproportionately high rate of non-response among young people to to the interview and self-administered questionnaire employed in this study and to interview surveys generally. If information about the

Table 22. *Age Characteristics for the Time Budget Diary Survey*

	BOTH STUDY AREAS	
	Numbers	*per cent*
TOTAL		
Persons contacted	296	100
Respondents	174	59
Non-respondents	122	41
AGE		
12–29 years contacted	139	100
Respondents	91	66
Non-respondents	48	34
30 Years and Over Contacted	155	100
Respondents	81	52
Non-respondents	74	48

recreation activities of young people—who, in general, have the largest amounts of available leisure time and leisure spending power—is not readily forthcoming through interviews or self-administered questionnaires, it may be that the investigator should seek this through the use of time budget diaries. Certainly, on the basis of the evidence from the present study, these would get a greater response than questionnaires.

One other point remains to be made about the response to the time budget diary. This concerns the distribution of diaries throughout the week. Diaries were to be kept for one day only and interviewers were instructed to divide their requests for them evenly throughout the week. In the event, one day of the week—Monday—was significantly under-represented (Table 23). The reason for this is most likely to be found in the pattern of interviewing. Since the diaries had to be kept from a midnight to a midnight, most interviewers would leave them to be completed for the next full day after the day of interview: that is, if the interview were held some time on Tuesday, then the contacts would be requested to keep the diary for Wednesday, from midnight Tuesday to midnight Wednesday. This means that, in all likelihood, those persons who kept diaries for a Monday were members of a household in which the interview had taken place on a Sunday. All of the interviewers were, however, married, and most had families. It is unlikely, therefore, that they were able to carry out as many interviews on Sundays as on other days of the week. Of course, interviewers did not necessarily have to ask contacts to complete the diary for the first full day after the day on which the interview was held; and, indeed, they were expressly asked to try to distribute

Table 23. *Response to the Time Budget Diary, by Day of the Week*

DAY OF THE WEEK	DIARIES REQUESTED		DIARIES REFUSED	DIARIES OBTAINED	DIARIES USABLE
	Total	per cent	per cent	per cent	per cent
Monday	30	100	50	50	47
Tuesday	45	100	42	58	53
Wednesday	40	100	45	55	50
Thursday	48	100	42	58	50
Friday	46	100	44	57	48
Saturday	47	100	36	64	57
Sunday	40	100	33	68	63
Total	296	100	41	59	53

their requests for diaries evenly throughout the week, and were provided with a checklist to help them in this. On the other hand, there would be a natural desire on the part of interviewers to get contacts to keep the diary for the day immediately following the day of interview, before their interest and curiosity had evaporated.

There is little more that need be added about the distribution of the diaries throughout the week. The rate of response—which ranged from a high of 68 per cent to a low of 50 per cent—was also lowest for Monday. It was highest for Saturday and Sunday. The overall response was 59 per cent, but a small number of these were unusable in the analysis because of large gaps in the information given. The final number of usable diaries obtained represented 53 per cent of the number requested, giving a wastage rate of 6 per cent in addition to the refusal rate of 41 per cent.

The relatively high level of overall response to the diary was

155

achieved without any special or unusual efforts to achieve this. There was, for instance, no suggestion that respondents would be paid for their efforts or that they would receive any other direct benefit to themselves. The most significant element in helping to obtain a high response was probably, in fact, the interviewer. The diaries (and self-administered questionnaires) were not sent through the post, but were delivered by the interviewers; and, most important, the interviewers also called back to collct them. There was an opportunity, therefore, for interviewers to persuade contacts to complete the diary. Furthermore, if, when the intervewers returned to collect the diaries, they had not been completed, they were instructed to try again—to give the contacts another day and date upon which to complete the diary. Since the day and date for completion were to be written on the face of the diary, it is possible to measure the numbers of diaries that were, in fact, completed at the second attempt (they will be ones which carry two dates, the first having been crossed out and replaced by the second). This exercise shows that 18 of the 174 diaries obtained were secured at a second, or subsequent, attempt.* In effect, these completions at the second attempt raised the overall response rate from 53 per cent to the final level of 59 per cent. Thus, the use of interviewers to deliver and collect the diaries probably had two main effects. Firstly, it is likely to have increased the level of the original response above the level that would have been obtained if delivery had been by post with respondents requested to post completed diaries back to the investigator. And secondly, it definitely helped to increase the overall response by providing the opportunity for contacts to be persuaded to complete the diary at a second attempt. Apart from this use of interviewers, however, no special efforts were made to secure an above-average rate of response. If, therefore, the achieved rate is considerably greater than average, it seems reasonable to attribute this to the use of interviewers.

Time Periods

The second major problem encountered in previous research with time budget diaries concerns the length of time for which diaries should be kept. Should contacts be asked to keep the diary for one day only, for several days (including a weekend), for a full week, or, perhaps, for longer periods? The problem is linked in part to the

* Although interviewers were only instructed to make two attempts to obtain a completed diary, there were, in fact, two cases where completion had been obtained at a third attempt.

problem of obtaining satisfactory response rates, because, prima facie, the longer is the period of time for which contacts are requested to keep the diary, the greater is the number of persons who are likely to drop out and, thereby, become non-respondents. The evidence from previous studies is contradictory on this point. The two American studies mentioned earlier used one-day diaries and achieved response rates of 72·5 per cent and 25 per cent. The only large-scale British study—by the British Broadcasting Corporation's Audience Research Department*—made use of a seven-day diary and secured a response of 58·5 per cent.

The scale of the present study precluded any attempt to test for the optimum period for which diaries should be kept. The total number of diaries that it was hoped to collect was too small for any such test to be fully effective. In practice, the choice lay between a period of one day only, one of several days, and one of a full week. The evidence from consultations with the investigators who carried out the two American studies suggested that the best chances of a high response lay in the use of a diary which requested information for a period of one day only. The evidence from the British study was confused and inconclusive. It was decided, therefore, to employ a one-day diary. But, to give some indication of differences between days of the week, the proposal was also made to instruct interviewers to spread the requests for diaries uniformly throughout the week.

This decision was also influenced by the fact that no incentives could be given to contacts to induce them to complete the diary. Chapin and Hightower, at the University of North Carolina, are currently experimenting with the payment of honoraria as a means of improving diary response rates. Neither this approach nor the introduction of a 'game' element with prizes could be considered for the present study. It may be, however, that future time budget studies in this country will be able to experiment with such methods as a means not only of achieving high response rates, but also of obtaining data for periods of more than one full day.

Time Intervals

The third major problem encountered in previous research with time budget diaries concerns whether or not the diary should be divided into specific time intervals, and, if so, what these are to be. Again, the evidence from previous studies was inconclusive on this. The British study used half-hour intervals, the Robinson and Converse

* See Chapter 2, pages 68–70.

study used one-hour intervals, while the Chapin and Hightower study did not use time intervals at all. Both American studies, however, sought information about the times at which each activity was begun and ended. Clearly, this latter approach provides the most useful way of obtaining unambiguous data about the length of time for which each activity was undertaken. But it still leaves the problem of deciding whether the diary should simply be laid out so that respondents begin recording at midnight on the first day and cease at midnight on the next, having listed consecutively all activities undertaken during the intervening period, as in the study by Chapin and Hightower; or whether it should be laid out in specific time intervals as well as including the opportunity for respondents to indicate the times at which activities are begun and ended, as in the Robinson and Converse study; and if the latter, what length should these time intervals be? An illustration of the two different approaches is shown in Figure 6.

There are sound arguments in favour of both of these systems. The major argument for the use of time intervals is that these provide a useful frame of reference for respondents; that without them, they would tend to 'lose track' of parts of the day and would be tempted to miss out activities with a very short duration—say, five or ten minutes—since they would tend to envisage these as being insignificant in the context of a full 24-hour period. With time intervals, however, such short-term activities would remain significant for the respondent because he would see them within the context of the time interval—say, the hour or half-hour—in which they take place; especially if, as requested, the respondent fills in the diary at regular intervals throughout the day rather than at a single sitting late in the day. Against this, however, is the argument that respondents are susceptible to suggestion and that, by introducing time intervals, they will obtain the impression that the day falls naturally into such intervals and will, therefore, make the duration of activities correspond broadly with the duration of the time intervals. It is argued in particular, that respondents will be confused in their recording of activities which encompass more than one time interval. This problem is avoided by the use of a diary with no time intervals.

The three previous time budget studies which had been examined in some detail gave no clue to the strength of these conflicting arguments. Moreover, the pilot survey for the present study was too small to effectively test them. In the event, therefore, the decision about which approach to adopt had to be based upon judgement. On balance, it was felt that the use of time intervals would be more helpful to respondents than their absence. A major factor influencing this decision was the statement made by Converse, in discussion, that the use of time intervals had not confused his respondents in their recording of activities which encompassed more than one time interval. The view was supported by the results of the small pilot survey carried out as part of the present study. This did not, of course, provide a solution to the argument that respondents are susceptible to suggestion and will record the duration of their activities to correspond with the duration of the given time intervals. It was decided, however, that this danger was preferable to the possibility that activities of a short duration would not be recorded at all. It should be stressed, however, that this decision was taken on the basis of judgement; it did not derive from the objective findings of previous research.

Having decided to make use of time intervals, there remained the problem of determining what should be the length of these. The choice effectively lay between intervals of one hour and of a half-hour, as these were the only ones that had been used in previous studies. Again, there was no clear evidence to suggest that one approach was obviously better than another. Bearing in mind, therefore, the argument that respondents could be induced to record the duration of activities to correspond with the duration of the given time intervals, it was decided to reduce the chances of this occurring, as far as possible, by utilizing the longer time interval rather than the shorter one. Accordingly, the diary was laid out in time intervals of one hour, as shown in the first illustration in Figure 6.

Although these decisions were taken largely on the basis of judgement, it was intended to test them by analysis of some of the data obtained from the survey. There were two main proposals: to analyse activities in terms of the length of time spent on each, on each occasion that it was undertaken; and to examine activity-occasions to see what proportion was recorded as being finished at the end of each (hourly) time interval on the diary. The former proposal would serve two purposes. First, it might help to indicate whether, in fact, respondents are susceptible to suggestion in respect of the recording of the duration of activities. In other words, if a disproportionate number of activity-occasions were found to have lasted about one hour, this would be prima facie evidence that there could be some substance in the argument. If, on the other hand, this were found not to be the case, then there would be good grounds for believing that the argument is spurious. Neither result would provide conclusive evidence, but both could provide a basis against which the findings from the second investigation could be cast. If a disproportionate number of activity-occasions were found to have lasted about one hour *and* a significant number of activity-occasions proved to have been recorded as finishing on the hour, then the probability would have been strengthened that the recording of the duration of activities is influenced by the time intervals into which the diary is divided.

1. The Time Budget Diary with Time Intervals

TIME PERIOD	ACTIVITY	TIME	
		Began	Ended
12.00noon	Lunch	12. 00	12. 40
	Washing up	12. 40	1. 00
1.00 p.m.			
	Reading Magazine	1. 00	1. 45
	Listening to the Radio		
2.00 p.m.	Gardening	1. 45	
			2. 45
3.00 p.m.	Made a cup of tea	2. 45	3. 00

2. The Time Budget Diary with no Time Intervals

ACTIVITY	TIME	
	Began	Ended
Lunch	12.00noon	12 .40
Washing up	12. 40	1. 00
Reading Magazine , Listening to the Radio	1. 00	1. 45
Gardening	1. 45	2. 45
Made a cup of tea	2. 45	3. 00

Figure 6. Examples of time budget diaries With and Without time intervals

If the opposite were found to be the case, then the opposite probability would have been strengthened. The second purpose in the analysis of the duration of activity-occasions was to see whether it could help to indicate the most suitable length of time intervals to be used in future diary studies—if of course the latter were found not to have significant detrimental effects anyway. If it were found, for example, that the great majority of activities lasted for about half an hour, then there could be a case for dividing the diary, in future studies, into time intervals of this length.

The results of the first exercise are shown in Table 24 and those of the second in Table 25. One particular point should be made in respect of these. It was noted earlier that the numbers of usable diaries obtained from the survey varied considerably between the seven days of the week. The first task, therefore, was to work out formulae whereby the figures for each separate day could be converted to a common base. This was then followed, in the case of Table 24, by all activity-occasions being classified according to their durations, the classes being at 15-minute intervals up to 90 minutes, and at 30-minute intervals thereafter.* The resulting values were then weighted. In the case of Table 25, each activity-occasion was classified into one of two groups, according to whether or not it was recorded as being completed on the hour. These values have not been weighted.

The data in Table 24 show that, of a total of 3,645 activity-occasions, more than half lasted for a period of 30 minutes or less—25 per cent for 15 minutes or less and 27 per cent for between 16 and 30 minutes. A further 22 per cent lasted between 31 and 60 minutes. Thus, the overall proportion of activity-occasions lasting for one hour or less was 74 per cent. The only significant variation from this pattern occurred for Sunday: in this case, the proportion of activity-occasions lasting for 15 minutes or less was only 15 per cent. (But even the figures for Sunday conformed to the overall pattern in respect of activity-occasions lasting for one hour or less—71 per cent as compared with the average for seven days of 74 per cent. Perhaps it is simply that people do not have to 'make haste' quite so much on Sundays as on other days!)

The proportion of activity-occasions lasting for between 46 and 60 minutes—that is, those which might be immediately affected by the use of one-hour time intervals in the diary—was relatively low, 12 per cent overall. While this does not prove that the use of such intervals has no effect upon the recording of activity durations, it certainly does not suggest that they have a major effect.

This latter conclusion is further supported by the data in Table 25. This shows the number of activity-occasions recorded as ending on the hour, as a proportion of the total number of occasions that could

---

* In fact, since respondents always recorded times to the nearest 5 minutes, each class really consisted of only three possible durations: the class 46–60 minutes, for example, included activity occasions lasting 50 minutes, 55 minutes and 60 minutes.

F   161

Table 24. Duration of Activity Occasions, By Day of the Week (Weighted)

DAY OF THE WEEK	Total		DURATION OF ACTIVITY-OCCASIONS (IN MINUTES)									180 and over
	No.	%	0-15 %	15-30 %	31-45 %	46-60 %	61-75 %	76-90 %	91-120 %	121-150 %	151-180 %	%
Monday	534	100	20	31	12	12	2	5	6	2	1	5
Tuesday	552	100	30	22	8	15	1	5	6	3	3	8
Wednesday	566	100	29	30	8	7	4	5	5	3	3	8
Thursday	515	100	26	28	9	11	2	4	4	3	2	11
Friday	525	100	27	24	8	15	3	3	5	3	4	8
Saturday	500	100	24	26	10	13	2	3	7	3	2	11
Sunday	453	100	15	29	10	18	5	8	3	2	2	8
Total	3,645	100	25	27	9	12	3	4	5	3	2	9

have been recorded—that is, the total number of diary-hours of respondents. It shows a value of 29 per cent, or an *average* of 7 hours in every 24. It is obvious that, for many people, there will always be a given number of activity-occasions which, by circumstance, end on the hour: the working day, and lunch breaks, for example, often begin and end on the hour for many workers. The salient question, therefore is whether the average of 7 such hours in every 24 is a true reflection of the actual situation, or whether it has been increased above the true average by a tendency among respondents to record activity-occasions as ending on the hour simply because the diary was laid out in hourly intervals. There can be no sure answer to this, but a

Table 25. *Activity-Occasions Ending on the Hour as a Proportion of Total Diary-Hours*

DAY	TOTAL DIARY-HOURS		ACTIVITY-OCCASIONS ENDING ON THE HOUR	
	No.	per cent	No.	per cent
Monday	336	100	108	32
Tuesday	576	100	163	28
Wednesday	480	100	132	28
Thursday	576	100	160	28
Friday	528	100	158	30
Saturday	648	100	186	29
Sunday	600	100	168	28
Total	3,744	100	1,075	29

reasonable estimate would be that it is not significantly above the true average. Thus, for example, a person whose working day begins at 9 a.m. and ends at 5 p.m. and whose lunch break lasts from 1 p.m. to 2 p.m.—an average office worker in any major city—will have at least four activity-occasions ending on the hour on each workday. It only requires that travel time to and from work should begin and end on the hour, to give a figure equal to the average shown for the present study. Of course, the figures shown in Table 25 do not refer solely to office workers and to workdays. Moreover, it is always doubtful logic to compare individual examples with an average. But, in the absence of more precise data, such an exercise does provide some kind of yardstick against which to compare the findings of Table 25. What is really needed is a controlled experiment in which the recorded activities of respondents could be matched against observed behaviour or objective evidence from other sources. Failing this, however, the balance of evidence from the present study must be that the use of time intervals in the design of the diary does not appear to have had a significant effect in causing respondents to record activities as beginning and ending concurrently with these time intervals. This conclusion is, however, based upon a value judgement, albeit a considered one. The whole question clearly warrants further empirical study.

As for the problem of which time intervals to use, the evidence in Table 24 clearly indicates that the majority of activity-occasions are of half an hour's duration or less. This would seem to imply that the time interval which would serve most usefully as a frame of reference for respondents would be the half-hour. This was, in fact, the length of interval used in the British Broadcasting Corporation's study in 1960, although there was no evidence to show that this particular level was chosen on the basis of any objective tests of alternatives. The only reservation that should be made in suggesting the half-hour interval concerns its possible effects in confusing respondents in their recording of activities which last for longer than one time interval. Converse stated that the use of one-hour intervals did not appear to have much confusing effect and that there were certainly few instances of large gaps in time sequences (although there were instances of small gaps of 5 or 10 minutes). But, with hourly intervals, the diary is only divided into twenty-four blocks: with half-hourly intervals it would consist of forty-eight blocks. The basic problem is to secure a satisfactory balance between the use of time intervals as a frame of reference for the respondent and the need to minimize the chances of respondents recording the duration of activities to correspond with the beginning and end of these intervals. The hourly intervals used in the present study appear to have largely achieved this. It may be, however, that half-hourly intervals could be used and still this balance would be achieved.

Coding and Analysis

The fourth major problem encountered in previous research with time budget diaries concerns the coding and analysis of the diary data. All of the previous studies examined have indicated that this is the most difficult problem of all, and the major obstacle to the use of time budget diaries on a large scale in social research. The basic problem is to devise a scheme whereby the free responses of the diarist can be translated into a form suitable for handling by electronic computers, without losing most of the variety and shades of difference in meaning which characterize the free response and constitute its chief advantage over the precoded answer. This is the same problem as occurs with the use of open-ended questions in interview and self-administered surveys. The major difference is that, in this latter case, free responses constitute a relatively small part of the total data obtained; in the case of the time budget diary, on the other hand, *all* of the data are in the form of free responses. What is required, therefore, is a coding system which will incorporate the largest possible number of activities, but still give comparability between individuals and classes of individuals.

In fact, there appear to be two separate but related problems to be tackled. The first is the construction of a system of codes for the recorded activities of the diarists. This raises all kinds of difficulties. Perhaps the most fundamental of these concerns the definition of an activity: when does some particular 'act' qualify to be called an 'activity?' This was a problem which continually occupied Chapin and Hightower. After considerable discussion, it was decided that this could only be satisfactorily determined on an *ad hoc* basis. Effectively, an act qualified to become an activity if sufficient numbers of respondents clearly conceived it as such. Another, equally difficult, problem concerns the grouping of activities: upon the basis of what criteria should activities be grouped together? This problem becomes acute when particular activities can be undertaken simply as a biological function, or for other purposes as well; the activity 'eating' for example, can be undertaken purely for purposes of subsistence or as part of a recreation experience. How, then, should it be coded? These are two examples of the kinds of difficulties encountered in the construction of a coding system for the diaries.

The second basic problem has to do with the construction of a system for transferring the coded data from the diary on to punched cards for mechanical handling. Unless this can be done satisfactorily, there will never be very great scope for the use of time budget diaries in recreation research—indeed, in social research generally—since it is only by mechanical handling that large numbers of diaries can be employed in a study. Manual handling and analysis restricts the number of diaries that can usefully be collected. Difficulties in this arise from the need to devise a system which caters equally for diarists with very different activity patterns. Some diarists will take part in a large number of activities in a given time period, others in a very small number; some will spend a long time engaged in particular activities, others only a short time. Essentially, the chosen system has to account for differences in the numbers of activities undertaken and in the length of time spent on activities.

165

In constructing a system of activity codes, the present study started with the advantage of having the experience of the two previous American studies as a guide.* Both of these studies had produced hierarchical coding systems. The study by Robinson and Converse had two main categories of activity—obligatory or non-leisure activities, and leisure or spare-time activities—which were sub-divided into a total of ninety-six basic activity-groups. Chapin and Hightower, in contrast, had nine major groupings which were divided into sixty-two basic activity-groups, some of which were further subdivided.† These two groupings proved to be an extremely valuable guide for the present study, though neither was wholly appropriate to a British context. Their chief value lay in their demonstration of the need for a tiered system of codes, with basic activity-groups divided into sub-groups.

This evidence that the coding system should be hierarchical also helped in tackling the problem of defining an activity. An examination of the thirty-eight completed diaries obtained from the pilot survey suggested that a three-tier coding system, similar to that used by Chapin and Hightower, should be adopted. The primary code would identify the *major category of activity*—for example, home and personal activities, work, recreation and so on. The secondary code would identify the *basic activity-groups* within these categories: for example, in the recreation category there would be groups for organized team games, outdoor sports, indoor sports, water-based activities, and so on. Finally, the tertiary code would identify *particular activities*; for example, within the activity-group for organized team games would be soccer, cricket, rugby, hockey, netball, and so on. By having a three-tier system of this kind, it was possible to add particular activities at the tertiary level on an *ad hoc* basis while the coding was actually in progress. If a particular act was mentioned frequently and was not already allocated a code, it could be given one from the unallocated tertiary codes. All previous recordings of this act, which would have been coded as 'other' or 'miscellaneous' activities, could then be recoded.‡

* The lack of any substantial methodological information about the B.B.C. study in this country ruled out the possibility of this being a helpful guide to the present study.
† See Chapter 1, pp. 56–57.
‡ This procedure is not, in fact, as laborious and time-consuming as might appear. The Survey Research Center, at the University of Michigan, has devised a system, based upon the attachment of a small card to schedules in which a free response has been coded as 'other', which enables subsequent recoding to be done relatively quickly and efficiently.

Reference was made, in constructing the primary codes, to both of the previous American studies, as well as to various general classifications of major human activities that have been advanced in recent medical, economic and other writings. Discussions were also held with many kinds of people from very different walks of life: indeed, the topic proved to be a major source of conversation at a wide range of social gatherings! Yet, from this wide diversity of sources a remarkably consistent general pattern emerged. Activities were seen, broadly, as being encompassed in nine major categories: (i) personal and family activities; (ii) home activities; (iii) work; (iv) education; (v) religious activities; (vi) social and cultural activities; (vii) recreation; (viii) travel; and (ix) shopping. Six of these categories compare directly with those used by Chapin and Hightower. The remaining three were included by them in other categories, while their own system had three categories not mentioned here: participation in club activities, participation in community service and political activities, and activities associated with food, shelter, medical and similar needs. All of these would be included here within one or other of the categories outlined above.

It was thought at first that these nine major categories could provide the primary codes for the present study. It soon became apparent, however, that this would not work. There were too many activities mentioned in the diaries obtained from the pilot survey which could have been included within two or more of these major groupings. Is gardening for example a home activity or a recreation? And what about visits to a church-based youth club or voluntary service group: are these religious, or social and cultural, or recreation? It seemed appropriate, therefore, to take these nine major categories as a starting point and to search for significant overlaps between them. At the same time, the opportunity was taken to remove 'travel' as a major category but to include it within other major categories according to its purpose. Thus, travel to and from work would be included as a basic activity-group within the major category of 'work'; travel to and from school would be included within the category of 'education'; and so on. As a result of this exercise, six primary codes were finally devised, as shown in Table 26.

Secondary codes were intended to identify basic activity-groups within major categories, while tertiary codes identified actual activities. Both sets of codes were constructed upon the basis of the evidence from the American studies, the findings of the pilot survey, and value judgement. They also included some activities identified on an *ad hoc* basis during the coding process itself. The full list of three-figure codes which were finally employed is given below in Table 26. It will be seen that in many cases there are spare codes at both the secondary and tertiary levels. This means that, in future large-scale studies, it

Table 26. *Activity Codes Employed for the Analysis of the Time Budget Diaries*

PRIMARY CODE	SECONDARY CODE	TERTIARY CODE	ACTIVITY
0			HOME AND PERSONAL
	00		HOMEMAKING
		000	Housework (unspecified)
		001	Washing, laundering, ironing
		002	Mending, sewing
		003	Preparing and serving food
		004	Washing dishes
		005	Vacuum cleaning, dusting, polishing
		006	Laying, lighting, cleaning fire
		007	Bedmaking
	01		HOME MAINTENANCE AND REPAIRS
		010	Maintenance, repairs (unspecified)
		011	Wallpapering, decorating
		012	Painting
		013	Odd jobs
	02		CHILD CARE
		020	Child care (unspecified)
		021	Feeding
		022	Bathing, washing
		023	Dressing, changing
		024	Putting to bed
		025	Reading to child
	03		EATING AT HOME
		030	Breakfast
		031	Lunch, Midday dinner
		032	Tea
		033	Evening dinner, supper
		034	Snack
		035	Morning tea
		036	Elevenses
		037	Other (e.g. drinks)

Table 26 (*continued*)

PRIMARY CODE	SECONDARY CODE	TERTIARY CODE	ACTIVITY
04			PERSONAL HYGIENE AT HOME
		040	Personal hygiene (unspecified)
		041	Washing
		042	Taking a bath
		043	Shaving
		044	Putting on make-up
		045	Washing hair
		046	Getting dressed
		047	Process of going to bed
		048	Preparing to go out
	05		LEISURE AND SOCIAL AT HOME
		050	Lesiure, social (unspecified)
		051	Entertaining visitors
		052	Reading
		053	Listening to radio, records tapes
		054	Watching T.V./home movies
		055	Hobbies (e.g. music, models)
		056	Games (e.g. cards, darts)
		057	Crafts (e.g. knitting, dressmaking)
		058	Playing with children
		059	Relaxing, resting, dozing
	06		HOME AND PERSONAL (MISCELLANEOUS)
		060	At home (unspecified)
		061	Care of pets, animals
		062	Gardening
		063	Work brought home
		064	School and college homework
		065	Club/group meeting in the home
		066	Letter writing/telephoning
		067	Home accounts
		068	Other activities at home
	07		SLEEP
		070	Asleep

169

Table 26 (*continued*)

PRIMARY CODE	SECONDARY CODE	TERTIARY CODE	ACTIVITY
1			WORK
	10		AT PLACE OF EMPLOYMENT
		100	Work
		101	Overtime
		102	Lunch, tea break
	11		TRAVEL TO AND FROM WORK
		110	Travel (unspecified)
		111	Travel on foot
		112	Travel by bicycle
		113	Travel by motor cycle/moped/ scooter
		114	Travel by car
		115	Travel by bus/coach
		116	Travel by train
		117	Travel by other means
	12		HOME-BASED EMPLOYMENT
		120	Work
		121	Business correspondence
2			EDUCATION
	20		SCHOOL
		200	School (unspecified)
		201	Lessons
		202	Assembly
		203	Plays, concerts, rehearsals
		204	Recreation, break
		205	Sport
		206	Exams
		207	Free period
	21		FURTHER AND HIGHER EDUCATION
		210	Classes and lectures
		211	Private work
		212	Tutorials
	22		EVENING CLASSES
		220	Evening classes
	23		EDUCATION-RELATED TRAVEL
		230	Travel (unspecified)
		231	Travel on foot

Table 26 (*continued*)

PRIMARY CODE	SECONDARY CODE	TERTIARY CODE	ACTIVITY
		232	Travel by bicycle
		233	Travel by motor cycle/moped scooter
		234	Travel by car
		235	Travel by bus/coach
		236	Travel by train
		237	Travel by other means
	24		EATING
		240	Tea, coffee, milk break
		241	Lunch break
3			SOCIAL, CULTURAL AND ENTERTAINMENT
	30		GATHERINGS (NOT CLUBS)
		300	Gatherings (unspecified)
		301	Visiting friends, relatives
		302	Parties
		303	Visit to the pub
	31		CLUB
		310	Club (unspecified)
		311	Specific interest club
		312	Sports club
		313	Old people's club
		314	Men's/women's club
		315	Youth club
		316	Community centre/church club
		317	Work-based social club
		318	Other social club
		319	Other club
	32		PUBLIC FACILITIES
		320	Museum, art gallery
		321	Library
	33		SPORTS
		330	Watching sport (unspecified)
		331	Watching Soccer
		332	Watching rugby
		333	Watching horse racing
		334	Watching greyhound racing

Table 26 (*continued*)

PRIMARY CODE	SECONDARY CODE	TERTIARY CODE	ACTIVITY
		335	Watching motor/motor-cycle racing
		336	Watching other sport
	34		ENTERTAINMENT
		340	Entertainment (unspecified)
		341	Theatre, pantomime
		342	Concert (all kinds)
		343	Discotheque
		344	Nightclub
		345	Dance
		346	Bingo
		347	Cinema
		348	Ice/roller skating (watching only)
	35		RELATED TRAVEL
		350	Travel (unspecified)
		351	Travel on foot
		352	Travel by bicycle
		353	Travel by motor cycle/moped/scooter
		354	Travel by car
		355	Travel by bus/coach
		356	Travel by train
		357	Travel by other means
	36		EATING OUT
		360	Breakfast
		361	Lunch, midday dinner
		362	Tea
		363	Evening dinner, supper
		364	Snacks
		365	Elevenses
	37		SOCIAL (MISCELLANEOUS)
		370	Going out (unspecified)
4			RECREATION
	40		ORGANIZED TEAM GAMES
		400	Soccer
		401	Rugby
		402	Cricket

Table 26 (*continued*)

PRIMARY CODE	SECONDARY CODE	TERTIARY CODE	ACTIVITY
		403	Hockey
		404	Netball
		405	Lacrosse
	41		OUTDOOR SPORTS
		410	Tennis
		411	Golf
		412	Outdoor bowls
		413	Archery
		414	Athletics
		415	Motor/motor-cycle/go-kart racing
		416	Scrambles
		417	Rallies
		418	Winter sports
		419	Flying, gliding, sky-diving
	42		INDOOR SPORTS
		420	Basketball
		421	Squash
		422	Badminton
		423	Table tennis
		424	Tenpin bowling
		425	Fencing
		426	Ice/roller skating
		427	Boxing/wrestling
		428	Judo/karate
		429	Keep fit/gymnastics
	43		WATER-BASED ACTIVITIES
		430	Swimming
		431	Fishing
		432	Surfing
		433	Water skiing
		434	Aqualung diving
		435	Sailing
		436	Rowing
		437	Canoeing
		438	Motor-boat cruising
		439	Messing around in boats
	44		OUTDOOR ACTIVITIES
		440	Mountaineering, climbing
		441	Hill walking, rambling

173

Table 26 (*continued*)

PRIMARY CODE	SECONDARY CODE	TERTIARY CODE	ACTIVITY
		442	Pot-holing
		443	Horse riding
		444	Hunting
		445	Cycling
		446	Camping, youth hostelling, Caravanning
		447	Picnicking
		448	Driving in the country
		449	Rambling
	45		RECREATION-RELATED TRAVEL
		450	Travel (unspecified)
		451	Travel on foot
		452	Travel by bicycle
		453	Travel by motor cycle/moped/ scooter
		454	Travel by car
		455	Travel by bus/coach
		456	Travel by train
		457	Travel by other means
	46		RECREATION (MISCELLANEOUS)
		460	Playing with the children
5			MISCELLANEOUS ACTIVITIES
	50		SHOPPING
		500	Shopping (general/unspecified)
		501	Christmas shopping
	51		SERVICES
		510	Laundrette
		511	Post office, letter box, collect pension
		512	Go to the garage
		513	Hairdresser/barber
		514	Other services
	52		TRAVEL RELATED TO MISCELLANEOUS ACTIVITIES
		520	Travel (unspecified)
		521	Travel on foot
		522	Travel by bicycle

Table 26 (*continued*)

PRIMARY CODE	SECONDARY CODE	TERTIARY CODE	ACTIVITY
		523	Travel by motor cycle/moped/scooter
		524	Travel by car
		525	Travel by bus/coach
		526	Travel by train
		527	Travel by other means
	53		OTHER MISCELLANEOUS ACTIVITIES
		530	Church
		531	Doctor/Dentist/visit to hospital (outpatients)
		532	Filling in diary
		533	Other miscellaneous activities (e.g. being interviewed)
6			
No Information			
	60		NO INFORMATION
		600	No information generally
		601	No information, but activity at home
		602	No information, but activity outside the home

will be possible to add codes for activities which may be significant in terms of a large study, but which were not mentioned by respondents to the present, relatively small study.

There is little more that need be said about the construction of the coding system. On the basis of the evidence from the two American studies, the findings of the pilot survey, and judgement, a system was constructed which took account of every activity mentioned by the 156 respondents who completed usable diaries. The system does have one ususual feature, however, which is worth particular mention. In addition to asking for information about what was being done, the diary also requested respondents to indicate where it was being undertaken and with whom. A separate coding system was devised to record the latter information which is shown in Table 27, but the former has been incorporated, in general terms, in the activity codes. That is, the system distinguishes between activities which take place inside the home and those which take place outside it. Thus, even activities within major categories—for example, recreation—will be coded under the primary category of *Home and Personal* if they take place within the home. For planning purposes, therefore, an easy and immediate distinction can be drawn, in analysis, between home-based activities and those which require other facilities or areas of land. If, however, more detailed locational information is desired, then a separate system of locational codes will be required.

The second basic problem in coding and analysis has to do with the construction of a system for transferring the coded data from the diary on to punched cards for mechanical handling. Essentially, the chosen system had to take account of two factors: differences in the numbers of activities undertaken by different individuals in any given

Table 27. *Company Codes Employed for the Analysis of the Time Budget Diaries*

CODE	COMPANY
0	No reply
1	Alone
2	Spouse
3	Spouse and child(ren)
4	Child(ren)
5	Parent(s) and/or brother(s) and/or sister(s)
6	Other relatives
7	Friend(s)
8	Workmates/colleagues
9	With a crowd

time period, and differences in the lengths of time spent on each activity by each individual. Furthermore, the problems caused by these two factors were often compounded by the manner in which information had been recorded by the diarists. Thus, for example, there were often small gaps present in the time-sequences recorded; and, sometimes, two non-parallel, but consecutive, activities were given a single time-span. An illustration of this kind of problem can be seen in Table 28. An entry of the kind shown here does not indicate the amount of time spent on each of the following activities: walking to the bus stop and waiting for the bus, travelling on the bus, and walking from the bus stop to the place of work. Examples of this kind occurred frequently—for example, 'eating' and 'washing up'—and complicated the calculation of activity durations. This error was also often coupled with a total loss of time in the recording: in the above example, the period of time between 'arrived at work' and 'commenced work' had not been accounted for. A reasonable assumption would be that this time had been spent in preparing for work, and it could, therefore, be coded accordingly. Similarly, the first problem could be solved simply by recording the whole time period with the general code for 'travel to work'. Obviously, there were many instances where adjustments of this nature had to be made if large numbers of the diaries were not to be discarded as incomplete and unusable. It was important, however, that a precise and consistent procedure should be laid down for the coding of blank periods and multiple activities.

Errors of the kind illustrated above merely served, however, to compound the difficulties arising from differences in the numbers of activities undertaken by individuals and in the length of time spent on each activity. What was being sought from the chosen system was

Table 28. *An Illustration of Two Common Recording Errors in Time Budget Diaries*

ACTIVITY	TIME	
	Began	*Ended*
Left home	8·00	
Arrived at work—by bus		9.00
Commenced work	9.15	

easy comparability between individuals and classes of individuals—for example, all persons below the age of 21 years compared with all persons above this age. Such comparisons would usually be made either for particular times of the day, or for the duration of particular activities. Thus, one might want to compare the numbers of persons below the age of 21 years who were watching television between 8 p.m. and 9 p.m. with the numbers of persons above this age who were doing so. Or, alternatively, the comparison might be made between the respective numbers who watched television for a period of at least one hour during a particular evening. The time-coding system had, therefore, to take account of both of these factors.

The general plan that was first proposed was to represent a particular section of the day on a separate punched card; but, within this, to record the duration of each activity undertaken rather than the time at which it was commenced. It was suggested that each card should represent a period of one hour, giving a total of twenty-four cards for each respondent-day. The attraction of this scheme was the ease with which it took account of the two sets of data indicated above as being of key importance. The duration of each activity undertaken during the hour would be actually recorded, in minutes, after the activity, while the time span within which these activities occurred—that is, the particular hour of the day—would be recorded in the identification code for each card. With each card containing a total of eighty columns, eight of which would be required for identification purposes, there would be considerable space for recording activities. Each activity would, in fact, require six columns—three for the activity code, two for its duration, and one for the company code (outlined earlier in Table 27). Thus, each card could take account of up to twelve activities; and since the evidence from the pilot survey had indicated that the maximum number of activities recorded during any single hour was five, there was clearly ample space to account for an hour on each card.

In principle, therefore, this general plan was adopted. In practice, however, two problems readily became apparent which called for modification of the general plan. The first of these concerned activities which overran the end of an hour. As was indicated in Table 25, there were, on average, only seven hours in twenty-four for which an activity was recorded as ending on the hour, leaving an average of seventeen hours in which the last activity undertaken would overlap into the next hour. How, then, should these activities be recorded? Several alternative schemes were considered. The first suggestion was that space be provided at the beginning of each card in which to record the time at which the first activity on that card was commenced. This was finally rejected, however, on the grounds that it complicated unnecessarily the general principle. Having decided not to record times at all but merely to have each card representing a particular hour in which activity-durations were recorded, it was thought that to now introduce some recording of times would tend to confuse coders. A second suggestion was that each card should carry the full duration of each activity. This also was rejected, on the grounds that there would then be values represented on an hourly card which would be in excess of sixty minutes. This would complicate the analysis of activities for a single hour. The whole point of having separate cards for each hour was that these could be run separately through the computer to give the pattern of activity during any particular hour of the day, without having to run through all other cards as well. Other alternatives were also considered, but only one fully satisfied the two key constraints—that the cards should give durations of activities within each hour, but that total durations should also be measurable. This system required that the final column on each card should be reserved to indicate whether or not there was an overlap, on to the next card, of the final activity on this card. In addition, two columns were reserved at the beginning of each card, immediately after the identification data, to record the duration of the overlap from the previous card. In considering total activity durations the computer could sum all overlaps; but in considering particular hours it could ignore them.

The other problem which became apparent arose from the need to record situations in which two activities, such as 'knitting' and 'watching television', were undertaken concurrently; or in which two consecutive activities, such as 'eating' and 'washing the dishes', were recorded with a single time span. The first decision that had to be made was how to treat the latter situation. The alternatives were basically twofold: either they could be recorded as concurrent activities, or the total time spent on them could be divided between the two of them in some predetermined and arbitrary proportion. In the event, it was decided to take the former course of action and to treat them as concurrent activities. This meant that the records of the respondents would not be subjectively adjusted in any way by the investigator. Furthermore, it was argued that, in giving the two activities a single time span, the diarist was indicating that, for practical purposes, they constituted a single activity anyway. Hence, to record them as concurrent, though they were not strictly this, would serve to emphasize this point.

Making allowance for concurrent activities in the coding system proved to be quite simple. The number of columns allocated to each activity was merely doubled so as to provide space for the recording of a concurrent activity. This reduced the total figure for the number of activities that could be included on one card, but the new figure was still more than adequate to cover the maximum likely number of activities.

One final alteration was made to the system before it was finally put into practice. The evidence of the pilot survey had shown that, for the majority of people, the first six hours of the day are largely inactive because they are asleep. This impression was confirmed by a rapid, though superficial, examination of the completed diaries from the main survey. It was proposed, therefore, that a single card should be used to cover these six hours, rather than having one card for each hour. Before accepting this proposal, however, an analysis was made of the activities of the few night workers in the survey during these six hours, to see whether the number of activities undertaken by them during this period could be accounted for on a single card.

179

This proved to be possible and therefore the proposal was adopted. As a result, adjustments had to be made to the numbers of columns made available for recording activity durations, since there was now the possibility, on the first card, of having a three-figure number—that is 360 minutes.

An example of the system that was finally employed is given in Figure 7. This has been completed for an hour taken from one of the

Subject	Punch	Col.	Subject	Punch	Col.	Subject	Punch	Col.
Respondent	0	1	Third	1	32	Sixth		62
Number	4	2	Activity	0	33	Activity		63
Card	0	3		0	34			64
Number	4	4	Concurrent	X	35	Concurrent		65
Household	0	5	Activity	X	36	Activity		66
Number	0	6		X	37			67
	9	7		0	38			68
Day	6	8	Duration	2	39	Duration		69
				0	40			70
Overlap	0	9	Company	8	41	Company		71
Duration	2	10						
	5	11	Fourth		42	Overlap	1	72
First	1	12	Activity		43			
Activity	0	13			44			
	0	14	Concurrent		45			
Concurrent	X	15	Activity		46			
Activity	X	16			47			
	X	17			48			
	0	18	Duration		49			
Duration	3	19			50			
	0	20	Company		51			
Company	8	21	Fifth		52			
Second	1	22	Activity		53			
Activity	0	23			54			
	2	24	Concurrent		55			
Concurrent	X	25	Activity		56			
Activity	X	26			57			
	X	27			58			
	0	28	Duration		59			
Duration	1	29			60			
	0	30	Company		61			
Company	8	31						

Figure 7. Code sheet for the time budget diaries

diaries actually obtained in the survey. It can be seen that eight columns are reserved for identification. The first two columns give the respondent's position in the household: 01 would be the head of household, 02 the housewife, and so on. The next two columns give the card number, which indicates the period of the day to which the card refers: 00 indicates the period 12 midnight to 6 a.m., 01 the period 6 a.m. to 7 a.m., then at hourly intervals until 18, which indicates the period 11 p.m. to 12 midnight. This card therefore refers to the period from 9 a.m. to 10 a.m. Columns 5–7 are used for recording the number of the household in the survey to which this respondent belongs. Finally, column 8 gives the day of the week to which the diary refers: 0 indicates Sunday, 1 is Monday, and so on, through to 6 for Saturday. The recording of the diary data begins in column 9. The first three columns indicate that the first activity has overlapped from the previous card for a period of twenty-five minutes: that is, it has already been going on for this length of time. Columns 12–14 show what this activity is, while the code X in columns 15–17 shows that there is no concurrent activity involved. Columns 18–20 indicate how long the activity goes on during this particular hour—in this case, thirty minutes. Finally, column 21 indicates with whom the activity is being undertaken. Space is then available for the same information to be given for up to five more activities. In fact, this respondent only took part in a total of three. The final column on the card, number 72, shows whether or not there is an overlap from this card to the next one: 0 means that there is no overlap, 1 means that there is. In this case, the third activity does overlap into the next hour.

Comment

This research has demonstrated that the major methodological problems associated with the use of time budget diaries for recreation research can be successfully overcome. There is no doubt, however, that they are more complicated, and involve more laborious coding operations, than interview and self-administered surveys. It may reasonably be asked, therefore, whether the method is worth the extra time, money and manpower that it requires. What, in fact, are the benefits obtainable from a time budget survey that cannot be obtained equally well from an interview or self-administered survey? Are there particular, unique data to be got from time budgets? And, if so, are these data useful for tackling definable recreation planning problems? Or are time budgets, as so far developed, an interesting research tool but one with little applied value? What, in other words, are the returns to be derived as compensation for the extra resources that are used in undertaking a time budget survey rather than using more-established social research techniques?

The particular value of time budget diaries in recreation research lies in the picture that they give of the relationships between recreation and other activities, especially as regards the length of time spent on recreation pursuits and their distribution throughout a day or longer period. These latter factors cannot be covered easily in an interview or self-administered survey (as witness the difficulties encountered in the pilot survey when the attempt was made to introduce a simple twofold time element—winter and summer). Yet, they have considerable implications for recreation planning. The length of time that people have available for different kinds of recreation activities, for example, will have direct implications for the distances that they can travel, or are prepared to travel, to seek facilities for these. This, in turn, has implications for the location and siting of facilities.* Again, the timing of activities throughout the day can help in the formulation of management policies for various kinds of recreation facilities. If public municipal parks, for example, are used most heavily between the hours of 12 noon and 2 p.m., it might be unwise to carry out major maintenance works in them during this time. These are just two examples of the kinds of use that can be made of time budget data. No attempt will be made here to analyse the actual data obtained from the present study. Its objectives were methodological—to suggest guidelines for the carrying out of future studies. This it has done. A system has been devised for transferring diary data on to punched cards for mechanical handling. A comprehensive code has been developed for activities. And suggestions have been made about the use of time intervals in the design of the diary.

The study would be incomplete, however, without any attempt to show how the analysis of diary data can be undertaken. An example of one way in which data might be examined has, in fact, already been shown in Table 24, which investigated the distribution of all activity-occasions in terms of their duration. This could also be done separately for major categories of activities, one of which, of course, would be recreation. Another example is given by the use of time-block diagrams, as shown in Figure 8. Taken from the data obtained in the two study areas, this illustrates the differences between Saturday and Sunday in the volume and distribution of leisure activities outside the home between the hours of 12 noon and 6 p.m. It is interesting to note how the pattern for Sunday is much more irregular than the one for Saturday. The proportion of respondents engaged in leisure activities outside the home during these hours reached a higher peak on Sunday, but it also rose and fell more sharply over relatively short periods of time. Of course, the data shown here refer to very small numbers of people and cannot in any

* This point has been developed further, into a hierarchical classification of facilities, in Chapter 10.

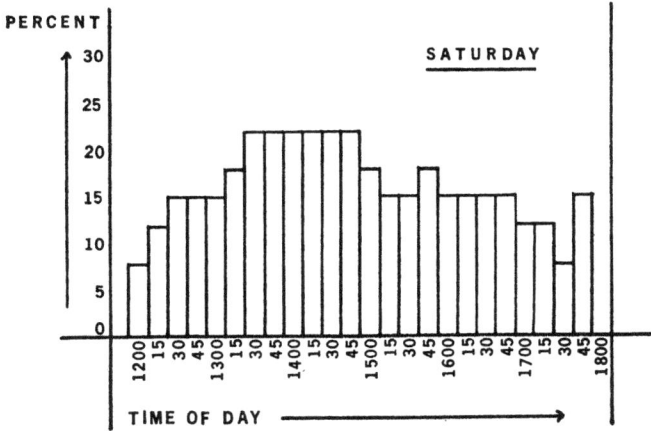

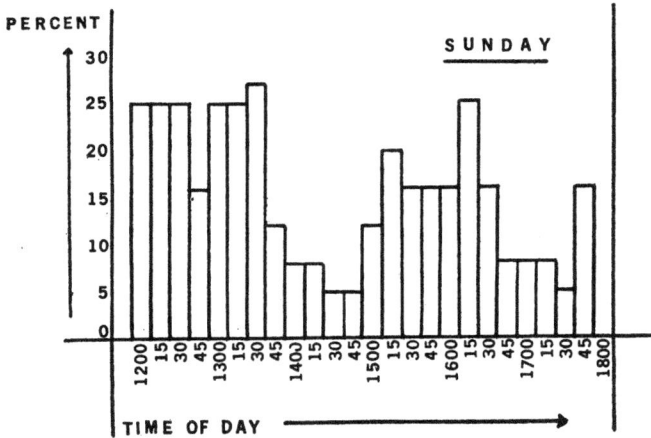

Figure 8. A time-block analysis

way be considered as being representative of the total population of the two study areas. It does illustrate, however, one of the main ways in which time budget data can be analysed for planning and administrative purposes. If, for example, the data shown here were

183

representative of a wider population, conclusions might be drawn about the optimum management policies for various kinds of leisure facilities on the two separate days, about optimum pricing policies for such facilities, and about the location and siting of additional facilities. Moreover, if it proved possible to provide this information for various sub-classes of the population—for instance, different income groups—there might then be scope for utilizing it within a predictive model of some kind. The application of time budget data to forecasting has received no attention to date, but it is certain that the problem will be increasingly considered in future research. For the meantime, however, the main value of such data appears to be for short-term—day to day, week to week and season to season—management purposes.

Chapter 8

Recreation Types

One of the primary objectives of the household and activities survey was to obtain the kind of data that would facilitate further testing of the concept of recreation types hypothesized by Proctor [43]. Respondents to the activities questionnaire were asked to indicate how many of 60 recreation activities they had ever undertaken during 1968. These data were then subjected to cluster and factor analyses to establish whether or not respondents could be grouped into types according to those activities in which they had participated. The purpose was to identify persons whose recreation activities could be grouped together on the basis of statistically significant relationships in rates of participation. That is, it could be argued that people are more likely to take part in several activities within a given group of activities than to take part in those which fall into different groups. Proctor's study had examined this concept, by using factor analysis, for 15 outdoor recreation activities.* The objective in the present study was to extend the scope of the concept, firstly, by applying two different kinds of analytical technique—cluster analysis as well as factor analysis—and secondly, by considering much greater numbers of activities.

The identification of definite and consistent recreation types could have considerable value for recreation planning. For example, such types could provide a more stable basis for recreation demand forecasting than individual recreation pursuits would do. This is because participation in individual pursuits could be expected to fluctuate more widely in response to changing parameters—such as, for example, climate and fashion—than participation in a group of pursuits. Again, knowledge of stable recreation types could help in the planning of recreation alternatives, or substitutes. That is, faced with a situation in which the resources necessary to provide a particular recreation facility are not available to him, the planner could, on the basis of established recreation types, provide an alternative facility which caters for a pursuit that falls within the same group as the pursuit that would have been provided for by the facility which he is unable to supply. The concept of recreation types would, thus, provide a much-needed element of flexibility in the

* See Chapter 2, pages 78–82.

185

programming and implementation stages of overall recreation planning.

Analytical Techniques

The construction of recreation types was attempted by means of two distinct techniques: cluster analysis and factor analysis. It is not intended here to present a detailed account of the workings of each of these techniques. A full outline of the cluster analysis technique is to be found in McQuitty [135], while a complete guide to factor analysis, for readers who are familiar with the necessary mathematics and statistics, is given by Harman [136]. All that will be given here is a brief description, in relatively non-technical terms, of the mechanics of the two techniques, which will enable non-statistical readers to grasp the essential procedures behind the construction of the various activity groups, or recreation types.

The starting point for the present discussion is a set of elementary definitions. Each recreation activity is designated as a *variable*. Each respondent to the activities questionnaire provides one *observation* on each variable: that is, the respondent has either undertaken the activity at least once during 1968, or he has not done so. If he has participated, then the value of the variable will be 1; if he has not done so, then its value will be zero. The extent to which respondents who participated in one activity also participated in another can be represented by a *correlation coefficient* between the two activities, or variables. This coefficient has three critical values. If every respondent who took part in, say, soccer also took part in cricket, then the correlation coefficient between the two activities will have a value of 1. If none of the respondents who participated in soccer participated in cricket, then the value of the coefficient will be zero. Finally, if all of the respondents who did *not* participate in soccer *did* participate in cricket, then the value of the coefficient will be −1. Obviously, these extreme values do not occur very often when, as in the present study, there are as many as 1,056 respondents. Most of the coefficients will have values lying somewhere between +1 and −1.

Both cluster analysis and factor analysis use these correlation coefficients to group activities, or variables, together. Examination of the coefficients should identify groups of activities which have relatively high correlation coefficients *among themselves*, but relatively low coefficients with activities outside the group, indicating that respondents tend to confine themselves to that set of activities, which, in turn, may reflect the influence of such factors as age, income, personality and life style.

186

Cluster analysis is a simple manual method of handling the set of correlation coefficients. There are several variations of the method, but the one that will be used here is known as McQuitty's elementary linkage method [135]. This works, broadly, as follows. The set of coefficients is first examined to find the one with the highest value. In the example (Figure 9), this is between soccer and cricket. All of the coefficients between soccer and the rest of the variables, and between cricket and the rest of the variables, are then examined to see if the highest coefficient of any other variable is with soccer or cricket. In this case, golf, table tennis and fishing all have their highest co-efficients with soccer, while there are no variables which have their

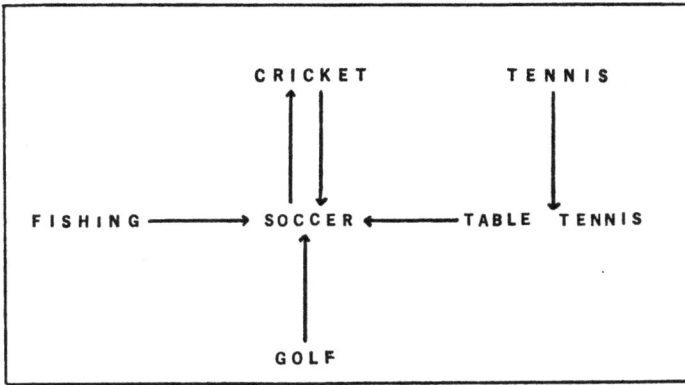

Figure 9. Construction of activity group by cluster analysis

highest coefficients with cricket. Thus, the activity group now com-prises soccer, cricket, golf, table tennis and fishing. The set of co-efficients is now examined again, to see if there are any variables which have their highest coefficients with these last three variables—that is, with golf, table tennis and fishing. This shows that there is one variable, tennis, which has its highest coefficient with table tennis. The procedure now would be to see if there are any other variables which have their highest coefficients with tennis. And so the process would continue until a closed system is obtained; that is, none of the variables inside the group has its highest coefficient with a variable, or variables, outside the group, and none of the variables outside the group has its highest coefficient with a variable, or variables, inside the group. This could happen with as few as two variables. In fact, in

187

the particular example shown here, the system becomes a closed one with six variables—soccer, cricket, golf, table tennis, fishing and tennis. Once one self-contained group has been established, the highest remaining coefficient is found and a new group started, co-efficients involving the original group now being ignored. In this way, all of the variables can be divided into mutually exclusive groups.

The major disadvantage of this method is that it takes account only of the *highest* coefficient between variables. Thus, for example, if the coefficient between soccer and cricket has a value of 0·536, while that for soccer and athletics has a value of 0·535, then soccer and athletics are almost as closely related as soccer and cricket; yet, cricket and athletics could end up in different groups. In fact, a variable could have its highest correlation with another variable in, say, Group I and very low correlations with all other variables in that group; in which case it will be placed in Group I, even though it may have high correlations with many more variables in another group. It is the *highest* correlation alone which determines the group into which a variable will be placed. It is possible to take some account of this problem by examining the *second highest* correlation coefficient as well, a procedure which has been adopted in the present study. In general, these second highest correlations tend to 'follow' the highest correlations and, thereby, make little difference to the final groups obtained. They do, however, provide a useful means of joining together small groups (of two or three variables only) to give larger groups.

Factor analysis overcomes this major weakness of cluster analysis by taking account of *all* of the coefficients and choosing the best groupings by statistical methods. The result is to produce 'factors' rather than groups. Most variables can be identified fairly definitely with *one* particular factor and, in this respect, they resemble groups produced by cluster analysis. But, in fact, *each* variable is related to *each* factor by a *factor coefficient*—although, if the analysis is successful, one of the factor coefficients is usually sufficiently greater than the others to indicate that the variable is closely identified with this one factor. The nature of the factors can be assessed by this identification of variables with single factors, but this assessment is also helped by the other factor coefficients. For example, it might appear that 'active' sports are identified with Factor I. Then, the idea that Factor I was an 'active' factor would be reinforced if 'inactive' sports (identified mainly with other Factors) could be shown to have very low, or even negative, factor coefficients for Factor I.

The Data

The data which were employed in the cluster and factor analyses were derived from the responses to the first question in the Recreation Activities Questionnaire which asked respondents to identify which of 60 listed activities he (or she) had ever undertaken during 1968, even if only once. In addition, each respondent was provided with the opportunity to list other activities that he had undertaken and which had not been included in the precoded list. These latter activities were then grouped, during the coding, into 12 categories—11 individual activities and one group for 'other activities'. This gave a total of 72 activities; but, during the preliminary analysis, it was found that one of these—lacrosse—had had no participants at all among the respondents. Thus, there were 71 possible recreation activities, for which each respondent was recorded as having participated or not participated. There were 1,056 respondents.

The initial cluster and factor analyses employed all 71 activities. But, for several reasons, two other sets of analyses were carried out using smaller numbers of activities. The first of these employed 59 activities; that is, all of the pre-listed and precoded activities except lacrosse. The reasoning behind this approach was that the 12 activities which had not been listed on the questionnaire but which had simply been recorded by respondents in the category of 'other activities' and had later been assigned a separate code were not wholly reflective of the experience of all respondents. The numbers of respondents who indicated participation in these activities might not have given a true picture. In other words, it was reasoned that these activities might have been mentioned only by those respondents who had participated in them fairly regularly, or who had good memories, or who had been particularly conscientious in answering the questionnaire. Other respondents who had actually participated in these particular activities, but only once or twice during the year, might not have bothered, or remembered, to record them. In the light of this reasoning, it was thought worthwhile to carry out separate analyses using only those activities which had actually been listed on the questionnaire seen by the respondents; and then to compare these analyses with those based upon 71 activities.

The second of these additional analyses employed only 40 activities. The reasoning behind this approach was simple. As has been indicated elsewhere in this report, the validity of statistical computations generally declines with decreasing numbers of observations, and becomes highly suspect when very small numbers are involved. That

189

is, a certain minimum *absolute* number within any particular 'cell' is necessary for valid statistical analysis to be undertaken. In the present case, it was decided that, while validity could still be obtained with smaller numbers, an arbitrary requirement of at least 20 participants in any activity would provide an interesting and statistically sound basis for further analysis. In other words, only those activities which had 20 or more participants would be included. There were 40 such activities.

To summarize, therefore, there were 1,056 respondents, each of whom was 'observed' as having participated or not participated in each of 71 recreation activities. Cluster and factor analyses were then carried out in respect of these observations for sets of 71, 59 and 40 activities.

The Cluster Analyses

The cluster analysis based upon 71 activities produced 14 groups, which are shown in Table 29. There were some unexpected relationships which emerged from this grouping process; but, in general, the activities within each group appear to be fairly homogeneous. Moreover, when the analysis was repeated—but this time using only the 59 precoded activities—there was virtually no difference in the groupings. Group XIII ceased to exist, since it was made up entirely of activities which had not been precoded. Apart from this, however, the groups remained the same—except, of course, that the other activities which had not been precoded were no longer present. This was so because all of these were activities which ended groups; that is, each of these activities had its highest correlation coefficient with another activity within its particular group, but no other activity within the group had its highest coefficient with one of these activities. It is worth examining each of the groups a little more closely to show the extent to which the activities within them are homogeneous—and, hence, the extent to which they are not.

Group I consists of 7 activities. All of these, with the exception of *Amateur Dramatics/Music*, are physically active pursuits. Participation in all of them is relatively cheap. All are, to some extent, group activities which are usually undertaken within a team or club setting —although *Cycling* could be an exception to this. All, with the exception of *Cycling*, are usually undertaken in a man-made, urban setting.

Group II consists of 9 activities, all of which are physically active sports. All are, by and large, individual activities rather than team

190

Table 29. *Cluster Analysis Groups Based Upon 71 Activities*

Group I
Rugby
Athletics
Basketball
Badminton
Keep fit
Cycling
Amateur dramatics/Music

Group II
Archery
Go-kart racing
Winter sports
Fencing
Surfing
Water skiing
Aqualung diving
Canoeing
Hunting

Group III
Hill walking
Rambling
Camping/Youth hostelling/
   Caravanning
Walking
Visit to museum/art gallery

Group IV
Soccer
Cricket
Tennis
Golf
Table tennis
Fishing

Group V
Hobbies/Do-it-yourself
Outdoor bowls
Motor racing
Motor-cycle racing
Scrambles
Rallies
Flying/Gliding/Sky diving
Squash
Boxing

Wrestling
Judo/Karate
Other activities

Group VI
Picnicking
Driving in the countryside
Gardening
Dining out
Visit to a pub or club
Bingo
Dancing

Group VII
Visit to a community or church
   centre
Old tyme dancing
Photography

Group VIII
Ice skating
Roller skating
Bird watching
Horse riding
Youth club

Group IX
Sailing
Rowing
Motor-boat cruising
Messing about in boats
Evening classes

Group X
Visit to a cinema
Visit to a theatre/concert
Visit to a library

Group XI
Hockey
Netball
Gymnastics

Group XII
Mountaineering
Pot-holing

Table 29. (*continued*)

Group XIII	*Group XIV*
Painting/Drawing/Sketching	Tenpin bowling
Going to a party	Swimming

pursuits. All, with the exception of *Archery*, involve some personal risk and danger. All require considerable skill; and all are quite expensive in terms of the cost of the equipment that the individual needs for participation.

Group III consists of 5 activities. The odd one out here is a *Visit to a museum/art gallery*. The remaining four activities are all unorganized outdoor pursuits which usually take place in a country-side setting. Participation in all of them is relatively cheap. The four outdoor activities all appear to be adventurous without being risky or hazardous, and little or no skill is required for participation in them. All of them can be individual or group activities. The presence of *Visit to a museum/art gallery* within this group cannot readily be explained. The only point that can definitely be made about it is that it was not a precoded activity, whereas the others were.

Group IV is made up of 6 activities, all of which (with the exception of *Fishing*) require a group of at least two persons for participation. Again with the exception of *Fishing*, all are physically active and competitive sports. All are usually inexpensive for participants—although, in some circumstances, participation in golf can be very costly. Some skill is an advantage to participants, but it is not necessary for participation.

Group V is the largest of all the groups, being made up of 12 activities. It is, perhaps, the most heterogeneous of the groups, although there is also considerable homogeneity between the activities. One of these consists of *Other activities*, about which little that is meaningful can be said. Of the remaining 11 activities, however, all are physically active pursuits—with the possible and occasional exception of *Hobbies/Do-it-yourself*. All, with the exception of *Hobbies/Do-it-yourself* and *Outdoor bowls*, involve some personal risk and danger. All require considerable skill; and, with one or two exceptions, all place a high premium upon speed and rapid reaction. Some are expensive for participants, but others are relatively cheap. Some are group activities, while others can be individual but are often not.

Group VI consists of 7 activities and is probably one of the most homogeneous of all the groups. All of the activities, except *Gardening*, are essentially social activities. All are relatively cheap for participants. Little or no skill is required for any of them, although some basic knowledge is probably necessary for *Gardening*. None of them need be very active physically, although *Gardening* and *Dancing* often are.

Group VII is made up of only 3 activities. The first two of these can readily be explained together, but the third—*Photography*—is certainly an oddity here. The other two are both social activities in which membership of a group is of paramount importance. Both are relatively cheap for participants; and neither requires much skill. The presence of *Photography* in the group, however, cannot be explained—at least not in terms of the characteristics that have generally been considered throughout this discussion. As with *Visits to a museum/art gallery* in Group III, the only point that can be definitely made is that *Photography* was not a precoded activity and the numbers of participants were very small.

Group VIII is, to all appearances, a rather odd group. The only major common thread is that 4 of the 5 activities within the group are predominantly, though not exclusively, young people's activities. All, except *Visit to a youth club*, require some degree of skill to enhance enjoyment, but all can be undertaken by persons with little or no skill. All except *Horse riding*, are relatively cheap for participants. All of them can be undertaken individually or within a group. All, except *Bird watching*, are usually physically active pursuits. The presence of *Bird watching* in the group is, at first glance, rather strange. There is, however, a strong suspicion that respondents have been facetious in their responses about this activity—a suspicion that is reinforced by the fact that this group is youth-oriented; *Bird watching*, as well as being a perfectly normal recreation activity, is also a slang euphemism among teenagers and young adult males for watching attractive girls!

Group IX consists of 5 activities. The odd one here is *Evening classes*, an activity which was not precoded on the questionnaire. The remaining four activities are all water-based pursuits; indeed, all are boating activities. All are at least moderately expensive for the participant. All are basically group activities. All require some amount of skill; and all, with the possible exception of *Motor-boat cruising*, are likely to be physically very demanding.

Group X is one of the most homogeneous of all the groups. It consists of only 3 activities, all of which are, to some extent, cultural pursuits. All are relatively inexpensive for the participant. All are usually indoor, urban activities. None requires a special skill or

G

knowledge, although this is often helpful for *Visits to a theatre/ concert.*

Group XI consists of three very physically active sports. All three are usually team activities, although *Gymnastics* emphasizes more than the other two the performance of the individual within the team. *Hockey* and *Netball* are largely restricted to females, and neither requires a special skill—although, in both cases, skill is an advantage and usually enhances enjoyment. All three activities are relatively inexpensive for the participant. *Gymnastics* fits less comfortably into this group than the other two; but it is worth nothing that it is an activity which was not precoded on the questionnaire.

Group XII consists of two activities which are very homogeneous. Both are physically demanding activities. Both can be done by an individual, but are usually undertaken within a group. Both involve considerable personal risk and danger. Both usually require a great deal of specialized equipment, making them moderately expensive for participants. Both require considerable skill.

The two activities in Group XIII cannot be readily explained in terms of the characteristics that have been cited throughout the rest of this discussion. Generally, there appears to be no common bond between the two activities. Both are activities which were not precoded on the activities questionnaire. Neither activity was recorded by many respondents, although it is suspected that *Going to a party* would have been mentioned by many more respondents if it had been a precoded activity. In the light of these points, it would probably be dangerous to attach much significance to this particular grouping.

Group XIV also consists of only two activities. Both of these are physically active sports. Both take place in capital-intensive structures although neither is very expensive for the participant himself. Both require some minimum level of skill for full enjoyment, but neither places a premium on skill. Both are usually undertaken in small groups, though either could be undertaken alone.

As was suggested earlier, these 14 groups appear to be generally homogeneous in respect of activities *within* groups. Certainly they provide the planner with a good indication of the particular activities which tend to go together—in the sense that people who tend to participate in one activity within a group will be more likely to participate in another activity within that group than in an activity within another group. For some purposes, however, it could be argued that there are too many groups. The range of alternatives open to a planning agency, for example, may not be as fine as this

194

particular set of groups requires. It may be that the agency is bound by law or custom to provide only a limited range of facilities and that this range cuts across several of the above groups. If, in this kind of situation, the agency has not the resources to provide, say, a golf-course and is unable to provide a facility which would cater for any of the other activities that are associated with golf (Group IV, Table 29), what other facility can it provide which will, at least in part, substitute for a golf-course? To answer this question requires broader groups than the ones obtained from the cluster analysis; and to produce these broader groups requires an analysis of homogeneity *between* the 14 groups outlined above. A possible approach to this would be by the identification of common characteristics within and between groups.

The first stage of this procedure is to examine activities within groups for major common characteristics. This is of course what has been done in the brief discussion of each separate group above. From this discussion it appears that there are at least eight major characteristics of the 71 activities which merit consideration. These are, first, the degree of skill required for the activity; second, whether or not it is a group activity; third, whether or not it is a physically active pursuit; fourth, the amount of risk or danger attached to it; fifth, whether it generally takes place in an urban or rural setting; sixth, cost to participants; seventh, whether or not it requires the use of water resources; and eighth, the degree of speed and dexterity required for the activity. There may of course be other major characteristics which these activities have, but these eight characteristics appear to be particularly significant. The second stage is then to compare the 14 groups on these characteristics, as shown in Table 30. Each group is examined to see whether, in general, it has or requires each of the eight characteristics. Following this, group correlations on the eight characteristics are drawn up, as shown in Figure 10. Finally, on the basis of these correlations, some preferred broader groups are identified. This final stage is shown in Table 31.

The result of this exercise was to produce three preferred broader groupings of the 14 cluster groups. The first of these, made up of Cluster Groups I, IV, VIII, XI and XIV, consists of activities which do not require a high level of skill from participants, although a basic level of skill will usually add to enjoyment; which are primarily group activities; which are physically active pursuits; which do not involve much personal risk or danger; which are usually not very expensive for participants, and which often take place in an urban setting. The second of the preferred broader groupings consists of Cluster Groups

195

Table 30. *Classification of Cluster Groups on Activity Characteristics*

CHARACTERISTIC	GROUPS WITH, OR REQUIRING CHARACTERISTIC	GROUPS WITHOUT OR NOT REQUIRING CHARACTERISTIC	GROUPS IN INTERMEDIATE POSITION
Skill	II; V; IX; XII	III; VI; VII; X	I; IV; VIII; XI; XIV
Group activity	I; IV; V; VI; VII; IX; XI; XII; XIV	II	III; VIII; X
Physically active	I; II; IV; V; VIII; IX; XI; XII; XIV	VI; VII; X	III
Risky or dangerous	II; V; XII	I; III; IV; VI; VII; VIII; X; XI; XIV	IX
Urban setting	I; IV; VII; X; XI	II; III; IX; XII	V; VI; VIII; XIV
Expensive for participants	II; IX; XII	I; III; IV; VI; VII; VIII; X; XI	V; XIV
Water-based	IX	I; III; V; VI; VII; VIII; X; XI; XII	II; IV; XIV
Speed, dexterity, rapid reactions	V; IX; XI	III; VI; VII; X; XII	I; II; IV; VIII; XIV

Note:
Following the line of the discussion in the text, Group XIII has been omitted from this analysis.

II, V, IX and XII. The activities within these groups are ones which generally require a high level of skill from participants; which are primarily group activities; which are physically active pursuits; which are often risky or dangerous for participants; which do not usually take place in an urban setting; and which are often very expensive for participants. The third broader grouping is made up of Cluster

1	11	111	1V	V	V1	V11	V111	1X	X	X1	X11	X1V	Cluster Groups
	2	3	7	3	4	5	6	2	4	7	3	5	1
		1	3	3	0	0	2	4	0	1	5	3	11
			2	1	5	5	4	1	6	3	3	1	111
				2	3	4	5	2	3	6	2	6	1V
					3	2	3	4	1	4	5	4	V
						7	4	1	6	4	3	3	V1
							3	1	7	5	3	2	V11
								1	4	5	2	5	V111
									0	3	5	2	1X
										4	2	1	X
											3	4	X1
												2	X11
													X1V

Note:
Figures in the squares indicate the number of characteristics on which the groups coincide in Table 30. For example, Groups I and IV coincide on 7 of the 8 characteristics.

Figure 10. Cluster group correlations on 8 activity characteristics

Groups III, VI, VII and X. The activities within these groups are ones which do not generally require any skill from the participant; they consist of both group and individual activities; they are in no way risky or dangerous for the participant; they are not very costly; and they do not require a great deal of speed or dexterity from participants. These activities are, in fact, largely passive, universal and social in character.

There is, thus, considerable homogeneity among the cluster groups

197

Table 31. Broader Groupings of the Cluster Analysis Groups

GROUPS CORRELATED ON 5 OF 8 ACTIVITY CHARACTERISTICS	GROUPS CORRELATED ON 6 OF 8 ACTIVITY CHARACTERISTICS	GROUPS CORRELATED ON 7 OF 8 ACTIVITY CHARACTERISTICS	PREFERRED BROADER GROUPS
I-VII-XIV	I-VIII	I-IV-XI	I-IV-VIII-XI-XIV
II-XII	III-X	IV-I	II-V-IX-XII
III-VI-VII	IV-XI-XIV	VI-VII	III-VI-VII-X
IV-VIII	VI-X	VII-VI-X	
V-XII	VIII-I	X-VII	
VI-III	X-III-VI	XI-I	
VII-I-III-XI	XI-IV		
VIII-IV-XI-XIV	XIV-IV		
IX-XII			
XIV-I-VIII			

Notes:
1. Each group within a preferred broader grouping must be correlated with *at least one* other group within that grouping on *at least* 5 of the 8 characteristics.
2. Following the line of the discussion in the text, Group XIII has been omitted from this analysis.

which make up the preferred broader groupings. Furthermore, with 69 activities distributed among the three groupings, there should be sufficient flexibility for the formulation of planning policy and for its implementation.

The cluster analysis based upon 40 activities produced 8 groups which, in their composition, strongly reinforced the groups obtained from the 71-activity analysis. In other words, the 31 activities that were eliminated as having less than 20 participants each were clustered, for the most part, in the 6 groups that ceased to exist. Only 5 of the 40 activities fell into different groups from the ones in which they had been placed by the 71-activity analysis. These were: hobbies/do-it-yourself, netball, outdoor bowls, visits to a community or church centre, and dancing. *Hobbies/Do-it-yourself* was now placed in the group clustered upon *Soccer* (Group A, Table 32), whereas previously it had been, itself, the focal activity for a group (Group V, Table 29). *Netball* moved from Group XI in Table 29, clustered upon *Hockey*, to Group B in Table 32, clustered upon *Rugby*. *Outdoor bowls*, which had been included in the group clustered upon *Hobbies/Do-it-yourself* (Group V, Table 29), was now, itself, the focal activity for a group which included *Tenpin bowling* and *Swimming* (Group C, Table 32). *Visits to a community or church centre* moved from being the focal activity for Group VII in Table 29 to being within the group clustered on *Picknicking* in Table 32 (Group G). Finally, *Dancing*, which had been included within the group clustered upon *Picknicking* (Group VI, Table 29), was now part of the group clustered upon *Visits to a cinema* (Group H, Table 32). Obviously, these changes had some small effects upon the structure of the cluster groups; but, in general, the composition of the groups themselves remained remarkably stable. While this does not prove that the derived groups for these 40 activities are, in any sense, 'correct', it strengthens the value that can be placed upon them.

The Factor Analysis

Unlike cluster analysis, factor analysis can yield as few or as many groups of activities as the investigator wants. The actual number of groups obtained will be equal to the number of factors employed in the analysis; and the number of factors employed will be determined by the investigator's knowledge of, or hypotheses about, the characteristics of the basic set of recreation activities which are the raw material of his analysis. Thus, for example, Proctor [43] began with data about rates of participation in a set of 15 outdoor recreation

199

activities. He then hypothesized that a factor analysis would show four basic 'recreation types'; that is, that there were four basic factors to be found in the 15 activities. These were: a 'backwoods' factor, an 'active' factor, a 'passive' factor, and a 'water' factor. The activities were then grouped according to their hypothesized

Table 32. *Cluster Analysis Groups Based Upon 40 Activities*

Group A	Horse riding
Soccer	Youth club
Cricket	
Tennis	*Group E*
Golf	Rowing
Table Tennis	Motor-boat cruising
Fishing	Messing about in boats
Hobbies/Do-it-yourself	
Other activities	*Group F*
	Hill walking
Group B	Rambling
Rugby	Camping/Youth hostelling/
Netball	Caravanning
Athletics	Walking
Basketball	
Badminton	*Group G*
Keep Fit	Picnicking
Cycling	Driving in the countryside
Amateur dramatics/Music	Gardening
	Dining out
	Visit to a pub or club
Group C	Visit to a community or church
Outdoor bowls	centre
Tenpin bowling	Bingo
Swimming	
	Group H
Group D	Visit to a cinema
Ice skating	Visit to a theatre/concert
Roller skating	Dancing

relation to these four factors. The factor analysis was then applied, and was found to substantiate the hypothesized groups—although with some minor modifications.

In the present study, however, the approach was somewhat different. No attempt was made to predict, or hypothesize, the number of basic factors that might characterize the sets of 71, 59 and 40 activities. Instead, several factor analyses were carried out with each of these three sets of activities and with varying numbers of factors. The 71-activity set was analysed with, successively, 4, 5, 6 and 8 factors, the 59-activity set with 3, 4, 5, 6 and 8 factors, and the 40-activity set with 4, 5, 6, 7 and 8 factors. The resulting groupings were then compared on the basis of some fairly general tests. The purpose was to discover whether any of the groupings appeared to be significantly 'better' than the others. The first, and most subjective, of the tests concerned the 'degree of reasonableness'. Which of the groupings that emerged appeared to be the most reasonable, in terms of the kinds of activities that were classified together in the groups? Here, the basic characteristics of activities, identified in Table 30, proved to be of general, though limited, use. The activities within each group could be examined for homogeneity in terms of the level of skill required, whether or not they are group activities, whether or not they usually take place in an urban or rural setting, and so on. The second test, also largely subjective, attempted to measure the extent to which one or more of the groupings could be said to be 'representative' of the others. The third test was entirely objective, being based upon the relative values of 'variance' for the groupings: the higher was the value of the variance for a grouping, the better it was statistically.

There were four factor analyses undertaken with the 71-activity set, none of which was immediately and obviously better than the others. On the test of reasonableness, the groupings based upon 4 and 5 factors were not very satisfactory. There was one factor in all of the four analyses which was not sufficiently correlated with any of the activities, with the result that each grouping contained, effectively, one less group than the number of factors employed. This meant that the 4-factor analysis produced only three groups, which consisted, respectively, of 26, 24 and 21 activities each. These groups were too large for them to be identified very strongly with one or other of the characteristics listed in Table 30. Broadly, Group I consisted of active team sports, Group II was made up of active individual and small-group pursuits, including a number of generally social activities; and Group III emphasized minority activities, together with several large-scale passive outdoor pursuits. There were, however, too many exceptions within each group for these generalizations to serve as identifying characteristics. The grouping based upon 5 factors, while somewhat better, also produced groups with considerable internal inconsistencies in terms of these characteristics. The groups derived from the analyses based upon 6 and 8 factors

Table 33. *Factor Analysis Groups Based Upon 71 Activities and 8 Factors*

	Factor Score
Factor 1 (Group I)	
Soccer	·779
Rugby	·596
Cricket	·696
Tennis	·508
Golf	·389
Athletics	·668
Basketball	·649
Badminton	·440
Table tennis	·614
Keep fit	·461
Swimming	·416
Fishing	·406
Rowing	·345
Messing about in boats	·336
Cycling	·591
Amateur dramatics/Music	·217
Youth Club	·414
Factor 2 (Group II)	
Rambling	·318
Picnicking	·651
Driving in the countryside	·609
Gardening	·370
Dining out	·602
Visit to a pub or club	·347
Visit to a community or church centre	·102
Visit to a cinema	·439
Visit to a theatre/concert	·479
Bingo	·079
Dancing	·281
Old Tyme Dancing	·108
Visit to a library	·189
Visit to a museum/art gallery	·075
Evening classes	·066
Factor 3 (Group III)	
Nil activities	—
Factor 4 (Group IV)	
Motor-cycle racing	·115

	Factor Score
Rallies	·668
Flying/Gliding/Sky diving	·695
Fencing	·660
Surfing	·184
Water skiing	·226
Motor-boat cruising	·332
	Factor Score
Factor 5 (Group V)	
Hobbies/Do-it-yourself	·172
Outdoor bowls	·288
Motor racing	·531
Scrambles	·560
Squash	·677
Photography	·181
Other activities	·342
Factor 6 (Group VI)	
Boxing	·713
Wrestling	·667
Judo/Karate	·408
Aqualung diving	·425
Going to a party	·411
Factor 7 (Group VII)	
Hockey	·508
Netball	·649
Ice skating	·481
Hill walking	·339
Pot-holing	·132
Bird watching	·244
Walking	·145
Gymnastics	·224
Painting/Drawing/Sketching	·326
Factor 8 (Group VIII)	
Archery	·446
Go-karting	·380
Winter sports	·518
Tenpin bowling	·350
Roller skating	·412
Sailing	·468
Canoeing	·445
Mountaineering	·185

Table 33. (*continued*)

Horse riding	·430	Camping/Youth hostelling/	
Hunting	·283	Caravanning	·278

were, however, much more homogeneous internally. The 8-factor analysis, in particular, produced groups which, in this context, could be described as reasonable (Table 33). Group I consisted primarily of active team and small-group sports which take place largely in an urban setting. Group II, in contrast, was made up of outdoor and indoor social activities, together with some cultural pursuits. There were no activities in Group III. The dominant characteristics of activities in Group IV were skill, speed and danger. Furthermore, most of these were outdoor countryside or water-based activities. Group V was a rather odd one, with no very obvious dominant features. It included *Hobbies* and *Motor racing, Scrambles* and *Outdoor bowls*. The emphasis in Group VI was upon physical-contact competitive sports, such as boxing and wrestling. Group VII was another unusual one; it consisted mainly of active pursuits, but ones with no very obvious links. There are grounds for suspecting, however, that this group included a disproportionate number of female respondents. Finally, Group VIII was very similar to Group IV, except that the emphasis here was more upon skill and less upon speed, danger and excitement. Most of the activities were outdoor ones, some of them, perhaps, meriting the description 'backwoods'—for example, hunting and mountaineering.

The test which attempted to measure the extent to which one or more of the groupings could be said to be 'representative' of the others was, in reality, a test of the extent to which groupings were found to contain groups which were similar in their composition. In this respect, the groupings for the 71-activity set could not be said to be very closely related. The only groupings which were reasonably comparable were those based upon 6 and 8 factors. Here, two groups within the groupings were entirely similar, while two other groups in the 6-factor analysis corresponded almost exactly with four groups in the 8-factor analysis.

The third test, the numerical value of variance, was not very conclusive (Table 34). The highest value was obtained for the 4-factor analysis, 39·9, while the lowest was obtained for the 5-factor analysis, 37·5. On the basis of the variance alone, the 4-factor analysis would have been the best, followed closely by the 6-factor analysis.

What emerged from the application of these tests, therefore, was a

203

rather indeterminate situation. In terms of their 'reasonableness', the groups produced by the 8-factor analysis appeared to be the best, followed by the groups derived from the 6-factor analysis. In terms of their comparability, the groups based upon 6 and 8 factors were again the best. Finally, on the basis of statistical variance, the groups based upon the 4-factor analysis were the best, followed closely by those derived from the 6-factor analysis.

The application of the same three tests to the 59-activity set produced much stronger and more positive results than their application to the 71-activity set had done. The groupings which most

Table 34. *Values of Variance for the Factor-Analytic Groups*

ACTIVITY SET	FACTORS	VARIANCE
71 Activities	4	39·9
	5	37·5
	6	39·5
	8	38·2
59 Activities	3	34·8
	4	40·7
	5	40·2
	6	40·4
	8	39·4
40 Activities	4	36·0
	5	38·6
	6	37·0
	7	38·9
	8	38·2

Note:
The higher the variance, the better is the factor grouping statistically.

satisfied the test of 'reasonableness' were those based upon 5, 6 and 8 factors. Again, as with the 71-activity set, the groups which emerged from the analyses based upon 3 and 4 factors were too large for them to be identified very strongly with any of the characteristics listed in Table 30. The groups from the 3-factor analysis consisted of 25, 18 and 16 activities, respectively; while those derived from the 4-factor analysis were made up of 22, 17, 12 and 8 activities, respectively. Some of the individual groups derived from the analyses based upon 5, 6 and 8 factors also included substantial numbers of activities, but, generally, homogeneity within the groups was more evident. When it came to the test of comparability, there was no doubt that the best groupings were those based upon 5 and 6 factors. Three of the groups in these two groupings were identical, while the remaining two in the 5-factor set made up the remaining three in the 6-factor

Table 35. *Factor Analysis Groups Based Upon 59 Activities and 5 Factors*

	Factor Score		Factor Score
Factor 1 (Group I)		Gardening	·323
Soccer	·581	Dining out	·597
Rugby	·469	Visit to a pub/club	·397
Cricket	·530	Visit to a community or	
Hockey	·489	church centre	·062
Netball	·524	Visit to a cinema	·466
Tennis	·568	Visit to a theatre/concert	·483
Golf	·320		
Athletics	·707	*Factor 3 (Group III)*	
Basketball	·650	Go-karting	·485
Badminton	·535	Surfing	·485
Table tennis	·629	Water skiing	·714
Ice skating	·516	Aqualung diving	·690
Roller skating	·454	Canoeing	·501
Keep fit	·497	Messing about in boats	·393
Swimming	·477	Mountaineering	·486
Fishing	·293	Pot-holing	·642
Hill walking	·362		
Bird watching	·262	*Factor 4 (Group IV)*	
Horse riding	·335	Archery	·212
Cycling	·620	Motor-cycle racing	·142
Amateur dramatics/Music	·243	Scrambles	·576
Youth club	·519	Rallies	·721
		Flying/Gliding/Sky diving	·696
Factor 2 (Group II)		Fencing	·582
Outdoor bowls	·298	Judo/Karate	·246
Tenpin bowling	·383	Motor-boat cruising	·304
Sailing	·266		
Rowing	·320	*Factor 5 (Group V)*	
Rambling	·404	Bingo	·108
Hunting	·129	Motor racing	·480
Camping/Youth hostelling/		Winter sports	·375
Caravanning	·314	Squash	·372
Picnicking	·620	Boxing	·444
Driving in the countryside	·609	Wrestling	·689

set. It was not difficult, therefore, to show that the 5-factor groups were, to a very considerable extent, representative of the 6-factor groups. Finally, on the test of variance, the best grouping was the one based upon 4 factors. But the variance for this set was not much greater than those for the sets based upon 5, 6 and 8 factors (Table 34). It appeared, therefore, that the best set from the 59-activity analyses was the one based upon 5 factors (Table 35).

Some of the most satisfactory of all the results were those obtained from the application of these three general tests to the set of 40

Table 36. *Factor Analysis Groups Based Upon 40 Activities and 5 Factors*

	Factor Score		Factor Score
Factor 1 (Group I)		*Factor 3 (Group III)*	
Soccer	·753	Netball	·526
Rugby	·649	Ice skating	·608
Cricket	·654	Roller skating	·566
Tennis	·488	Horse riding	·516
Athletics	·751	Youth club	·430
Basketball	·726		
Badminton	·478		
Table Tennis	·569	*Factor 4 (Group IV)*	
Keep fit	·557	Visit to a pub or club	·338
Swimming	·345	Bingo	·280
Fishing	·339	Dancing	·205
Cycling	·529		
Amateur dramatics/Music	·250		
Other activities	·192	*Factor 5 (Group V)*	
		Golf	·449
Factor 2 (Group II)		Outdoor bowls	·418
Picnicking	·689	Tenpin bowling	·602
Driving in the countryside	·667	Rowing	·490
Gardening	·352	Motor-boat cruising	·441
Dining out	·671	Messing about in boats	·441
Visit to a community or		Hill walking	·278
church centre	·166	Rambling	·283
Visit to a cinema	·473	Camping/Youth hostelling/	
Visit to a theatre/concert	·509	Caravanning	·280
Walking	·001	Hobbies/Do-it-yourself	·070

activities. The groupings which most satisfied the test of reasonableness were those based upon 5 and 8 factors. In particular, these groupings produced fairly well-marked distinctions between active sports, social and cultural pursuits, youth-oriented activities and passive outdoor pursuits. When it came to the test of comparability, the groupings based upon 5 and 6 factors were again similar—although not as obviously as was the case with the 59-activity sets. The 5-

factor grouping was, however, still fairly representative of the 6-factor grouping. This could not be said of the groupings based upon 7 and 8 factors. Finally, on the test of variance, the best groupings were those based upon 5, 7 and 8 factors. It appeared, therefore, that, for the 40-activity set as well, the best grouping was the one based upon 5 factors (Table 36).

This discussion has led to the suggestion that the 'best' factor-analytic groups are: for the 71-activity set, those based upon an 8-factor analysis; for the 59-activity set, those based upon a 5-factor analysis; and for the 40-activity set, also those based upon a 5-factor analysis. It is freely admitted, however, that the basis for this decision has been largely subjective. The application of two of the three tests hinged very closely upon the author's definition of what is 'reasonable' and upon his interpretation of what is 'representative'. It is believed that these tests have been applied equally to all of the factor-analytic groupings; but it is not, thereby, contended that they have been objective, scientific tests. The factor analyses, themselves, represent entirely objective statistical techniques for classifying the recreation activities into groups. The tests which were employed for choosing between the resultant groups represent the author's considered judgements. It is likely that a fully objective choice between the different factor groupings could only be made by correlating each group within each grouping with the socio-economic data derived from the survey and then to test for significance between groups, a task which would constitute a full research study in itself.*
There is, however, one final exercise that can be done with the data that have been considered here, and which could be particularly useful for current planning. In all, there were 17 groupings of activities prepared for this study—3 cluster groupings and 14 factor groupings. As these were being examined it became obvious that there were some activities which were always to be found together in the same groups. This suggests that these activities are particularly closely correlated— at least on the basis of the present data. It will be worth identifying some of these activities.

The Cluster and Factor Analyses Compared

Obviously, an investigation of the stability of activity groups as

---

* The computer calculations alone represent a considerable undertaking: the factor analysis programme itself takes around 20 minutes to run, while each run through the survey data takes about 15 minutes, and at least 60 runs would be required!

between the 3 cluster analyses and the 14 factor analyses can only be carried out for those activities which were employed in *all* of these analyses; that is, for the 36 activities which were precoded on the survey questionnaire and which also had more than 20 participants each. The procedure for this investigation was a simple one: merely to record how many times a number of activities appeared together in the same group. No attempt was made to discover how often these activities were *directly* correlated as compared with the number of times they were correlated *through various other activities*. Instead, it was proposed to eliminate any activity which did not appear within the particular group being considered at least 14 times out of the possible 17. In this indirect way, a high degree of association between the activities within the group was demanded.

The first apparently stable group consisted of four activities— soccer, cricket, table tennis and tennis. The first three of these appeared in the same group in every one of the 17 analyses. Tennis was associated with the other three activities 15 times. Although it did not quite meet the numerical requirements, golf was also fairly closely related to this group, being associated with the other four activities 13 times.

The second stable group embraced six activities—rugby, athletics, basketball, keep fit, badminton and cycling. The first four of these were grouped together in all of the 17 analyses. The last two were associated with the first four activities 16 and 15 times, respectively, and with each other 14 times.

The third stable group was composed of four activities—roller skating, ice skating, youth club and horse riding. The first three of these appeared in the same group 16 times. The fourth was associated with the first 15 times and with the other two 14 times.

The final group also consisted of four activities—picnicking, driving in the countryside, gardening and dining out. The first and the third of these appeared in the same group 16 times. All four of them were grouped together 14 times.

The full list of these apparently stable groups is to be found in Table 37. What they and the cluster and factor analyses have shown is that people can be grouped into recreation types on the basis of the kinds of recreation activities in which they participate. The analyses in the present study have not shown that any particular set of groups is necessarily the 'best', if only because they have been based exclusively on 'width' of activity; but it has demonstrated that some particular activities almost always go together. Further work will need to be carried out to show how these recreation types are correlated with different socio-economic groups within the population. This work will require considerable resources, in both money and manpower. Much of the statistical material that will be needed is,

Table 37. *Some Relatively Stable Recreation Groups*

Group I	Group III
Soccer	Roller skating
Cricket	Ice skating
Table tennis	Youth club
Tennis	Horse riding
Group II	Group IV
Rugby	Picnicking
Athletics	Driving in the countryside
Basketball	Gardening
Keep fit	Dining out
Badminton	
Cycling	

Note:
See the text for a full discussion of how these groups were derived.

however, available from the present study; for example, there is more socio-economic information available than from any previous recreation study in this country. In the meantime, the present discussion has served to lay the guidelines along which further studies can progress.

Chapter 9
Profile Data

In attempting to establish guidelines for the collection and analysis of data about the profile characteristics of respondents to recreation surveys, there are two groups of problems to be tackled. The first relates to the kinds of profile characteristics about which information should be obtained and, perhaps, more important, which indicators of these to use. Thus, for example, we need to know whether information should be sought about the educational backgrounds of respondents; and, if so, whether this should relate to, say, the terminal school age, or the type of school last attended, or the number of years of further education undertaken. The second problem concerns the ways in which the data about the chosen characteristics and indicators should be grouped for analysis. A major objective of the household and activities survey was to seek solutions, in some depth, to each of these three problems.

As a prior consideration, however, it will be useful to re-state here the reasons why data about the profile characteristics of respondents should be collected in recreation surveys. There are, essentially, two reasons. The first is to facilitate comparisons between the findings of different studies; the second, to provide the background data about respondents that are generally used as inputs in models and systems that attempt to forecast future levels of recreation activity. The general evidence is that many profile characteristics are highly correlated with recreation behaviour: to such an extent, in fact, that they can be assumed to be major causal variables. Thus 'if a way can be found of grouping the population in terms of its recreation patterns, then . . . we should be in a clearer position to make meaningful statements about the ways in which recreation demands are generated by these identifiable groups' [14]. In most previous recreation research, such groupings of the population have been based largely upon socio-economic characteristics of one kind and another. It was shown, however, in Chapter 8, that such groupings can also be based upon recreation activity types; but even with this kind of grouping, there will still be a need to identify major socio-economic characteristics with which to correlate these recreation types for forecasting purposes.

210

The Profile Data

There has been little difficulty in assessing, on the basis of previous studies, the kinds of profile characteristics about which it is considered essential to have data. The major categories which would give, prima facie, comparability with other studies, both in recreation and more generally, are sevenfold: age; sex; marital status; family or household composition; education; income; and occupation or social class. In addition, there are five characteristics about which information has often been obtained in previous recreation studies, although there has been much less unanimity among researchers in respect of these. They are: ownership and use of a motor car; type and tenure of housing; length of paid annual holiday; ownership of selected household equipment; and ownership or use of selected recreation equipment.

Since the purpose of the present study was to lay down guidelines for the collection of profile data in future studies, it was considered imperative, in designing the survey, that no very basic assumptions should be made concerning which of these characteristics should be included in the survey questionnaire, and which should be excluded. It was proposed, therefore, to obtain at least some information about all of them. In the event, an error in the final preparation of the survey documents meant that one subject which had been included in the questionnaire used for the pilot survey was omitted from the questionnaire employed in the main survey. In consequence, no information was obtained in respect of the length of paid annual holiday received by each respondent. Questions were included, however, which sought information about each of the eleven other characteristics listed above.

A more difficult set of decisions was posed when it came to the question of determining which of the many alternative indicators of these characteristics should be measured. It was noted in Chapter 1, for example, that there are at least eight different indicators relating to occupation, ranging from whether or not the respondent was employed to the kind of job he actually did and the length of his official working week.* Moreover, this list in no way exhausts all of the possibilities. Other indicators might be, for instance, whether or not he has any persons working under him, or whether or not he is required to do shift work. In a similar way to this, it would be possible to use a number of different indicators of education, housing and ownership or use of various classes of goods. Clearly, in any particular

* See page 44.

Table 38. *Profile Characteristics and Indicators*

CHARACTERISTIC	INDICATORS CONSIDERED FOR TESTING	INDICATORS ADOPTED FOR TESTING
1. AGE	Age	Age
2. SEX	Sex	Sex
3. MARITAL STATUS	Marital status	Marital status
4. HOUSEHOLD COMPOSITION	Number of persons in household	Number of persons in household
5. EDUCATION	Type of school last attended	Type of school last attended
	Operator of school last attended	Operator of school last attended
	Sex structure of school	Sex structure of school
	Terminal school age	Terminal school age
	Further education	Further education
	Further education qualifications	Further education qualifications
6. INCOME	Personal income	Personal income
	Form of payment of income	Form of payment of income
7. OCCUPATION	Employment status	Employment status
	Socio-economic group	Socio-economic group
	Length of official working week	Length of official working week
	Length of actual working week	Length of actual working week
	Length of usual working week	Length of usual working week
	Shift working	Shift working
	Saturday working	Saturday working
	Any qualifications for job done	
	Opportunities for overtime work	
8. MOTOR CAR OR MOTOR CYCLE	Ownership or regular use of a car/motor cycle	Ownership or regular use of a car/motor cycle
	Ownership of a car/motor cycle	
	Regular use of a car/motor cycle	

9. HOUSING	Type of dwelling Length of residence Garden or no garden Owned or rented Age of dwelling	Type of dwelling Length of residence Garden or no garden
10. RECREATION EQUIPMENT	Possession or regular use of items Possession of items Regular use of items	Possession or regular use of items
11. HOUSEHOLD EQUIPMENT	Possession of various items	Possession of various items

survey, it would be impossible to seek information about all of these items. If the investigator were to attempt to do so, he would either have to restrict the number of questions that he could ask about the subject matter of the survey itself, or else he would have to lengthen the questionnaire to a size which would significantly reduce his potential response rate. In these circumstances, he would look for guidelines as to which of the alternative indicators of each characteristic are the most useful to include in his survey. The purpose of the present study was, of course, to determine these guidelines; but, in order to do this, data were collected about a much larger number of different indicators of each of the chosen characteristics than would be desirable in an ordinary survey. Even here, however, some indicators had to be excluded while others were included, a process for which some consistent criterion of judgement was necessary. In the event, it was decided that the best criterion was to include those indicators which, on the basis of previous studies, appeared to have the strongest associations with recreation activity. The alternative indicators of each characteristic were ranked 'crudely' on this basis, the number to be included in the survey then being determined upon the basis of judgements about the maximum acceptable length of the questionnaire and the necessity to cover some aspect, at least, of each of the eleven characteristics. The list of characteristics and indicators considered, and those chosen for testing, is given in Table 38. This list is of course not exhaustive; but it does encompass a wide range of profile indicators. It shows that data were collected for testing in respect of 25 indicators out of a total of 34 that were considered.

In addition to the problem of choosing which indicators of each characteristic to use, a problem arose concerning the choice of alternative ways of grouping the data about each indicator, for both collection and analytical purposes. In part, the problem of how the data were to be collected was one of questionnaire and survey design; and, in part, it was bound up with the proposed methods of analysis of the data. To the extent that data are collected in specified groups, they can only be analysed in those groups or in larger combinations of them. They cannot be broken down into smaller groups for analysis. If on the other hand the data are collected in the form of individual units, then these can later be amalgamated into any groups that the investigator wishes to use. An example will suffice to illustrate this point. Respondents could be asked to indicate the age-group into which they fall from a series such as the following: 0–4 years, 5–9 years, 10–15 years, 15–19 years . . . 60–64 years, 65 years

214

and over. Or alternatively, they could be asked to give their actual age. In the first case, correlations between recreation activity and age can only be calculated for the given age-groups or larger combinations of them (such as 0–14 years, 15–29 years and so on). In the second case, however, correlations can be calculated for each individual age year, or for any groups that the investigator wishes: for example, 0–6 years, 7–11 years, 12–15 years. This logic suggested that the best approach would be to collect information in the smallest possible units and then, in analysis, to combine these into any desired groups. This was therefore adopted as the ideal procedure; although there were, unfortunately, some operational constraints upon this approach, which will now be briefly discussed.

The pilot survey showed that respondents are especially reluctant to provide information about their *actual* incomes, but that they are more easily persuaded to give an indication of this by placing themselves within specified income *groups*. This has indeed been a particular problem in social research generally for a considerable time. The main task in this respect therefore was to devise income groups which would serve two somewhat conflicting functions: each group should encompass as small a range of income as possible so as to provide us with groups which could be adequately tested for significance; at the same time, they had to be large enough to convince respondents that they were being asked only to place themselves within a range and not to give, in a devious way, their actual incomes. The groups finally used consisted largely of differentials of £2.50 per week (for example, 'more than £5 up to £7.50 per week', 'more than £7.50 up to £10 per week', and so on). Even despite this attempt to balance the need to obtain detailed data with the desire to obtain any data at all, the question about income had the highest level of non-response of all the factual question asked in the survey.

The guiding principle, then, for the collection of profile data was that these should be obtained at the smallest possible level of detail, so that groups could be built up at the analysis stage to test particular hypotheses about their relationship to recreation behaviour. The proposal for the analysis stage itself was to use the unit of collection as the unit of analysis: for example, since data about the ages of respondents had been collected in the form of single years, the analysis of the correlations between age and recreation activity should also be made for single years. Unfortunately, there were also some operational constraints upon this approach. The absolute numbers of respondents falling within some groups were too few for a meaningful statistical analysis of the usual two-way tabulation type to be undertaken. For example, information about the marital status of respondents was collected in the form of five groups—single, married, separated, divorced and widowed. It was discovered at the analysis stage, however, that there were insufficient numbers of respondents within each of the two groups 'separated' and 'divorced' for them to be treated as distinct groups for statistical analysis. Instead, they had to be included within an enlarged group, 'separated, divorced and widowed'. In the same way, there were insufficient numbers of persons within each individual age-year for these to be analysed separately. Instead, the analysis had to be made for two-year age-groups, viz. 12–13 years, 14–15 years, 16–17 years, and so on.* This was in fact an example of the kind of problem encountered in many previous studies, such as the *Pilot National Recreation Survey* [6] and discussed in Chapter 1. In the experimental study it proved possible, in most cases, to utilize more detailed groupings in the analysis than had been possible in previous studies; for example, two-year age-groups instead of five-year groups. We were not able, however, to be as detailed as we had hoped.

The discussion so far can be summarized by saying that the purpose in collecting and analysing profile data in the kind of detail employed here was to attempt to determine which indicator, or indicators, of any particular profile characteristic is, or are, most significantly correlated with recreation behaviour and, hence, should be included in future surveys. A second purpose was, in the case of some of the indicators, to investigate the differences in recreational activities between particular groups. The next stage of the discussion focuses upon the kinds of recreation data with which these profile characteristics were correlated.

The Recreation Data

Obviously, any attempt to discover which profile characteristics are significantly correlated with recreation behaviour—that is, to the extent that it may reasonably be presumed that they are causal influences—required that the measure of recreation behaviour which is being employed should be as broadly-based as possible. On the other hand, it would also be useful to have some indication of the significance of such characteristics in influencing detailed recreation behaviour. In view of these two desired features, it was proposed to adopt two separate recreation measures for correlation with each

* Although, even these groups were not entirely valid in nonparametric analyses.

profile indicator. These were, firstly, the number of recreation activities ever undertaken during 1968 (even if only once) and, secondly, the frequency of participation in the particular activity which was undertaken *most often* during 1968. Both of these, it is suggested, are reasonable criteria against which to measure significance.

The first criterion—number of recreation activities ever undertaken during 1968—measures the total range of the recreation experiences of the respondent over a fairly long period. It emphasizes the *breadth* of recreation demands. It encompasses both the casual participant who, by taking part in an activity perhaps only once during the year, places an irregular, but nonetheless real, pressure upon facilities, and the regular participant. It has the disadvantage of course that it gives an undue importance to the 'unattached' person who takes part casually in a large number of activities, since the person who takes part in one or more activities on a regular basis may reasonably be assumed to take part in fewer activities over-all. The second criterion, however, will reverse this bias—at least in part. It measures the *depth* of demand, the frequency of participation in the particular activity which was undertaken most often during 1968. In other words, it measures the frequency with which the demands for particular facilities are expressed. The use of both sets of data may help us to avoid spurious measures of significance that could emerge from the use of one or the other only.

There are of course several other possible measures of recreation activity or behaviour. It would have been possible, for example, to use the 'popularity' of activities as a measure, by taking the numbers of people whose chosen major activity fell within each of the cluster and factor groups established in Chapter 8. The problem here, however, was, as indicated in that chapter, that the composition of these groups changed, sometimes considerably, with changes in the numbers of factors employed and the numbers of activities included in the analysis. It is possible that the degrees of correlation could also change with changes in the composition of these groups; and since it is difficult to say that any particular set of groups is 'best', it would be unwise to use them for purposes of establishing the significance of profile characteristics as 'determinants' of recreation activity or behaviour. Other measures were also rejected for similar reasons, or else because the data could not be easily obtained from the survey. Thus, the significance of the profile indicators listed in Table 38 has been measured against the two indicators of recreation activity outlined above. The first measures the breadth of the respondent's recreation activity; the second measures its depth.

The Analysis

The procedure in the analysis was, of course, to compare the data for each of the two measures of recreation activity to each of the profile indicators that had been selected for test. In the discussion which follows, the profile indicators will be referred to as the independent variables, while the two measures of recreation activity will be designated as the dependent variables.

The first problem encountered in preparing the tests was that, in many cases, the dependent and independent variables would have different scales of measurement [137]. *Nominal* scales are ones where the data are merely classified into groups. There is no suggestion of rank in the data, no indication that one group is of a 'higher' or 'lower' order than another. An example of a variable measured on a nominal scale would be sex; it is divided into two unranked groups—male and female. Other examples would be marital status, type of school last attended and socio-economic group. *Ordinal* scales are ones which do imply some order of ranking. One item is 'higher' or 'lower' or 'better' than another. An example of a variable measured on an ordinal scale might be the order of popularity of a particular recreation activity: the most popular activity would have a value of 1, the second most popular a value of 2, and so on. None of the variables employed in the analysis which follows used this type of scale. *Equal interval* or *ratio* scales are more precise ordinal measures. Not only is one value 'higher' or 'lower' than another, but it is also known by how much the one exceeds the other. An example of a variable measured on an equal interval scale would be the number of persons in the household.

The fact that many of the independent variables were measured on a different scale from those in which the dependent variables were measured would not, in itself, prohibit their being compared so as to establish their correlations. There are several well-established statistical tests for comparing variables with the same and different scales of measurement. For example, if the two variables to be compared were both nominal, then the appropriate test is a chi-square; if a nominal scale was being compared with an ordinal one, a Spearman or Kendall Test would be appropriate; and if the comparison were between a nominal scale and an equal interval one, then a Kruskall–Wallis test would be appropriate. Thus, the existence of different scales of measurement in the independent and dependent variables was no obstacle to their being compared in order to seek correlations [138].

218

There were, however, good reasons for wanting all of the variables to be measured on the same scale. One was ease of computation. A major purpose of the analysis of the profile data was to measure the *relative* efficiency of the different independent variables as 'determinants' of the two dependent variables. If these independent variables are measured on different scales, then different tests would have to be used in correlating them with the dependent variables. This would in turn make the comparisons between the independent variables themselves less satisfactory. In order to obtain some idea of the relative efficiency of the different independent variables, it would be desirable to have all of them measured on the same scale. Fortunately, this problem can be easily solved by 'downgrading' those variables measured on an ordinal or equal interval scale to a nominal one. Thus, the equal interval measure of the *length of the respondent's official working week* can be downgraded to a nominal measure by grouping the responses in some such way as follows:

1. Less than 40 hours = Short week
2. 40 hours = Normal week
3. More than 40 hours = Long week

The main aim when dividing a variable into nominal groups like this is to ensure that the number of observations falling in any group does not fall below a statistically significant number (when the chi-square test is used, the expected frequency in any 'cell' should not fall below 5). Within this constraint the investigator is free to divide the variable in any way he thinks fit. Generally, he aims to keep certain groups distinct: for example, adolescents on the age-scale, the 40-hour week on the length of working week scale, and so on. When he is interested in comparability with other studies, or with official statistical sources, the groups used in these sources will usually be adopted.

The proposal, then, was to express the 25 independent variables—the profile indicators—and the two dependent variables in the form of nominal scales of measurement; and then to compare the correlations between each of the independent variables and the two dependent variables by means of chi-square tests. In fact, 16 of the independent variables were already measured on a nominal scale as a result of the way in which data about them had been collected. One of the dependent variables was also expressed in this form. The remaining 9 independent variables and 1 dependent variable were converted into nominal groups on the basis either of groups used in previous studies or judgements as to the most useful divisions, from the point of view of statistical efficiency or research interest. The final groups used for each variable are shown in Table 39. Each of these is worth some further brief discussion.

1. *Age.* Traditionally, age has been measured in five-year groups or in multiples of five-year groups. Thus, the Census employs groups which go up in units of five years from '0–4 years' to '65 years and over'. Previous studies have suggested, however, that such groups may not be particularly relevant to changes in recreation behaviour. In particular, the use of five-year groups would mean that the critical period in most people's lives when they go through their most rapid and fundamental changes—adolescence and early adulthood—would be covered by, at most, only three groups: 15–19 years, 20–24 years and 25–29 years. Furthermore, it is quite possible that behavioural changes *within* these groups could be more significant than changes *between* them; for example, the difference between the 18-year-old and the 19-year-old might be much greater than the difference between the 19-year-old and the 20-year-old. Yet, with five-year age-groups, the first two would be included within the same group. The main objectives, therefore, in devising the age-groups for use in this study were, firstly, to examine the significance of traditional five-year groups and, secondly, to examine potential alternative groups, at least for persons between the ages of 12 and 25 years. Unfortunately, it was not possible to employ single-year groups for persons between these ages, since, for many of them, there were insufficient absolute numbers of persons for valid statistical analysis. Two-year age-groups were, therefore, used—although strictly speaking, statistical validity was still not wholly maintained. Thus, age was examined twice: first, in the traditional groups based upon five-year units or multiples of five-year units; second, in the two-year groups for persons between the ages of 12 and 25 years.

2. *Sex.* The two groups used to examine the significance of sex in influencing recreation activity were the obvious physiological ones—male and female.

3. *Marital status.* It had been hoped that marital status could be examined within a fivefold grouping; single, married, separated, divorced, and widowed. Unfortunately, there were insufficient numbers of respondents in the 'separated' and 'divorced' categories for a valid statistical analysis to be made of these. These were, therefore, combined with widowed persons into one group, giving a threefold grouping: single; married; and separated, divorced and widowed.

4. *Number of persons in the household.* The grouping used here is

Table 39. *Nominal Groups for the Variables*

VARIABLE	NUMBER OF GROUPS	LIST OF GROUPS
1A. Age—first classification	9	12–19; 20–24; 25–29; 30–39; 40–49; 50–59; 60–64; 65–69; 70 and over
1B. Age—second classification	14	12–13; 14–15; 16–17; 18–19; 20–21; 22–23; 24–25; 26–29; 30–39; 40–49; 50–59; 60–64; 65–69; 70 and over
2. Sex	2	Male; Female
3. Marital status	3	Single; Married; Separated, Divorced and Widowed
4. Number of persons in the household	6	1 person; 2 persons; 3 persons; 4 persons; 5 persons; 6 or more persons
5. Type of school last attended	5	Primary, Elementary, Council; Secondary Modern; Grammar; Technical, Comprehensive, Bilateral; Public, Independent, Other
6. Operator of School last attended	3	Local Education Authority; Roman Catholic; Other group
7 Sex structure of school	2	Co-educational; Single sex
8. Terminal school age	5	Under 14; 14; 15; 16 and over; Still in school
9. Further education	2	Yes; No
10. Further education qualifications	2	Higher Education, Professional, Vocational; Others
11. Personal income (after deductions at source)	7	Up to £5 per week; Over £5 up to £7.50; Over £7.50 up to £10; Over £10 up to £12.50; Over £12.50 up to £15; Over £15 up to £20; Over £20
12. Form of Payment	2	Weekly, Monthly, Other
13. Employment Status	6	Unemployed; Retired; Employed; Still at school or college; Housewife; never employed
14. Socio-economic group	6	S.E.G.s 1, 2, 3, 4 and 13—employers, managerial and professional persons; S.E.G.s 8, 9, 12 and 14—skilled and self-employed workers; S.E.G.s 5 and 6 —non-manual workers; S.E.G.s

221

Table 39. (*continued*)

VARIABLE	NUMBER OF GROUPS	LIST OF GROUPS
		7, 10 and 15—personal services, semi-skilled and agricultural workers; S.E.G. 11—unskilled manual workers; S.E.G.s 16 and 17—Armed Forces and others
15. Length of official working week	4	Up to 39·9 hours; 40 to 40·9 hours; 41 hours and over; None (and No Reply)
16. Length of Actual working week	3	Up to 39·9 hours; 40 to 40·9 hours; 41 hours and over
17. Length of usual working week	3	As for Number 16
18. Shift working	2	Yes; No
19. Saturday working	4	Never work Saturdays; occasionally to One-in-two: Work every Saturday; other arrangement
20. Ownership or regular use of a motor-car or motor-cycle	2	Yes; No
21. Type of dwelling	3	Semi-detached: terraced; Other
22. Length of residence	4	Up to 5 years; 5–9 years; 10–14 years; 15 or more years
23. Garden or no garden	2	Yes; No
24. Possession or regular use of Recreation equipment	5	Nil items; 1 item; 2 items: 3 items; 4 or more items
25. Possession of household equipment	—	Not analysed
Number of activities ever undertaken during 1968	5	0 activities; 1–2 activities; 3–4 activities; 5–9 activities; 10 or more activities
Frequency of participation in activity done most often during 1968	8	Daily, Every night; Most nights, 4 or 5 times per week; 2 or 3 times per week; Once per week; Every Weekend, Most Weekends; Once or twice per fortnight; Once or twice per month; Less than once per month

Note: All variables included a group for 'No Reply/Don't know,' in addition to the groups shown.

the 'standard' one that is used in most British housing surveys.

5. *Type of school last attended.* The data were collected for each type of school separately; but, again, there were insufficient numbers within some groups for them to be separately tested. These were therefore combined with other groups. The five groups which emerged emphasized the major educational changes in Britain since the Education Act, 1944.

6. *Operator of school last attended.* Lack of sufficient numbers within some individual categories again meant that some categories had to be combined. The threefold grouping emphasizes, firstly, the overwhelming importance of the local education authorities and, secondly, the fact that the only religious group in Britain which is actively expanding its schools on a relatively large scale is the Roman Catholic Church.

7. *Sex structure of school.* The grouping was the obvious twofold classification into coeducational and single sex.

8. *Terminal school age.* The focus of attention here was really the change in the school leaving age and the numbers of children who stay on at school after reaching the official leaving age. It had been hoped to use actual age throughout; but, again, lack of numbers within some groups meant that all persons staying on at school beyond the (current) official leaving age were placed in one group—16 years and over. If the surveys had been carried out in different areas, or nationally, then more detailed age-groupings of older school-leavers might have been possible.

9. *Further education.* This was a simple nominal measure, covering those who had received some further education after leaving school and those who had not.

10. *Further education qualifications.* These data were collected in considerable detail. There were, however, so few persons who had obtained any further education qualification at all that only two groups were possible. The distinction was based upon whether or not the qualification obtained was directly related to the respondent's occupation. Hence, one group encompassed qualifications that were, broadly, 'vocational', while all the other qualifications were placed in the remaining group.

11. *Personal income.* Reference has been made earlier in this chapter to the reasons why income data were sought from respondents in the form of groups rather than actual income. The same basic groups were used in the analysis, except that for statistical reasons, some of the highest groups were combined into a single group.

12. *Form of payment of income.* Two groups were used; those who

223

were paid weekly; and those who were paid monthly or on some other basis, such as authors living on royalties and retired persons living on interest payments and dividends.

13. *Employment status.* The six groups represent the basic range of possibilities. There are no further alternatives.

14. *Socio-economic group.* All respondents were placed in one of the Registrar-General's 17 socio-economic groups by reference to the latter's *Classification of Occupations*, 1966. It was then found that some of these groups included insufficient numbers for adequate statistical analysis. It was therefore decided to combine these 17 groups into six larger ones. These large groups follow those employed in the Census and other official studies.

15. *Length of official working week.* In the data collection, coding and transfer to punched cards, this information was given in terms of the actual number of hours. In the analysis, however, this had to be reduced to a nominal measure. The proposal was to use four groups, focusing attention upon the '40-hour week' which was, at the time, a kind of standard against which Trade Unions, in particular, set collective bargaining objectives. Respondents were, therefore, grouped into those for whom the official working week was less than 40 hours, those for whom it was 40 hours, and those for whom it was more than 40 hours. The fourth group encompassed those persons who had no official working week.

16. *Length of actual working week.* The groups here were the same as for the preceding variable, except that there was no fourth group, since there was no employed person who did not have an actual working week. The term 'actual working week' refers to the number of hours worked in the week prior to the interview.

17. *Length of usual working week.* The groups used here were exactly the same as those used for measuring the length of the actual working week.

18. *Shift working.* Two groups were used; those who did shift work and those who did not.

19. *Saturday working.* Again, for analytical purposes it was necessary to combine the groups in which the data were collected into larger groups for the significance tests. The essential distinction to be made was between those for whom Saturday working was customary, those for whom it was occasional, and those who never had to work on a Saturday. This led to the formulation of four groups; never work Saturday; work occasional Saturdays to work one-in-two Saturdays; work every Saturday; and have other arrangements (for example, milkmen, who often work six Saturdays in seven).

20. *Ownership or regular use of a car or motorcycle.* There were two groups; those with the use of a car or motor cycle, and those without.

21. *Type of dwelling.* Because of the physical structure of the two areas in which the study took place, there were only two dwelling types with sufficiently large numbers of respondents—semi-detached and terraced houses. All other types were combined into a single group.

22. *Length of residence.* Although data were available for the actual numbers of years that respondents had lived in their present dwellings, the decision to use a nominal measure required groupings. The four groups used correspond to those which have been used in several recent British housing surveys.

23. *Garden or no garden.* This involved a simple twofold division into those respondents who had a garden and those who did not.

24. *Possession or regular use of recreation equipment.* Information was sought about the respondent's access to eleven different classes of recreation equipment—either in the form of possession or regular use—ranging from a tape recorder and/or record player to underwater swimming equipment. Respondents were classified into five groups, according to the number of these classes of goods to which they had access.

25. *Possession of household equipment.* Respondents to the household questionnaire were asked to indicate which of four items were found in the household. The four items were a television, washing machine, refrigerator and telephone. The straight counts indicated that, with the exception of a telephone, these items were now standard equipment in most households; so much so that they were unlikely to be significantly correlated with differences in recreation behaviour. It was decided, therefore, not to proceed with an analysis of the relationship between possession of these goods and the two dependent variables.

Dependent Variable No. 1. Tabulations were drawn up to show the numbers of respondents who had engaged in various numbers of activities, from zero to 71, during 1968. These showed that the highest number of activities undertaken was 28 (by one person), but that the majority of respondents had taken part in 10 or less activities. The largest concentrations were in 5 activities or less. In the light of this evidence, the first dependent variable was classified into five groups: no activities undertaken, 1–2 activities, 3–4 activities, 5–9 activities, and 10 or more activities.

Dependent Variable No. 2. The data for the second dependent

H

Table 40. Tests of Significance for the Profile Variables
Significance*

INDEPENDENT VARIABLE	DEPENDENT VARIABLE No. 1			DEPENDENT VARIABLE No. 2		
	Both Areas	Billesley	All Saints	Both Areas	Billesley	All Saints
1A. Age—first classification	2	2	2	2	2	2
1B. Age—second classification	2	2	2	2	2	2
2. Sex	2	2	2	2	2	2
3. Marital status	2	2	2	2	2	2
4. Number of persons in the household	2	2	2	0	0	0
5. Type of school last attended	2	0	2	2	0	2
6. Operator of school last attended	0	2	0	0	0	0
7. Sex structure of school	2	2	2	0	0	0
8. Terminal school age	2	2	2	0	0	0
9. Further education	0	2	0	0	0	0
10. Further education qualifications	2	0	2	0	0	0
11. Personal income	2	2	2	0	0	0
12. Form of payment of income	2	2	0	0	0	0
13. Employment status	2	2	2	2	2	2
14. Socio-economic group	2	2	2	2	2	2
15. Length of official working week	2	0	2	0	0	0
16. Lenth of actual working week	2	0	2	0	0	0
17. Length of usual working week	2	0	0	0	0	0
18. Shift working	0	0	0	0	0	0
19. Saturday working	0	0	0	0	0	0

20. Ownership or regular use of a car or motor cycle	2	2	2	2	2	2
21. Type of dwelling	2	0	0	2	2	0
22. Length of residence	2	2	2	0	0	0
23. Garden or no garden	2	0	0	0	0	0
24. Possession or regular use of recreation equipment	2	2	2	0	0	0

* Significance: 0 means not significant at the 5 per cent level.
  1 means significant at the 5 per cent level.
  2 means significant at the 1 per cent level.

Dependent Variable No. 1 = number of activities ever undertaken during 1968.
Dependent Variable No. 2 = frequency of participation in activity undertaken most often during 1968.

227

variable—frequency of participation in the activity undertaken most often during 1968—had already been collected in the form of groups. This had arisen because, although the interest was in *frequency* of participation, the pilot survey had shown that respondents were rarely able to place a precise figure upon frequency. They were much more likely to state that they had participated 'once a week' or 'every weekend' than to give a figure, such as '15 times'. When the respondent is being asked to cast his mind back over a period of a year, he cannot be expected to remember in great detail. On the basis of the replies to the pilot survey, therefore, eight groups had been established and used in collecting the data in the main survey. These groups ranged from 'daily/every night' at one extreme to 'less than once per month' at the other. These same groups were used for the analysis.

These, then, were the groups into which the dependent and independent variables were organized for the analysis. The relationships between each independent variable and the two dependent variables were then measured by means of chi-square tests on two-way contingency tables.* The results were expressed in one of three forms: either the correlations were found to be significant at the 1 per cent level of probability; or they were significant at the 5 per cent level of probability; or they were *not* significant at the 5 per cent level. Some independent variables were then further examined for differences between the groups into which they had been divided. The method used for this was an examination of *average activity rates* for each group, based upon the first recreation variable—the number of activities ever undertaken during 1968.

The Findings

The result of the tests of significance between the variables are given in Table 40. This indicates that, for the two areas taken together, nine of the twenty-four profile variables were significantly correlated with both measures of recreation activity. Moreover, all of these correlations were significant at the 1 per cent level of probability.†
In addition, there were nine profile variables that were significantly correlated with the first recreation activity measure only—that is, the

---

* Non-respondents were excluded from this analysis.

† Indeed, there were no profile variables which were correlated *only* at the 5 per cent level of probability; all variables, whether correlated with one or both of the recreation variables, were either significant at the 1 per cent level or were not significant even at the 5 per cent level.

number of activities ever undertaken during 1968. In contrast, there were no profile variables that were significantly correlated with the second recreation activity measure only—the frequency of participation in the activity undertaken most often during 1968. This leaves six profile variables which were not significantly correlated with either of the two recreation measures. An example of the testing— between marital status and the first recreation variable—is given in Table 41.

In general, the results of these significance tests were confirmed when the same tests were applied to the data for the two survey areas separately. In the case of the first recreation variable, there were seven differences between the two areas, three of which had to do with

Table 41. *Tabulations of Marital Status by Number of Activities Ever Undertaken during 1968*

| MARITAL STATUS | NUMBER OF ACTIVITIES EVER UNDER- TAKEN DURING 1968 | | | | | TOTAL |
	None	*1–2*	*3–4*	*5–9*	*10 and over*	
Single	4	25	18	74	81	202
Married	52	187	149	272	42	702
Separated, divorced, widowed	35	71	23	22	1	152
Totals	91	283	190	368	124	1,056

Degrees of Freedom = 8. Chi-square = 295·754.
Significant at the 1 per cent level of probability.

the length of the working week. The length of the *official* working week was significantly correlated with this variable in the All Saints area, though not in the Billesley area or in the two areas taken together. In contrast, both the length of the *actual* working and the *usual* working week were significantly correlated with this variable in the All Saints area *and* the two areas taken together, but not in the Billesley area. The other variables where correlations differed between individual areas or between one area and the two taken together were the *sex structure of the school, the form of payment of income, type of dwelling* and *ownership of a garden*. In the case of the second recreation variable, there were only five differences which emerged when the data for the two survey areas were analysed separately. The most important of these were the *length of the actual working week* and the *ownership or regular use of recreation equipment*. In both cases, correlations with the recreation variables were significant at the 1 per cent level for the two areas taken together, but were not significant, even at the 5 per cent level, for each area separately. These will obviously require further analysis in future studies.

What has emerged then is that there are nine profile variables which, at least for the two survey areas taken together, are significantly correlated with both the 'breadth' and the 'depth' of recreation experience and which would appear, therefore, to be particularly important for forecasting purposes. These consist of three demographic variables—age, sex and marital status;* two occupation variables—employment status and the length of the actual working week; one education variable—the type of school last attended; one housing variable—type of dwelling; the motor car variable—ownership or regular use; and the recreation equipment variable—also ownership or regular use.

The nine variables that were correlated only with the first measure of recreation activity—the breadth of the respondent's recreation experience—consisted of one demographic variable—the number of persons in the household; two education variables—further education and terminal school age; two income variables—personal income and form of payment of income; two occupation variables—socioeconomic group and the length of the usual working week; and two housing variables—the length of residence and the possession of a garden. Some, or all, of these variables could be useful for forecasting and planning purposes if the particular focus of interest is the width of the population's recreation activity.

Finally, there are the six profile variables which were not significantly correlated with either of the two measures of recreation activity and which would appear, therefore, to be of no use for forecasting purposes. These consisted of three education variables—the operator of the school last attended, the sex structure of the school and the further education qualifications obtained; and three occupation variables—the length of the official working week, shift working and Saturday working.

The implications of these findings and the suggested guidelines for the collection of profile data in future studies will be discussed in the final section of this chapter. Prior to this, however, a brief discussion will be made of the validity of the groups into which the nine highly

* Both groupings of age were significant, although, as indicated earlier, some of the frequencies in the finer groupings do not meet the full requirements of statistical rigour—but that is not too serious.

significant profile variables were classified; that is, the nine variables that were significantly correlated with both measures of recreation activity. As indicated earlier, the test of validity was an examination of differences in *average activity rates* between groups; that is, differences between groups in the average number of activities ever undertaken during 1968. This is by no means the only possible measure of differences between groups; nor it is necessarily the most sophisticated statistically. But, for the purpose of providing broadly based guidelines, it has the merit that is both statistically sound and easily carried out. It is fairly safe to assume that, for tables in which the variables have been shown to be related by the chi-square tests, the large differences between groups in these average activity rates must be statistically significant. For present purposes, therefore, differences in average activity rates have been used as the sole criterion for judging the validity of the groups employed. Some suggestions for further, more sophisticated, statistical tests have, however, been made in the final chapter of this report.

Two alternative sets of *age-groups* were examined. The first consisted of groups made up on the basis of the traditional five-year intervals, but with some necessary modifications. The second employed more detailed two-year groups for respondents below the age of 30 years, in order to test the hypothesis that there are significant differences between persons within the five-year groups below this age. The figures for each group in both classifications are given in Table 42. What emerges from an examination of the traditional groups is a major difference in the average activity rate between respondents aged 12–19 years and those aged 20–24 years; the average for the former group is 10·5 activities, while for the latter it is 7·0 activities. The differences between other groups are much smaller and, in some cases, it is doubtful that they are significant. Generally, however, what emerges from the examination of traditional age-groups is major differences between groups on either side of the following points: 20, 30, 50 and 60 years. When the examination of the detailed two-year groups is added to this, some further major differences emerge. The most important of these is the differences between respondents aged 12–13 years and those aged 14–15 years; the average rate for the former group is 12·1 activities, while for the latter it is 9·7 activities. There are also major differences between the groups 18–19 years and 20–21 years, and between the groups 20–21 years and 22–23 years. All of this suggests that key dividing ages are 13, 19, 21, 23, 30, 50 and 60 years.

The groupings by *sex* indicated a clear difference in average activity

231

rates between males and females. Male respondents were considerably more active, having an average rate of 6·1 activities. Females, in contrast, had an average rate of only 4·1 activities.

The examination of *marital status* groups showed major differences between the three groups employed. The average activity rate for single persons was 9·0; for married persons it was 4·3; and for separated, divorced and widowed persons it was 2·1.

Table 42. *Average Activity Rates for Various Age Groups*

AGE-GROUP (years)	AVERAGE ACTIVITY RATE*
1. *Standard classification*	
12–19	10·5
20–24	7·0
25–29	6·6
30–39	5·2
40–49	4·8
50–59	3·8
60–64	2·5
65–69	2·3
70 and over	1·5
2. *Detailed classification for*	
12–29 years	
12–13	12·1
14–15	9·7
16–17	10·4
18–19	10·1
20–21	8·3
22–23	5·6
24–25	6·8
26–29	6·1

* Average Activity Rate—average number of activities ever undertaken during 1968 by respondents within each group.

Differences were, also, generally significant between *employment status* groups. The average activity rate was highest, not surprisingly, for respondents still at school or college—a value of 11·2. Employed persons participated, on average, in 5·6 activities; housewifes in 3·2 activities; and retired persons in 1·8 activities. The remaining two groups—unemployed persons and those never employed—consisted of too few persons for valid statistical analysis.

Differences between the three groups used to measure *the length of the actual working week* were not very clear. In particular, the

232

difference between respondents who worked a 40-hour week and those who worked for *more* than 40 hours was much smaller than the difference between those who worked a 40-hour week and those who worked *less* than 40 hours. The average activity rate was 4·7 for respondents who worked less than 40 hours, 5·8 for those who worked 40 hours, and 6·3 for those who worked more than 40 hours.*

Of the five groups used to measure *the type of school last attended*, two were very similar. The average activity rate for respondents whose last school attended was a Primary, Council or Elementary school was 3·0; the figure for Public, Independent and Other schools was 3·6. All others showed clear and major differences. The figure for those from Secondary Modern schools was 5·9; for those from Grammar schools it was 7·2; and for those from Technical, Comprehensive and Bi-lateral schools it was 9·2.

Differences were fairly substantial between the two major groups used to measure *type of dwelling*. The average activity rate for respondents from semi-detached houses was 5·9; while for respondents from terraced houses it was 4·1.

The ownership or regular use of a motor car was measured in terms of two groups only—those respondents who had access to a car (or motor cycle) and those who did not. The former group participated in an average of 6·8 activities; the latter in an average of 4·2 activities.

Average activity rates were very clearly and consistently related to the final variable to be examined—*ownership or regular use of recreation equipment*. For respondents with access to none of the listed items, the average activity rate was only 2·6. This rate rose almost proportionately with the number of items available to a level of 8·7 for respondents with access to four or more items of equipment.

Recommended Guidelines for Future Studies

The major purpose in undertaking this research project and, in particular, the analysis of the relative significance of different profile variables in 'determining' recreation behaviour, was 'to provide guidelines for wider studies at the national and, more particularly, the regional and subregional levels'. The findings of the analysis will not make it possible for us to lay down precise regulations about which profile variables should be included in future studies and which

---

* It is, incidentally, interesting to note that the relationship is the exact opposite to what might be expected. The average activity rate rises with a *rise* in the length of the working week!

233

excluded. It is doubtful that we should want to do this anyway, even if the results of the present study enabled us to do so beyond any reasonable doubt; for it is certain that the relative importance of the different profile characteristics in influencing recreation behaviour will change over the long run. As more and more schoolchildren go on to further education after school, for example, the strength of this variable in formulating behaviour is likely to change significantly in relation to other variables. What is being sought here, therefore, is not a list of absolute standards to be applied in all future studies for the next ten or twenty years; but, rather, a set of ground rules which will facilitate comparability between future studies and which will provide some systematic data for use in forecasting models of one kind and another. Those people directing studies during the next ten years or so should not be restricted to collecting only the data that will be specified below. On the contrary, they should be encouraged to collect additional profile data wherever appropriate. But, equally, they should be strongly advised, persuaded and, wherever possible, required to collect data about, at least, those data which are specified in the guidelines. This is absolutely necessary if we are to obtain comparability and a systematic base for forecasting in different regions, subregions and, even, cities.

A necessary corollary of establishing guidelines, however, is that they should be subject to fairly regular review. Ground rules cannot be established for posterity. They are, by their nature, rules of behaviour or procedure that relate to a particular society at a particular time. They should change as society changes. This is, indeed, a fundamental tenet of, for example, political organization; without regular and well-founded changes in its ground rules a political system will atrophy. The guidelines that are suggested here will be relevant for a period of, perhaps, ten years or so; thereafter, they are likely to be increasingly outmoded and irrelevant. It is recommended, therefore, that this particular aspect of the present study—that is, the relative significance of different profile variables in affecting recreation behaviour—should be repeated at intervals of not more than about ten years.

The first set of variables about which recommendations should be made is, obviously, those which were found to be significantly correlated with both depth and width of recreation activity. These are the nine variables that were discussed in detail in the previous section of this chapter. It is proposed that data about *all* of these should be collected in future studies (Table 43). For five of them, it appears appropriate to employ the groups used in this study. The other four,

234

Table 43. *Recommended Guidelines for Future Studies: Profile Variables*

PROFILE VARIABLE	NUMBER OF GROUPS	LIST OF GROUPS*
1. AGE	8	(1) 12–13 years (2) 14–19 years (3) 20–21 years (4) 22–23 years (5) 24–29 years (6) 30–49 years (7) 50–59 years (8) 60 years and over
2. SEX	2	(1) Male (2) Female
3. MARITAL STATUS	3	(1) Single (2) Married (3) Separated, Divorced, Widowed
4. EMPLOYMENT STATUS	6	(1) Unemployed (2) Retired (3) Employed (4) Still at School or College (5) Housewife (6) Never Employed
5. LENGTH OF ACTUAL WORKING WEEK	2	(1) 40 hours or less (2) More than 40 hours
6. SOCIO-ECONOMIC GROUP	17	Individual Groups 1–17
	or 6	(1) S.E.G.s 1, 2, 3, 4 and 13 (2) S.E.G.s 8, 9, 12 and 14 (3) S.E.G.s 5 and 6 (4) S.E.G.s 7, 10 and 15 (5) S.E.G. 11 (6) S.E.G.s 16 and 17
7. TYPE OF SCHOOL LAST ATTENDED	5	(1) Primary, Elementary, Council (2) Secondary Modern (3) Grammar (4) Technical, Comprehensive, Bi-Lateral (5) Public, Independent, Other

235

Table 43. (*continued*)

PROFILE VARIABLE	NUMBER OF GROUPS	LIST OF GROUPS*
8. TERMINAL SCHOOL AGE	7	(1) Under 14 years (2) 14 (3) 15 (4) 16 (5) 17 (6) 18 (7) Over 18
9. PERSONAL DISPOS-ABLE INCOME	7	(1) Up to £5 per week (2) Over £5 up to £7.50 per week (3) Over £7.50 up to £10 per week (4) Over £10 up to £12.50 per week (5) Over £12.50 up to £15 per week (6) Over £15 up to £20 per week (7) Over £20 per week
10. TYPE OF DWELLING	7	(1) Detached house (2) Semi-detached house (3) Terraced house (4) Bungalow (5) Self contained flat, maisonette (6) Other flat, bedsitter, rooms (7) Prefab.
11. OWNERSHIP OR REGULAR USE OF A CAR OR MOTOR-CYCLE	2	(1) Yes (2) No
12. OWNERSHIP OR REGULAR USE OF SELECTED RECREA-TION EQUIPMENT	5	(1) Nil Items (2) 1 Item (3) 2 Items (4) 3 Items (5) 4 or more Items

* For discussion of groups consult the text.

however, warrant some further discussion. They are age, length of actual working week, type of school last attended, and type of dwelling.

The results of the examination of conventional age-groups suggested that the key margins between groups occurred at the ages of 20, 30, 50 and 60 years. In addition, the analysis of the detailed two-year groups for respondents aged between 12 and 25 years indicated three other important divisions, between 13 and 14 years, between 21 and 22 years, and between 23 and 24 years. However, these findings will have been influenced, at least in part, by the groups that were used themselves. The problem is not unlike the proverbial 'chicken-and-egg' conundrum; which is cause and which effect? Thus, for example, no significant difference was found between the groups 30–39 years and 40–49 years. But we do not know whether there might be significant differences between sub-groups within these groups which would suggest, say, two quite different final groups, such as 30–35 years and 36–49 years, or, even, three or more groups. Tests were not undertaken for differences within these groups, mainly because restrictions of time, resources and computer availability dictated that all sub-groups could not be examined and judgement, based upon previous research, suggested that the more important sub-groups to be examined were those within the five-year groups spanning the ages 12–29 years. Here, the analysis demonstrated fairly conclusively that some major differences do exist between these micro-groups.

In the light of this evidence, it is recommended that future studies employ, at least, the eight groups shown in Table 43. Five of these groups cover the 18-year span between 12 and 29 years of age; the remaining three cover persons aged 30 years and over. It is further recommended, however, that the *collection* of data should preferably be in the form of asking respondents to give their date of birth (month and year) so that analysis could be undertaken of more detailed groups if thought necessary or desirable.

In the case of the three groups used to measure the length of the respondent's actual working week, the results of the analysis, while establishing differences between groups, were less satisfactory than for any of the other eight variables examined. In particular, the validity of the distinction between those persons who worked a 40-hour week and those who worked *less* than 40 hours per week is questionable. There was no very clear difference between these two groups, whereas the difference between those who worked a 40-hour week and those who worked *more* than 40 hours was fairly obvious. In view of this it is recommended that a twofold classification

237

between those who work *40 hours or less* and those who work *more than 40 hours* is probably adequate. This variable, however, obviously needs further analysis.

Five groups were used in analysing the significance of the type of school last attended as a determinant of recreation behaviour. The examination of average activity rates indicated, however, that there was no very clear difference between respondents whose last school attended was a Primary, Elementary or Council school and those for whom it was a Public, Independent or Other school. There is no obvious reason why this should be so. It is possible, of course, that the similarity between the two groups is fortuitous—although it appears for both survey areas separately as well as for the two areas taken together. Until, however, further testing has been done, it will be best to recommend that these two groups should remain separated rather than be amalgamated. The remaining three groups were quite clearly different from each other and from these two groups.

In examining the significance of the type of dwelling in influencing recreation activity, only three groups were used—semi-detached house, terraced house and other dwelling. The data had, in fact, been collected in seven groups: detached house, semi-detached house, terraced house, bungalow, self-contained flat or maisonette, other flat, bedsitter or rooms and prefab. Unfortunately, there were insufficient numbers of respondents in five of these groups for them to be separately tested. They were therefore amalgamated together in a single group. A major reason why there were relatively few respondents in these groups was, of course, because the survey took place in two relatively small areas of Birmingham. Had the areal base of the study been wider—for example, the whole of the City— then it is likely that a more uniform distribution of respondents over the seven groups would have been obtained. We cannot say, of course, that there would have been significant differences between the seven groups in respect of the recreation variables. But, equally, it would be inadequate to recommend the three groupings used here for all future studies. As a compromise, therefore, it is recommended that the sevenfold grouping be used in future studies until further research has suggested better groups.

Consideration can now be given to the nine variables that were correlated significantly with only one of the recreation variables— the number of activities ever undertaken during 1968. It is recognized that, for organizational and technical reasons associated with the conduct of social surveys, it will not be possible to recommend that data should be collected about *all* of these variables in future studies. On the other hand, it would be useful to have a few of them included in future work so as to act as a check upon the present findings. Furthermore, the present analysis had, perforce, to be limited to an analysis of correlations between the profile variables and only two measures of recreation activity, depth and width.* It is possible, however, that there would have been some differences in the relative prominence of variables if other measures of recreation activity had been employed; in particular, if the analysis had been made of 'types' of activity. There are three of the nine variables that were significantly correlated only with width of activity which previous studies have suggested would also be significantly correlated with 'types' of activity undertaken. In addition, these are variables which are usually included in other, non-recreation studies and which would, therefore, provide a good basis for comparability. It is therefore recommended that these three should also be included in future studies. They are *personal income, terminal school age* and *socio-economic groups.*

The data about personal income should refer to income after all deductions made at source—that is, essentially, personal disposable income. Several previous studies have concluded that this is the most satisfactory measure.† As for the groups to be used, these are defined to some extent by the fact that the data have to be collected in group form in order to avoid excessively high rates of non-response. The groups used in the present study showed clear differences in average activity rates only among the higher groups. It is not recommended, however, that the lower groups be amalgamated —at least, not for the collection of the data—since they do give comparability with other studies.

The groups used to measure terminal school age all showed major differences from each other in respect of average activity rates. It is recommended, therefore, that these groups be used, with the exception that the group '16 years and over' be divided into several groups, such as '16 years', '17 years', '18 years', and 'over 18 years'. The only reason that this constituted a single group in the present study was because of the lack of numbers for valid statistical analysis of the smaller divisions. In future studies, however, it should be useful to analyse the recreation data in terms of these more detailed groups. If the analysis should then show that there are no significant

* Some of the effects of this limitation are discussed more fully in the Epilogue.
† For a wider discussion of the findings of previous studies, see T. L. Burton and G. E. Cherry, *Social Research Techniques for Planners*, George Allen & Unwin, 1970, Chapter 5.

differences between the various groups above the age of 15 years, they can be added together to make a single group '16 years and over'.

Finally, it is recommended that the analysis of socio-economic group be undertaken wherever possible, in respect of individual groups. Where a lack of numbers makes this impossible, the groups can be amalgamated into the five social classes (plus the odd groups, 16 and 17) that have been generally used in previous research. The analysis from the present study in respect of the first recreation variable indicated significance for the three classes for which sufficient absolute numbers of respondents were obtained.

To summarize, it is recommended that, in future studies, information should be collected about twelve profile variables. Three of these are demographic variables—*age, sex* and *marital status*; three are occupational—*employment status, socio-economic group* and the *length of the respondent's actual working week*; two are concerned with education—*type of school last attended* and *terminal school age;* one relates to income—*personal disposable income*; one is a housing variable—*type of dwelling*; one measures mobility—*ownership or regular use of a car or motor cycle*; and the final one covers the *ownership or regular use of various items of recreation equipment*. These variables and the groups in which it is recommended they be analysed are listed in Table 43.

It should be emphasized once again, however, that these recommendations merely constitute a set of guidelines for future research. The evidence from the present study strongly supports the choice of these particular variables; but that evidence is limited in its scope. Further testing, by other studies and by additional analyses of the data collected in this study, will help to refine and strengthen these recommendations. A discussion of some potential directions for further work will be found in the Epilogue.

Part Three
The Measurement of Supply

Chapter 10
Compiling an Inventory of Opportunity

It was part of the purpose of this research project to consider methods of measuring the supply of recreation facilities as well as the demand for them. Furthermore, the physical restriction of the demand survey within two selected areas of the city and the proposal to investigate the interrelationships of demand and supply in these areas required that a clear and detailed inventory be drawn up of available facilities within the two areas. The review of recent studies pointed to some of the major difficultes that have been encountered in past attempts to compile inventories of supplies. Essentially, the problems have been twofold: on the one hand, some facilities have not been listed at all; on the other hand, there have been some facilities which have been listed more than once. The present chapter will consider some of the difficulties that have arisen from these problems by outlining the methods that were used to compile an inventory of available supplies in the two study areas. It also includes a discussion of other methods that were considered for use, but which, in the final instance, were not employed.

The interest here is, of course, with opportunity and not simply with supply. This implies that consideration must be given to limitations placed upon the use of facilities by such factors as location, management and policy. It is unlikely that restrictions deriving from location will be very important, since the two study areas are, relatively, quite small. The furthest distance that any inhabitant of either area would have to travel in order to reach a facility within the same area is approximately 2·5 miles. It is probable, however, that restrictions imposed by the times at which facilities are available for use will have a significant effect. And, perhaps even more important, careful note will need to be taken of situations in which facilities are reserved for the exclusive use of particular groups of people only, such as private sports clubs. It is in these kinds of situations that the concept of opportunity is so much more meaningful than the concept of supply.

A Classification of Recreation Opportunity

It is pertinent, at this point, to consider the problems of classification and grouping of recreation facilities, since one of the major elements in classification is opportunity: 'The classification of recreation facilities should be directly related to the classification of demands, since facilities are designed to cater for demands' [8]. That is to say, a categorization of supply is only useful if it is related to a demand which it is capable of satisfying: which is merely another way of saying that we should classify opportunity rather than supply.

Opportunity is determined by a number of factors, but there are two which are particularly important: the location of facilities (and, hence, the distance and time necessary to reach them) and the period of time available for recreation. Other factors are management policy, economic constraints, family and community customs and modes of life, and so on. The importance of these other factors will vary from one place to another, and in some situations they may be equally as important as location and available recreation time. But these two latter factors will be of critical importance in *all* situations. It is, therefore, worth considering them in further detail.

The most important point to be made about location and available recreation time is that they are interdependent variables in determining opportunity. The longer is the period of available recreation time, the more flexibility is possible in the location of facilities. Conversely, the shorter is the period of available recreation time, the more rigid are the requirements for the location of facilities. This, of course, assumes that the length of each period of available recreation time is the primary constraint, and that the location of facilities can be adjusted in line with this. In most cases this is probably a reasonable assumption, but there are situations in which the location of facilities is fixed. In such cases opportunity can only be measured if we know the lengths of the different periods of recreation normally required, and available, for the kinds of activities which can be undertaken at these fixed facilities.

This twofold concern with the location of facilities and available recreation time has led most investigators to adopt a basic twofold classification: on the one hand, user-oriented facilities; on the other, resource-based facilities. Some studies, such as those by the O.R.R.C.[38] and Clawson [18], have produced more detailed classifications; but even these have had, as an underlying division, the distinction between those facilities for which location is determined primarily by the distribution of population and its available recreation time, and those for which location is a function of the distribution of natural resources.* User-oriented facilities are located close to users and are based upon whatever resources, natural and artificial,

* Not only natural resources, of course; some man made resources (e.g. Stonehenge) would belong here.

244

can be made available at these locations. Resource-based facilities, on the other hand, are located wherever outstanding natural resources happen to exist. In the former case location is determined by the demand for facilities; in the latter case, by the supply of resources.

This primary twofold classification of facilities can be further subdivided by reference to the distribution of available recreation time. The time budget studies outlined earlier in Chapter 7—and other studies, by the British Travel Association [2, 6]—have suggested that periods of time available for recreation fall, broadly, into five groups; first, *very short periods* of up to about an hour; second, *short periods* of up to a few hours, usually in the evenings after work and school or as a half-day; third, *a full day*, sometimes during the week but more usually at weekends; fourth, *periods of a few days*, mainly at weekends which are extended by Bank Holidays; and fifth, *periods of a week or more* as part of annual holidays. These five distinct categories of recreation time have precise implications for the location of facilities. The analysis of the time budget diaries showed that very short periods of recreation time tend to be used up either in the home or in the immediate locality of the home—for example, in a neighbour's home or a nearby playground. Short periods of a few hours or a half-day tend to be used up in activities in the wider district in which the home is located or, if travelling time is not excessive, in the town or city centre. Sometimes, a half-day is used for short distance travel out of the town or city into nearby rural areas. A full day (in this context, a period of about ten hours or more) is almost invariably used for trips away from the town, to coast or countryside. Periods of a few days tend to be used either as an opportunity to travel a considerable distance from home and stay away overnight, or as successive periods of a full day: these full days then being used for trips away from home but with no overnight stay, or, in turn, being made up of several successive short periods of recreation time—a morning, an afternoon and an evening—with people usually returning to the home between each period. Finally, recreation periods of a week or more as a part of annual holidays place virtually no restrictions upon the location of activities.

These five categories of recreation time are not, of course, mutually exclusive. It has already been noted above, from the time budget studies, that some people may choose to take a full day's recreation in the form of several short periods. Similarly, others may choose to take a period of a few days' recreation in the form of several successive full days. In other words, people may choose to take the longer periods of recreation time in the form of several successive shorter periods. Moreover, the distinction between one category and another is not always very clear: this is especially so with the short periods and the very short periods. A housewife may have a short period of several hours of recreation time available during a weekday afternoon while her baby sleeps, but, because she must be present in case of emergencies, she may effectively think of this as a very short period and use it as such. Qualifications of this kind, however, do not invalidate the concept of a fivefold classification, but merely act as a caution against interpreting it too rigidly.

The identification of five broad categories of available recreation time and of the general ways in which each is used has made it possible to construct an overall classification of opportunity—that is, of facilities capable of satisfying a demand. This classification has six divisions, shown in Table 44 in relation to the five categories of recreation time. The table also includes examples of the kinds of facilities that would be envisaged at each opportunity level. The classification is hierarchical, ranging from the locality to the national level. No attempt has been made to suggest optimum sizes of population for each opportunity level, for two main reasons. In the first place, each opportunity level, while obviously having spatial implications, was not conceived as a distinct physical area of ground. Each derives from a concept of periods of recreation time of differing lengths and the location of activities undertaken during these periods. The schema is based, therefore, upon time–distance constraints rather than upon optimum population sizes. Secondly, at least at the regional and town levels, the optimum size of population to be served can be determined, in large measure, by the size, siting and design of facilities provided; it is, in other words, variable.

The kinds of facilities that would be provided at each opportunity level will depend upon other factors in addition to the period of recreation time available. In particular, there will be an important part to be played by economic considerations. Some facilities which are used mainly for short periods could, for example, be provided at either the neighbourhood or district level; or, again, at either the district or town level. Where this kind of flexibility exists, particular attention can be devoted to economic and other considerations. Indeed, in the commercial sector, economic viability is a primary concern. As a result, many commercial facilities will only be provided at the town or city level, since it is only at this level that economies of scale are sufficiently high to assure economic viability. In the public sector, where facilities are usually operated at a loss

246

anyway (at least in direct monetary terms), the objective may be simply to minimize losses; and this may require that a facility be provided at one level rather than another. Thus, for example, a small swimming pool may only be viable, in these terms, at the district level, even though the type of use made of it—for short periods

Table 44. *A Classification of Recreation Opportunity*

OPPORTUNITY LEVEL	TIME–DISTANCE CONSTRAINT*	AVAILABLE RECREATION TIME	EXAMPLES OF FACILITIES
Locality	½ mile 10 minutes	Very short periods Short periods	Children's play spaces
Neighbourhood	Up to 2 miles Up to 20 minutes	Short periods	Park Tennis courts Sports pitches
District	Up to 3 miles Up to 30 minutes	Short periods Half-day	Branch library Swimming pool Social centre
Town/City	Up to 4–5 miles Up to 30–45 minutes	Short periods Half-day	Major Sports centre Large commercial facilities Cultural facilities
Regional	Up to 25–30 miles About 1–1½ hours	Half-day Full day Several days	Outdoor water areas Airfields Race tracks
National	None	Full day Several days Annual holiday	Resource-based facilities

* Time–Distance Constraint is a maximum figure in time or distance: which figure is operative will depend, of course, on mode of transport.

of recreation—means that it could, in principle, be provided at either the neighbourhood or the district level.

This classification provides a potentially useful structure for planning purposes. It has the merit that it is based upon an observed pattern of periods of recreation time of differing lengths and upon the location of activities undertaken during these periods. Its use as a planning tool would obviously require more detailed consideration of the economic constraints upon the provision of various facilities at different opportunity levels. Further work also needs to be done to assess the validity of the crude values given to the time–distance constraint at each opportunity level. The figures given here were based partly upon the findings of the time budget studies, partly upon other studies—such as those by Burton [11] and Wager [47]—and partly upon intuition. A major priority for further research must clearly be to test and refine this concept further.

The inventory of opportunities in the two study areas, shown in detail in Chapter 11, has been compiled with the above classification in mind. The size of each area is such that opportunities *within* them could only occur at the locality, neighbourhood and district levels. The remainder of this chapter will be taken up with a discussion of the methods used to compile the inventory at each of these three levels within each area. The methods employed were, essentially, twofold: the use of documents and the use of a demand survey. Each will be discussed separately below.

Documents

Documents are likely to be the major source of data in compiling an inventory of recreation opportunities in any particular area. They can be supplemented by other techniques, such as postal survey and observation, but they will undoubtedly provide the basic data for the inventory. It was suggested in Chapter 1 that documents are of two main kinds—continuous and discontinuous records—and that they can suffer from two major sources of bias—selective deposit and selective survival. In the context of an inventory of existing opportunities, the second source of bias is unlikely to be of very great significance. Selective deposit—or, more exactly, selective recording of data—is likely, on the other hand, to be of major importance. Some facilities will certainly not be recorded at all; while others will be recorded in several different documents and may, on occasion, be recorded more than once in the same document.

The primary sources to consult when compiling an inventory within a particular area are the continuous records of the public authorities in that area; in particular, the local council. Most local government authorities, at the rural district level and above, keep at least general lists of the facilities provided by public agencies within their boundaries. In most authorities these lists are contained in the annual reports of each department of the local authority, such as the Parks

248

Department and the Baths Department. In a few very large authorities, however, these lists are collected together in a single volume, often prepared for publicity purposes, which can be obtained from the council offices. The City of Birmingham has such a summary volume. The City Council has established its own statistics department, which publishes an *Annual Abstract of Statistics* [90], with sections on area and climate, population, births, marriages, deaths, employment, transport and communications, housing, and so on. The section on miscellaneous matters includes the following six tables:

(i) Stock of books and registered readers at, and borrowings from, lending and reference libraries.

(ii) Attendances at various sections of the City of Birmingham Museum and Art Gallery.

(iii) Bathers in various sections of public baths.

(iv) Sports facilities provided by the City in parks and recreation grounds.

(v) Recreational facilities in individual public parks, playing fields and recreation grounds administered by the City.

(vi) Number and area of allotments under Corporation control.

Only one of these tables (No. 5) proved to be useful for compiling the inventory of opportunities within the two particular areas with which this study is concerned. The remaining tables provided information about demand only; or, alternatively, gave information about facilities in the form of totals for the whole city. These tables would obviously be very useful for other studies, but were of no help for the present one. The fifth table, on the other hand, provided very detailed information about facilities within individual public recreation areas. The actual data for the two study areas are shown in Chapter 11.

In addition to this comprehensive volume of statistics for the whole city, an examination has been made of the individual publications of separate departments of the city council. Most of these documents have been prepared for publicity purposes, and consist of timetables and similar material. Thus, for example, the timetables for the Baths Department include a list of all the swimming baths in the city, times of opening and admission charges. From this it was ascertained that neither of the two study areas has a swimming bath within its boundaries, but that each has one within a distance of about one mile. By a similar process, it was discovered that neither area has a branch public library, but that each has one located within less than a quarter of a mile of its boundary.

The official publications of the city council provide a useful list of all facilities made available by it for public recreation; and, in the few cases where data are missing or ambiguous, they can be supplemented by observation or by a postal inquiry to the relevant department, as was done in this study. These publications do not, however, provide information about facilities belonging to private associations, voluntary groups and commercial organizations. In relatively small towns this information can often be obtained by reference to local newspapers, Citizens' Advice Bureaux, local trading organizations, and so on. Thus, for example, a complete list of local cinemas can be compiled from the advertisements of programmes in the local newspaper. Again, branch libraries usually have notice boards devoted to information about local voluntary groups and forthcoming local events. In a similar way, church notice boards carry information about social clubs and organizations linked to the church. All of these are documents that can be consulted by the simple, though often tedious, process of visiting such places as churches and libraries. In a small area, this process may not be very time-consuming. In a large area, however, such as the whole of the City of Birmingham, this procedure is wholly impracticable. Some other approach would be necessary.

Fortunately, many large cities have one or more organizations which publish semi-official directories containing information of very diverse kinds about the city. These directories are semi-official in the sense that they usually contain detailed information about the constitution of the city council, its departments, members and officers, and have been (tacitly) recognized as authoritative by the city council. The most useful and comprehensive directory for Birmingham is published annually by the city's leading newspaper, the *Birmingham Post* [88]. This includes sections on the City Corporation, the law courts and magistrates, churches and religious congregations, welfare and health services, transport and travel, and so on. There are two sections, in particular, which were helpful in compiling the inventory of recreation opportunities: those on *cultural activities and entertainments*, and *sports, pastimes and clubs*. These two sections gave detailed information about music and art societies, theatres, cinemas, sports clubs, community associations and other voluntary groups throughout the city. The entries included information pertaining to the addresses of secretaries of clubs and organizations, and the places at which meetings were usually held.

These, then, were some of the kinds of documents used to compile the inventory of facilities in the two study areas. They were immensely useful and provided a significant base of data about facilities, which could then be augmented by data obtained in other ways. Nobody, of course, will know of all the available documents which list facilities and organizations; on the other hand, it is not difficult to discover them. The obvious first place to visit when compiling an inventory of facilities within a town or city is its Central Reference Library. Many of the documents that were used in compiling the inventory of opportunities in the two study areas were first consulted at the Reference Library in Birmingham. The information obtained from these documents gave a basic picture of the numbers and kinds of opportunities provided by the local authority for the general public. In addition, they gave details of some opportunities that are provided by community associations, voluntary groups and commercial organizations. The documents consulted included the City's *Annual Abstract of Statistics* [90], the *Birmingham Post* and the *Evening Mail*, the telephone directory, various publications of the Baths, Education, Museum and Art Gallery, Parks, Smallholdings and Allotments, and Public Libraries Departments of the City Council, and the *Birmingham Post Year Book and Who's Who* [88]. In addition, notice boards were examined at the Branch Library in each area and at various churches. Despite this, however, there was a relative dearth of data obtained about the kinds and volume of facilities provided by private groups, voluntary associations and commercial organizations; and the information that was obtained was usually much less detailed than the information obtained about local authority opportunities. It was obvious that an alternative method was necessary in order to secure data about these kinds of opportunities.

Several ways of doing this were considered. Maps of the city were examined—in particular, the City's *Development Plan* [91]. This provides a comprehensive statement of land use throughout the city, as at the time of its compilation, and includes proposals for changes in land use for a given period ahead. The maps for each section of the city are therefore in two parts: the Town Map, which shows the existing state of land use at the time the Plan was compiled, and the Programme Map, which shows proposals for changes in land use. The major weakness of the Plan is that it was drawn up during the 1950s and approved by the Minister of Housing and Local Government in December 1960. The Town Map was therefore likely to be considerably out of date by 1968, while there was no way of knowing, from the Plan itself, how far the proposals in the Programme Map had been implemented. The Plan was very useful, however, as a base

251

map for showing the existing opportunities cartographically once their existence had been established by alternative methods.

Other methods that were considered were aerial photographs, observation and postal survey. One major argument against all three approaches was the cost and labour involved. But there were other, and more important, conceptual arguments against each method. Aerial photographs—and, indeed, photographs taken from satellites (which, paradoxically, are usually incomparably better)—are extremely useful for showing major categories of land use; for example, open space as against housing or transportation. They cannot distinguish, however, between different uses of buildings; for example, whether a building is used as a cinema, a tenpin bowling centre, or a bingo club. Yet, this is precisely the kind of information that was required. The chief value of aerial photography as a method of compiling an inventory of recreation facilities would seem to lie in rural areas, where the concern is to identify outdoor opportunities. Coppock [100] is employing this approach in his survey of tourism in the Borders.

Observation was also considered as a potential method, but similar arguments hold against this. In addition to the prohibitive scale of costs and labour that would have been required, the method also suffers from the same kind of difficulties, though on a lesser scale, as aerial photography. It is often not possible to discover what activities take place within a building merely by noting its exterior. A sports hall could be laid out for a variety of different activities, or for one only; a community hall might, or might not, have a stage. These problems could be overcome by the observer actually entering buildings and noting what activities take place. This, however, is very time-consuming. In general, observation is potentially the most satisfactory and comprehensive approach, as was demonstrated by Sir Dudley Stamp's mammoth land use survey between the two world wars, *The Land of Britain* [140]. For the present study, however, limitations upon resources ruled out this possibility. A general observation was made, however, of each area by means of several car trips, and this was useful in supplementing some ambiguous data obtained from documents; but this was the only kind of observation employed.

Consideration was also given to the possibility of undertaking a postal survey to inquire from organizations and groups about the kinds of opportunities that they made available to the general public and to exclusive groups. The simple—and insoluble—problem in this case was to decide to whom the questionnaire should be sent.

Certain national commercial organizations, such as Mecca Limited and Top Rank Limited, would be obvious organizations to be surveyed. But a preliminary search of the telephone directory when the proposal was first considered suggested that it would be difficult, if not impossible, to identify small-scale local commercial enterprises which were, effectively, providing recreation opportunities. Moreover, the difficulties of obtaining a statistically satisfactory response rate to postal surveys—outlined in Chapter 1—suggested that the results of such a survey would be unlikely to justify the time and resources devoted to it. Postal inquiries were, however, directed to some local authority departments to throw light upon ambiguities encountered in compiling the inventory from documents; but a formal postal survey was not undertaken.

Demand Surveys for Determining Supply

Having rejected the use of aerial photography, observation and a postal survey as suitable ways of compiling the inventory, the problem of accounting for facilities provided by private and voluntary groups and commercial organizations remained. It was therefore decided to test whether it might be possible to compile an inventory of these from replies to particular questions in the demand survey. Since the concern was with opportunity, or effective supply, it could be argued that this would be made apparent through a demand survey; if a particular facility was not mentioned by any person in the survey, then it could reasonably be assumed to be ineffective. The implicit assumption here is, of course, that the size of the sample is sufficiently large to give an adequate coverage of the population of the area and to provide a reasonable chance of a facility being mentioned at least once. The original sample for the household and activities survey in the two study areas covered 1-in-8 households, and the numbers of completed questionnaires represented approximately 9 per cent of the total population of each area. There is of course no indication that such a sample is sufficient to provide a reasonable chance of any facility being mentioned at least once. Samples as small as one-tenth of this, proportionately, have, however, been accepted in surveys of other kinds of facilities: for example, housing surveys. In these circumstances, it can reasonably be hoped that the sample was, if not totally comprehensive, at least sufficient to enable the identification of the majority of facilities.

The activities questionnaire employed in the household survey was therefore designed to include two sets of questions about recreation

Table 45. Recreation Facilities Identified from the Demand Survey, by Type

FACILITY	BILLESLEY STUDY AREA*	ALL SAINTS STUDY AREA*	ELSEWHERE	TOTAL
A. CITY COUNCIL				
Open spaces	1	1	14	16
Golf courses	0	0	3	3
Allotments	0	0	0	0
Public libraries	0	0	0	0
Swimming baths	1	1	6	8
Reservoirs, lakes, canals	0	0	4	4
Concert halls	0	0	1	1
B. VOLUNTARY ORGANIZATIONS				
Community centres	2	1	7	10
Youth clubs	2	1	10	13
Church clubs	2	1	10	14
Arts centres	0	0	1	1
C. PRIVATE GROUPS				
Social clubs	4	1	13	18
Works clubs	2	3	23	28
Old people's clubs	0	1	3	4
Men's clubs	0	2	7	9
Women's clubs	1	0	2	3
Specific interest clubs	0	1	14	15
Other clubs	0	1	4	5
Golf courses	2	0	1	3
Sports clubs	0	0	12	12
Sports stadia	0	0	13	13

D. COMMERCIAL ORGANIZATIONS				
Public houses	5	15	31	51
Bingo clubs	1	2	3	6
Cinemas	1	2	10	13
Skating rinks	0	1	2	3
Theatres	0	0	1	1
Ballrooms	0	0	6	6
Tenpin bowling centres	0	0	1	1
Discotheques	0	0	1	1
Nightclubs	0	0	3	3
Restaurants	0	0	6	6
E. OTHER FACILITIES				
Total facilities	24	34	17	17
Facilities previously identified from documents	8	5	229	228
Facilities newly identified	16	29	†	†

* Includes facilities within the Study Area and those within approximately ONE mile of its boundary.
† Not applicable.

255

places. In the first set of questions, respondents were asked, first, to indicate which activity they had taken part in most often during 1968 and, second, to state whether this was undertaken regularly at one particular place, and, if so, to give the name and location of that place. In the second set of questions they were asked, first, to indicate whether they took part in any activities as a member of a club and, second, if so, to give the name of each club, the kinds of activities for which it catered and its location. In this way it was hoped to obtain information about commercial and social facilities available for general public use, such as dance halls and social and community centres, and about those which were available for the use of members only, such as private sports clubs and firms' sports and social clubs.

The results of this approach are set down in Table 45. This shows that 24 facilities were identified from the demand survey as being within or immediately surrounding the Billesley Study Area, 8 of which had already been identified from the documents discussed earlier. In the All Saints Study Area 34 facilities were mentioned in the demand survey, 5 of which had previously been identified from the documents. (In addition, 229 facilities were mentioned which were located elsewhere in the city, giving a total of 298 facilities identified through the demand survey.) By relating these facilities to location and by examining their availability to the general public, an inventory of opportunity can be constructed. This has been done, in detail, in Chapter 11.

It is obvious that the demand survey proved to be an extremely valuable source of information about the numbers and kinds of opportunities available within and immediately surrounding the two Study Areas—and, indeed, in other parts of the city as well. It is equally obvious, however, that this approach is by no means fully comprehensive and that it cannot be considered as an alternative to the use of documents. It should be seen, rather, as a complementary approach. This point can be best illustrated by comparing the numbers of each type of facility identified from the demand survey with those identified from documents. This has been done in Table 46. What this shows is that certain kinds of facilities, such as sports and social clubs, are only likely to be identified at all from a demand study.* None of the sports and social clubs and few of the commercial facilities in the two Study Areas which were identified from

* Given sufficient resources, it might be possible, of course, to identify such facilities by means of observation or postal survey, or a combination of such methods.

256

the demand survey had been identified from documents as well. On the other hand, some facilities such as public open spaces, although they could be identified from a demand survey, are more likely to be identified in full from documents. There are in the Billesley Study Area,* for example, seven public open spaces covering a total area of about 220 acres and including soccer, rugby and cricket pitches, putting and bowling greens, tennis courts, children's playgrounds, and fishing and boating-lakes. Yet only one of these open spaces was identified by respondents to the demand survey. In the All Saints Study Area there are eight such open spaces, one of which was identified from the demand survey. No doubt this reflected, in part, the way in which questions about facilities included in the demand survey were phrased, and alternative forms of questioning could perhaps have yielded more specific information about open spaces. But, short of turning the demand survey into one which was concerned largely with the respondent's knowledge of facilities—a very different kind of survey—it is unlikely that this problem could have been wholly solved.

The joint use of documents and a demand survey provides a much more comprehensive inventory of facilities than the use of either method alone. A total of 47 facilities were identified within and immediately surrounding the Billesley Study Area, 24 from the demand survey and 31 from documents. Only 8 facilities were identified from both sources. In the All Saints Study Area there was a total of 48 facilities, 34 identified from the demand survey and 19 from documents. Only 5 facilities in this area were identified from both sources. But while the numbers of facilities identified by the joint use of the two methods are clearly much greater than the numbers identified by the use of either method alone, there can be no suggestion that the two methods together provide a fully comprehensive inventory. There is little doubt that some facilities will not have been identified by either method. On the other hand, the use of a demand survey does appear to give a substantial increase in the numbers of facilities identified; and, more important, it provides a significant source of information about social clubs, sports clubs and commercial facilities, the very kinds of facilities for which documents are least satisfactory as sources of information. From this viewpoint, the experiment of using a demand survey to compile an inventory of supply can be considered a success. It is by no means established, however, that this approach would be equally successful for other

* This refers to facilities within the Study Area itself *and* those within approximately ONE mile of the boundary of the Study Area.

Table 46. Recreation Facilities Identified from the Demand Survey and from Documents, By Type

TYPE OF FACILITY	BILLESLEY STUDY AREA*			ALL SAINTS STUDY AREA*		
	Demand survey	Documents	Both sources	Demand survey	Documents	Both sources
A. CITY COUNCIL						
Open spaces	1	7	1	1	8	1
Golf courses	0	1	0	0	0	0
Allotments	0	10	0	0	2	0
Public libraries	0	1	0	0	1	0
Swimming baths	1	1	1	1	1	1
Reservoirs	0	0	0	0	1	0
B. VOLUNTARY ORGANIZATIONS						
Community centres	2	2	2	1	1	1
Youth clubs	2	0	0	1	0	0
Church clubs	2	7	2	1	3	0
C. PRIVATE GROUPS						
Social clubs	4	0	0	1	0	0
Works clubs	2	0	0	3	0	0
Old people's clubs	0	0	0	1	0	0
Men's clubs	0	0	0	2	0	0
Women's clubs	1	0	0	0	0	0
Specific interest clubs	0	0	0	1	0	0
Other clubs	0	0	0	1	0	0
Golf courses	2	1	1	0	0	0

D. COMMERCIAL ORGANIZATIONS

Public houses	5	0	0	15	0	0
Bingo clubs	1	0	0	2	0	0
Cinemas	1	1	1	2	2	2
Skating rinks	0	0	0	1	0	0
Total facilities	24	31	8	34	19	5

* Includes facilities within the Study Area and those approximately within ONE mile of its boundary.

259

studies. The present study had the major advantage that it was conducted within two relatively small areas, but with a relatively large sample survey. The reasonable assumption could, therefore, be made that most facilities are highly likely to be mentioned at least once by respondents. The smaller is the sample, proportionately to the total population of an area, the lesser the degree of certainty with which this assumption can be made.

To summarize, then, the inventory of opportunities available in the two Study Areas was compiled from two major sources—from documents and from a demand survey. These two approaches were supplemented, occasionally, by observation or by a postal enquiry to the relevant person or body. The two methods enabled facilities to be identified from which opportunities were assessed by reference to such factors as location, times of operation, whether or not they were available for general public use, and so on. The full inventory of opportunities in each Study Area is given in Chapter 11, which sets out to examine interrelationships between supply and demand. The present chapter has been concerned only to consider the methods of compiling such an inventory. The results have indicated that demand surveys can, in particular circumstances, be a useful complement to documentary sources for this purpose, but that, in all probability, a fully comprehensive inventory could only be compiled by means of a costly and time-consuming observation study.

Chapter 11
Demand-Supply Relationships

The major factor influencing the choice of study areas for the household and activities survey was the proposal to investigate the interrelationships between recreation demand and supply: in particular, to examine the extent to which demand is a function of supply (or, more correctly, the extent to which consumption is a function of opportunity). It was this objective which led to the decision to select two areas which were broadly similar in their socio-economic structure, but which contrasted significantly in their supplies of recreation facilities. It was hypothesized that, by matching two areas on the basis of certain socio-economic variables, but differentiating them on the basis of available recreation opportunities, it would be possible to minimize the differences in the effects of these 'causal' variables in shaping patterns of recreation behaviour and, thereby, to gain an insight into the effects of differences in the availability of opportunities. The way in which the socio-economic matching of the two chosen areas was carried out has been described in Chapter 5, while the approach to the compilation of an inventory of opportunities has been outlined in Chapter 10.*

What emerged from the socio-economic matching procedure was the selection of two areas for study which compared closely on five out of six socio-economic characteristics. These were, first, the Shevky–Bell typology of social rank and family status; second, the proportion of households sharing a dwelling; third, the proportion of the population which consisted of immigrants; fourth, the average numbers of persons per room; and fifth, the proportion of the population that had moved into the area during the five years up to 1966 (the latest year for which all of these kinds of data were available). The sixth characteristic, on which the two areas compared badly, was a crude measure of housing standards, showing the proportion of households in each area having exclusive use of four basic utilities—hot water, fixed bath, w.c., and cooking stove. It was not suggested that these six characteristics are, directly, major determinants of patterns of recreation behaviour. It was believed, however, that if the two areas could be matched on the basis of these six characteristics, then the two populations would be broadly similar in their

---

* Pages 117–124 and 243–260, respectively.

socio-economic composition. This, in turn, would suggest that the major socio-economic influences upon recreation behaviour could be assumed to be similar in the two areas; and, therefore, that any differences in patterns of recreation behaviour between the two areas would stem from other causes—in particular, differences in available opportunities.

It should be stated at the outset that this attempt to isolate the effects of opportunity upon consumption was, largely, unsuccessful. This was so for three main reasons. Firstly, as indicated in Chapter 10, it proved impossible to compile an inventory of recreation opportunities which included *all* facilities available in the two study areas. There is little doubt that the inventory of facilities operated by the Birmingham City Council is fully comprehensive. On the other hand, there is equally little doubt that the inventories of facilities provided by private, voluntary and commercial organizations are not fully comprehensive. This means that any attempt to relate activity to opportunity can only be made with complete confidence for those activities which make exclusive use of facilities provided by the City Council. Of course, it would be possible to analyse activity–opportunity relationships for other facilities; but the degree of confidence that can be attached to these will depend upon the extent to which the inventory of opportunities in respect of these particular facilities can be considered to be comprehensive.

The second reason for the lack of success stemmed from the fact that activity–opportunity relationships had to be expressed for individual activities rather than for groups of activities, since the data relating to opportunities were usually expressed in terms of individual facilities. Thus, for example, the inventory of opportunities provided by the City Council identified the exact numbers of soccer pitches available in each of the two areas. The obvious and logical procedure then would have been to compare the levels of participation in soccer, however measured, between the two areas. The problem was that the absolute numbers of respondents that had participated in soccer were too small for any definite significance to be attached to the differences between the two areas. This was true not just for soccer, but for most of the 71 activities covered in the demand survey. Differences of 3 or 4 per cent in the proportions of respondents participating in particular activities could not be attributed to differences in available opportunities, since the percentage differences themselves were not necessarily statistically significant. They could have been real differences between the two sets of respondents; but they were more likely to have been the result of random sampling error.

The third reason for the lack of success lies in the structure of the sample populations in the two areas. In spite of the attempt to identify areas which were broadly similar in their socio-economic structure, there were some significant differences in the socio-economic composition of the two sample populations. It is not difficult, with hindsight, to explain this. The selection of the two study areas was made on the basis of data obtained from the *Sample Census*, carried out in April 1966. The data for the two sample populations, on the other hand, were obtained from the household and activities survey carried out more than two years later, in November and December 1968. Both study areas had experienced population changes between these two dates; but the All Saints area, in particular, had undergone significant change. This area is located within one of the oldest industrial parts of the city. In consequence, it had, during this period, received increasing priority for redevelopment. Indeed, some whole streets in the area had already been designated for demolition and had been compulsorily purchased by the City Council—a fact which had helped to lower the rate of response to the survey in this area. A more important effect of this, however, was that the All Saints area tended to attract a more mobile population than the Billesley area; although it should be stressed that this was true only for certain parts of this study area. As a whole, the population of the All Saints area was only marginally more mobile than that of the Billesley area. It was sufficiently more so, however, for greater changes to have taken place in the composition of the latter; and hence, for the two sample populations obtained in the 1968 survey to differ more significantly than the two populations recorded in the 1966 Census. Moreover, some of the most important of these differences occurred for socio-economic characteristics which the analysis in Chapter 9 has shown are significantly correlated with recreation activity. Thus, any differences in rates of participation in particular activities between the two areas could be the result of differences in the socio-economic structure of the two sample populations; or equally, the result of differences in available recreation opportunities; or, most likely, the result of some combination of these two forces.

None of these three problems is, by itself, an insuperable obstacle to a reasonably reliable analysis of activity–opportunity relationships. If, for example, the only difficulty were the incompleteness of the inventory of opportunities, then the analysis could have been restricted to those activities for which the inventory could be assumed to be largely, though not wholly, complete. While the results could not be held to be 100 per cent accurate, they would certainly have a

263

strong probability of accuracy. Similarly, if the only difficulty were the relatively small absolute numbers participating in particular individual activities, then it might be possible to amalgamate activities and opportunities into larger groups—for example, organized team games instead of the individual activities of soccer, rugby, cricket, hockey and so on. There would be difficulties in this procedure in terms of the relative weights to be given to different facilities when compiling a larger group, 'organized team game opportunities'. Does a hockey pitch for example carry the same value as a soccer pitch? In spite of such difficulties, however, some such larger groupings of activities and opportunities might be tried. Furthermore, even if statistical significance in activity rates between areas cannot be positively established, it could be argued that, where *all* or *most* of the differences operate in the same direction, then even though individually they are not significant, the one area is more 'active' than the other. Finally, if the only difficulty were the differences in the socio-economic composition of the two sample populations, then, provided that these differences were not too many and too great, they could be accounted for by the use of a composite weighting factor. When these three problems exist together, however, it is doubtful that attempts to offset them of the kind suggested here would be very worth while or practicable. The resulting activity–opportunity relationships, given the weighting, the grouping, and the incompleteness of the inventories of opportunities, would probably be subject to such a wide margin of possible error as to be of questionable value for practical planning purposes. Too many assumptions would have had to be made for each adjustment to the basic data.

Yet, despite all of the difficulties encountered, it would not be true to say that the attempt to identify activity–opportunity relationships was a total failure. For a very few activities, the inventory of opportunities was reasonably comprehensive, the numbers of respondents sufficient, and the biasing effects of socio-economic differences between the two samples relatively limited, so that a broad, but useful, analysis of activity–opportunity relationships could be made. The results are not as strong, statistically, as had been hoped; but they provide a sufficient basis for some interesting speculation about the nature of the relationships. Moreover, since this book is concerned to consider methods rather than results, it will be worth while to follow through the analysis, stage by stage, so as to observe and judge the rationale behind the overall approach. There are, essentially, four stages: first, to identify the actual differences between the two areas in respect of the available recreation opportunities; second, to outline the major differences between the two areas in patterns of recreation activity; third, to consider the significance of socio-economic differences between the two sample populations; and fourth, to determine, as far as possible, the extent to which reported differences in patterns of recreation behaviour between the two areas derive from the differences in known available opportunities rather than from socio-economic differences between the two sample populations.

The Inventory of Opportunities

Employing the approach and techniques described in Chapter 10, an inventory was drawn up of the available recreation facilities in the two study areas. This is shown, for each area separately, in Tables 47 and 48. Facilities are identified and listed in four main categories, according to the type of operator: Birmingham City Council, voluntary organizations, private groups, and commercial organizations. Within these categories, each facility is identified by type, location and opportunity. Types of facility range from open spaces (within which detailed facilities are noted, such as soccer and cricket pitches and children's playgrounds) to public houses, cinemas and bingo clubs. Location is measured on a simple two-part scale: W indicates that a facility is located within the study area itself, while O indicates that it is located outside the study area but within approximately one mile of its boundary. The type of opportunity is determined by reference to the classification outlined in Table 44 in Chapter 10. In this case, the classification is based upon a value judgement about the catchment area that each particular facility is assumed to serve. The result is that all of the facilities fall into one or other of two groups—neighbourhood and district.

Perhaps the most important differences between the two areas are to be found in the category of facilities operated by the City Council. There are 20 such facilities in the Billesley area, as compared with 13 in the All Saints area. Billesley has seven open spaces, covering a total area of 220 acres, 130 acres of which are located within the study area itself. These open spaces incorporate 17 soccer pitches, 2 rugby pitches, 9 cricket pitches, 14 grass and hard tennis courts, 3 bowling and putting greens, 5 children's playgrounds, and 2 boating and fishing lakes. In contrast to this, the All Saints area has eight open spaces encompassing a total area of 112 acres—about half the Billesley acreage. Moreover, only 2 acres of this are actually located within

Table 47. Recreation Facilities in the Billesley Study Area

FACILITY		OPPORTUNITY	LOCATION (See note)
A. FACILITIES OPERATED BY THE CITY COUNCIL			
1. Billesley Common: 73·6 Acres	Open space, including 7 cricket pitches 12 soccer pitches 1 rugby pitch 2 hockey pitches 9 grass tennis courts 1 children's playground	Neighbourhood and district	W
2. Chinn Brook: 31·5 acres	Open space, including 1 children's playground	Neighbourhood	W
3. Daisy Farm: 24·1 acres	Open space, including 1 bowling green 2 cricket pitches 4 soccer pitches 1 rugby pitch 1 putting green 3 hard tennis courts 1 children's playground	Neighbourhood and district	W
4. Sarehole Mill: 9·2 acres	Open space	Neighbourhood	O
5. Swanshurst Park: 44·2 acres	Open space, including 1 soccer pitch 1 putting green 2 hard tennis courts	Neighbourhood and district	O

6. *The Dingles: 21·5 acres*	Open space boating fishing 1 children's playground	Neighbourhood	*O*
7. *Trittiford Mill: 15·3 acres*	Open space, including boating fishing 1 children's playground	Neighbourhood and district	*O*
8. *Cocks Moors Woods*	Golf course, 18 holes	District	*W*
9. *Warstock Lane*	Allotments	Neighbourhood	*W*
10. *Maypole Lane*	Allotments	Neighbourhood	*W*
11. *Highters Heath Lane*	Allotments	Neighbourhood	*W*
12. *Prince of Wales Lane*	Allotments	Neighbourhood	*O*
13. *Greenaleigh Road*	Allotments	Neighbourhood	*O*
14. *Colebourne Road*	Allotments	Neighbourhood	*O*
15. *Barn Lane*	Allotments	Neighbourhood	*O*
16. *Howard Road East*	Allotments	Neighbourhood	*O*
17. *May Lane*	Allotments	Neighbourhood	*O*
18. *Hollybank Road*	Allotments	Neighbourhood	*O*
19. *Highfield Road*	Public library	District	*O*
20. *Institute Road, Kings Heath*	Swimming baths	District	*O*

267

Table 47. (*continued*)

FACILITY		OPPORTUNITY	LOCATION (See note)
B. FACILITIES OPERATED BY VOLUNTARY ORGANIZATIONS			
21. *Community Centre* Yardley Wood Road	Community centre	Neighbourhood and district	W
22. *Community Hall* Daisy Farm Road	Community centre	Neighbourhood	W
23. *Kings Heath Technical School*	Youth club	Neighbourhood and district	O
24. *Highers Heath School*	Youth club	Neighbourhood and district	O
25. *Methodist Church* Trittiford Road	Church club	Neighbourhood	W
26. *Holy Cross Church* Beauchamp Road	Church club	Neighbourhood	W
27. *Wesleyan Church* Sladepool Farm Road	Church club	Neighbourhood	W
28. *Roman Catholic Church* Glenavon Road	Church club	Neighbourhood	W
29. *Baptist Church* High Street Kings Heath	Church club	Neighbourhood	O
30. *Gospel Hall* Glastonbury Road	Church club	Neighbourhood	O

31. *St. Peter's Church* Highfield Road Hall Green	Church club	Neighbourhood	O
C. FACILITIES OPERATED BY PRIVATE GROUPS			
32. *E57* Alcester Road	Social club	Neighbourhood	W
33. *Carnegie* Trittiford Road/Chinn Brook Road	Social club	Neighbourhood	W
34. *British Legion* Hollybank Road Yardley Wood	Social club	Neighbourhood and district	O
35. *Co-operative Hall* School Road	Social club	Neighbourhood and district	O
36. *Civil Service Sports Club* Alcester Road	Works club	District	W
37. *Birmingham Transport Club* Wheeler's Lane	Works club	District	O
38. *Gay Hill* Hollywood	Golf club	District	O
39. *Moseley Golf Course* Hollywood	Golf club	District	O
40. *Child Welfare Centre* Highfield Road	Young wives' club	Neighbourhood	O
D. FACILITIES OPERATED BY COMMERCIAL ORGANIZATIONS			
41. *Prince of Wales* Maypole Lane	Public house	Neighbourhood	W

269

(Table 47. *continued*)

FACILITY	OPPORTUNITY	LOCATION (See note)
42. *Horse Shoe* Alcester Road South	Public house	W
43. *Valley Hotel* Haunch Lane	Public house	O
44. *Maypole Hotel* Alcester Road	Public house	O
45. *Bagnall Arms* School Road	Public house	O
46. *Kingsway* Kings Heath	Cinema	O
47. *Tudor Club* Haunch Lane	Bingo club	O

Note:
For Location, *W* means within the Study Area itself; *O* means outside the Study Area but within approximately ONE mile of its boundary.

Table 48. *Recreation Facilities in the All Saints Study Area*

FACILITY	OPPORTUNITY	LOCATION (See note)
A. FACILITIES OPERATED BY THE CITY COUNCIL		
1. *Musgrave Road:* 2·3 acres Recreation ground	Neighbourhood	W
2. *Brookfields:* 1·1 acres Children's playground	Neighbourhood	O
3. *Burbury Street:* 4·3 acres Recreation ground, with 1 children's playground 1 supervised play centre	Neighbourhood	O
4. *Tower Street:* 1·3 acres Recreation ground	Neighbourhood	O
5. *Handsworth Park:* 63·3 acres Open space, including 3 hard tennis courts 3 grass tennis courts 1 netball pitch 1 putting green 2 bowling greens boating 1 children's playground	Neighbourhood and district	O
6. *Summerfield Park:* 34·3 acres Open space, including 2 soccer pitches 4 hard tennis courts 6 grass tennis courts 1 putting green 2 bowling greens 1 children's playground 1 supervised play centre	Neighbourhood and district	O

271

Table 48. (continued)

FACILITY		OPPORTUNITY	LOCATION (See note)
7. Black Patch: 4·0 acres Warley (approx)	Recreation ground	Neighbourhood	O
8. Anderton Road: 1·0 acre (approx)	Recreation ground	Neighbourhood	O
9. Edgbaston Reservoir	Part open space, with fishing	District	O
10. Perrott Street	Allotments	Neighbourhood	O
11. Oxhill Road	Allotments	Neighbourhood	O
12. Soho Road Handsworth	Public library	District	O
13. Monument Road Ladywood	Swimming baths	District	O
B. FACILITIES OPERATED BY VOLUNTARY ORGANIZATIONS			
14. Ladywood Community Centre Monument Road	Community centre	Neighbourhood and district	O
15. Brookfield and Ladywood Boys Club George Street West	Youth club	Neighbourhood and district	W
16. St. Peter's Church Spring Hill	Church club	Neighbourhood	W
17. New Testament Church of God George Street	Church club	Neighbourhood	O

18. *St. Patrick's Church* Dudley Road	Church club	Neighbourhood	*O*
19. *St. Francis Church* Hunters Road	Church club	Neighbourhood	*O*
C. FACILITIES OPERATED BY PRIVATE GROUPS			
20. *Silver Lining Club* Park Road	Old people's club	Neighbourhood	*W*
21. *Birmingham Prison Officer's Club*	Works club	District	*W*
22. *The Mint Works Club* Icknield Street	Works club	District	*W*
23. *Summerfield Hospital Social Club* Western Road	Works club	District	*O*
24. *CIU Working Man's Club* Reservoir Road	Men's club	Neighbourhood and district	*O*
25. *Rotten Park Gardens Working Man's Club* Barford Road	Men's club	Neighbourhood and district	*O*
26. *The Beeches* Skipton Road	Specific interest club (epileptics)	District	*O*
27. *Monte Carlo Club* Soho Road	Social club	Neighbourhood and district	*O*
28. *Ridgway Georgian Club* Soho Hill	Other club	Neighbourhood and district	*O*
D. FACILITIES OPERATED BY COMMERCIAL ORGANIZATIONS			
29. *The Hydraulic* Lodge Road	Public house	Neighbourhood	*W*

273

Table 48. (*continued*)

FACILITY		OPPORTUNITY	LOCATION (See note)
30. *Abbey Vaults* Lodge Road	Public house	Neighbourhood	W
31. *The Royal Exchange* Park Road	Public house	Neighbourhood	W
32. *Welcome Tavern* Park Road	Public house	Neighbourhood	W
33. *The Prince George* Crabtree Road	Public house	Neighbourhood	W
34. *Lamb Tavern* Clissold Street	Public house	Neighbourhood	W
35. *Brookfield Tavern* Hingeston Street	Public house	Neighbourhood	W
36. *Duke of York* Hockley Hill	Public house	Neighbourhood	W
37. *Sir Charles Napier* Roseberry Street	Public house	Neighbourhood	W
38. *The Gates* Icknield Street	Public house	Neighbourhood	W
39. *The Laurels* Hingeston Street	Public house	Neighbourhood	W
40. *The Commercial Inn* Prescott Street	Public house	Neighbourhood	W

41. *Rose and Crown* Hingeston Street	Public house	Neighbourhood	W
42. *The Prince* Prescott Street	Public house	Neighbourhood	W
43. *Rose Villa Tavern* Warstone Lane	Public house	Neighbourhood	W
44. *The Palladium* Soho Road	Bingo club	District	O
45. *Mawley's* Dudley Road	Bingo club	District	O
46. *Olympic* Spring Hill	Roller skating rink	District	W
47. *ABC* Soho Road	Cinema	District	O
48. *Grove* Dudley Road	Cinema	District	O

Note:
For Location, *W* means within the Study Area itself; *O* means outside the Study Area but within approximately ONE mile of its boundary.

the study area itself. These eight open spaces incorporate 2 soccer pitches, 16 grass and hard tennis courts, 6 bowling and putting greens, 6 children's playgrounds, and one boating lake. Thus, the Billesley area has nearly twice as much acreage of open space as All Saints and many more specific facilities within them; in particular, it has many more soccer and cricket pitches. On the other hand, despite its considerably smaller acreage, the All Saints area has marginally more tennis courts and putting greens. In addition to these open spaces, each area has one public library and one swimming bath, while Billesley has ten allotments and All Saints has two. Finally, Billesley has one 18-hole public golf course, whereas there are none in All Saints.

As indicated earlier, it is particularly important to note these differences between the two study areas in respect of the facilities operated by the City Council, because this is the only group of facilities for which the inventory can reasonably be assumed to be fully comprehensive. Most of the data for these facilities were obtained from official sources—Departmental lists, maps and plans —supplemented by direct observation. In the case of facilities provided by private, voluntary and commercial organizations, the data were obtained largely through the demand survey, or from newspapers, advertisements, notice boards and similar sources. There is less certainty, therefore, about the extent to which the lists are comprehensive; which, in turn, means that less significance can be attached to activity–opportunity relationships identified for these categories of facilities.

There appear to be few differences between the two areas in the availability of opportunities provided by voluntary organizations. The Billesley inventory shows two community centres and two youth clubs, as compared with one of each in the All Saints lists. There are also more church clubs listed for Billesley than for All Saints.

The same pattern is evident for opportunities provided by private groups: there appear to be more of these in the Billesley area than in the All Saints area. There are, in particular, more social clubs in the Billesley list. The most significant difference here, however, lies in the availability of facilities for golf. The Billesley area has two private golf clubs, each with an 18-hole course. This means that, including the public golf course listed under facilities operated by the City Council, the Billesley area has three 18-hole golf courses, as compared with none in the All Saints area.

The pattern for opportunities provided by commercial organizations is the reverse of that shown for the other three categories. Here, the All Saints inventory has identified many more facilities than has the one for Billesley. The former lists 15 public houses, 2 bingo clubs, 2 cinemas and a roller skating rink. In contrast, the Billesley list includes only 5 public houses, 1 cinema and 1 bingo club. It is highly likely, of course, that there are more than just 5 public houses in and around the Billesley area. On the other hand, it is equally likely that, whatever may be the absolute numbers involved, there are more public houses in and around the All Saints area than there are in and around the Billesley area. The former is a much older and more established part of the city, in which industrial and residential areas sit cheek by jowl and where the working man's tavern, as much a lunch-time venue as a night-time one, occupies many street corners. Billesley, on the other hand, is a newer area, almost wholly residential, and one in which the pub is frequented mainly at night.

This, then, is the broad pattern of recreation facilities in the two study areas; Billesley with a very much greater acreage of public open space, and, generally, more of those facilities provided by voluntary organizations and private groups; All Saints with more public houses and, generally, a greater supply of those facilities provided by commercial organizations. It is, however, worth emphasizing once more that these inventories represent the best available information about recreation opportunities. And, while they are considerably more detailed than is normally available for this kind of study, they are in no sense fully comprehensive.

Recreation Activity in the Study Areas

In general, the volume of recreation activity was higher for the Billesley area than for the All Saints area. The proportion of respondents who had ever participated during 1968, even if only once, was higher for almost every activity for the Billesley sample than for the All Saints sample. The only clear exceptions were *visits to a pub or club* and *visits to a community or church centre*. For the former activity, the proportion of respondents who had participated during 1968 was 52 per cent in Billesley and 58 per cent in All Saints. The proportions for the latter activity were 5 per cent and 9 per cent, respectively. For virtually all other activities, however, the proportions were higher for the Billesley sample than for All Saints. Of course, for many activities the absolute numbers of participants were too few for any statistical significance to be attached to the percentage differences in participation between the two areas. But the fact that levels of participation were higher in the Billesley sample for sixty-six of

277

the seventy-one recorded activities suggests that the *breadth* of recreation activity was greater for the Billesley sample than for the All Saints sample. This suggestion is supported by two other items of data: first, the proportion of respondents who reported that they had participated in none of the seventy-one activities; and second, the numbers of activities reported as having been undertaken by respondents.

The proportion of respondents that had participated in none of the seventy-one activities was 13 per cent in All Saints, compared with 5 per cent in Billesley—a difference which is just significant at the 5 per cent level of probability. The data relating to the numbers of activities ever undertaken during 1968 show that 58 per cent of respondents in Billesley had participated in five or more different activities during the year, as compared to only 33 per cent of respondents in the All Saints sample. The figures for the proportions of respondents who had participated in two or less activities illustrate the differences between the two areas even more dramatically; these were 25 per cent in Billesley and 48 per cent in All Saints (Table 49).

The differences between the two areas in respect of the *depth* of recreation activity are less dramatic, though still statistically significant. The frequency of participation in the activity undertaken most often during 1968 was generally higher in Billesley than in All Saints: 72 per cent of respondents in the Billesley sample participated once a week or more often, compared with 62 per cent in the All Saints sample. In contrast, the proportion that had participated less than once a month was only 6 per cent in the former sample, compared with 15 per cent in the latter (Table 49).

These two measures of the breadth and depth of recreation activity are useful for illustrating the broad scale of recreation participation in the two study areas. But, in order to show how activity varies with opportunity, detailed data are required about specific recreation activities. This has been shown, for ten activities, in Table 50. Rates of participation in each activity have been measured in two ways: first, the proportion of respondents that had ever participated in each of the selected activities during 1968 (designated *P1* in the Table); and, second, the proportion of respondents that identified each selected activity as one of the three activities undertaken most often during 1968 (designated *P2* in the table). The ten selected activities are those which were the most popular in both areas, in terms of the numbers of respondents that had participated in them at least once during 1968. (The relative popularity of the ten activities differed slightly between the two areas; but, in both areas, the same ten

278

activities were the most popular.) What the analysis shows is that, for at least five of the activities, the differences between the two areas are not statistically significant. If we take the *P1* measure, then the differences are significant for five activities—gardening, driving in the countryside, visits to the cinema, picnicking, and visits to a pub or club—the first four of which were more popular among the Billesley sample, while the last was more popular with the All Saints sample. If the *P2* measure is used, then the differences between the two areas are significant for only two activities—gardening and visits to a pub

Table 49. *Recreation Activity in the Two Study Areas*

MEASURE OF ACTIVITY	BILLESLEY		ALL SAINTS	
	No.	*per cent*	*No.*	*per cent*
1. NUMBER OF ACTIVITIES EVER UNDERTAKEN DURING *1968*:				
0	31	5	60	13
1–2	117	20	166	35
3–4	101	17	89	19
5–9	252	42	116	25
10+	86	15	38	8
Total	587	100	469	100
2. FREQUENCY OF PARTICIPA- TION IN ACTIVITY UNDER- TAKEN MOST OFTEN:				
Once a week or more often	423	72	290	62
Between once a week and once a month	101	17	84	18
Less than once a month	37	6	71	15
No reply	26	5	24	5
Total	587	100	469	100

or club—the former being more popular with the Billesley sample, the latter with the All Saints sample.

The general picture, then, shows a greater breadth and depth of recreation activity among respondents in Billesley than among those in All Saints. In the case of individual activities, levels of participation, however measured, tend to be greater for Billesley than for All Saints; but, with the exception of a very few activities, the differences between the two areas are not statistically significant. In other words, while the differences between the two areas could reflect real differences in the behaviour of respondents, they could equally reflect a random sampling error. Furthermore, even in the case of activities where the differences in participation are significant, it has not been established that the cause of these is the difference in available recreation opportunities between the two areas, rather than, say, differences in the socio-economic composition of the two sample populations. Before this can be determined, it will be necessary to analyse the socio-economic structure of the two samples to see whether there are any significant differences between them and, if so, whether these are major influences upon recreation activity.

Table 50. *Participation in Selected Recreation Activities*[1]

| | BILLESLEY | | ALL SAINTS | |
ACTIVITY	*P1*	*P2*	*P1*	*P2*
Gardening	*63*	*39*	*28*	*16*
Visit to pub or club	*52*	*29*	*58*	*44*
Driving in the countryside	*50*	27	*30*	21
Visit to a cinema	*46*	17	*38*	20
Picnicking	*36*	9	*20*	5
Dining out	33	8	27	11
Swimming	24	9	15	6
Visit to a concert or theatre	24	5	19	8
Bingo	21	12	20	14
Dancing	12	7	11	8

Notes:
1. Figures which are significantly different between the two areas, at least at the 5 per cent level of probability, are shown in italics.
2. *P1* = percentage of respondents that had participated in the activity at least once during 1968.
3. *P2* = percentage of respondents identifying the activity as one of the three undertaken most often during 1968.

The Sample Populations

It was clear during the earliest stages of the analysis that there were some major differences in the socio-economic composition of the two sample populations. This was to be expected, since it would be virtually impossible ever to match two areas perfectly, The purpose of this analysis was not, therefore, to establish whether or not there were any socio-economic differences between the two samples; but rather, to ascertain whether or not the differences which would inevitably occur were significant ones. It is, of course, on this point that much of the success or failure of the activity–opportunity analysis would turn. If the two populations were found to be largely similar, then a reasonable case could be made for attributing any major differences in recreation activity to differences in the availability of recreation opportunities. If, on the other hand, the two samples should exhibit major socio-economic differences, the analysis would be more complicated and the findings less assured; it would then be necessary to determine whether these differences were ones which significantly influenced recreation activity and, if so, in what ways and to what extent. All of this meant, of course, that in comparing the two samples, particular attention should be devoted to the eighteen profile characteristics which the analysis in Chapter 9 had shown were significantly correlated with the breadth and depth of recreation activity.

Normally, in comparing the importance of any differences between the characteristics of two samples, the concern would be only with those particular characteristics for which the differences between the two samples were statistically significant; in this case, only six variables—type of school last attended, type of dwelling, ownership or regular use of various items of recreation equipment, socio-economic group, form of payment of income, and ownership of a garden. But, for the purposes of a detailed activity–opportunity analysis, *any* differences in respect of these eighteen recreation-related profile variables will be important. It does not matter whether the differences between the two samples in the profile variables themselves are significant or not: all that this means is that there is a (given) probability that the differences between the two samples are —or are not—real differences, rather than a result of random sampling error. What matters is whether there are any differences *at all* between the two samples. If there are, then, depending upon the strengths of the correlations, there will be resulting differences, of varying amounts, in the patterns of recreation activity between the two samples. Obviously, the more significant are the differences in the profile characteristics, the more important it will be to establish accurately the effects of these differences upon recreation activity; but, ideally, the effects of all differences should be established.

Unfortunately for present purposes, the two sample populations did, in fact, differ considerably. They exhibited some differences in respect of all of the eighteen recreation-related profile variables. A brief general summary of the differences follows: first, the significant differences and then the others.

The major differences between the two samples in respect of the *type of school last attended* were that the All Saints area had, proportionately, more persons whose last school attended had been a Primary, Elementary or 'Council' school, while the Billesley sample had more persons from a Secondary Modern school; 41 per cent of

Billesley respondents had finished their schooling in a Primary, Elementary or 'Council' school, as compared with 54 per cent of All Saints respondents. In contrast, 39 per cent of Billesley respondents had last attended a Secondary Modern school, as compared with only 29 per cent of respondents in the All Saints sample. The proportion of respondents that had last attended a Grammar, Technical, Comprehensive or Bi-Lateral school was also greater for the Billesley sample than for All Saints—13 per cent compared with 7 per cent— a difference which, unlike the others, was not statistically significant.

The greatest difference between the two sample populations occurred in respect of *type of dwelling*. The proportion of respondents living in a semi-detached house was 65 per cent for the Billesley sample and only 2 per cent for the All Saints sample. In contrast, 22 per cent of Billesley respondents lived in terraced houses, compared with 93 per cent of All Saints respondents. Other differences in type of dwelling were not significant.

The major difference in respect of the *ownership or regular use of various classes of recreation equipment* occurred in the proportions of the two populations that had access to none of the items listed. In Billesley, 9 per cent of respondents reported that they had none of the recreation goods listed; in All Saints the proportion was 27 per cent. In all the other groups—1 item, 2 items, 3 items, and 4 or more items—the proportions were higher for the Billesley area than for All Saints: but for no group was the difference between the samples found to be significant.

There were two major differences between the samples in the distribution of respondents by *socio-economic group*. In Billesley, 30 per cent of respondents fell into socio-economic groups 8, 9, 12 and 14, and 26 per cent into groups 5 and 6. The corresponding figures for All Saints were 39 per cent and 15 per cent, respectively. Other differences between the two samples were not significant.

The differences in the *form of payment of income* were that 92 per cent of employed respondents in the All Saints sample were paid on a weekly basis, compared with 83 per cent of the Billesley sample. The proportions that received payment in some other form were 8 per cent and 17 per cent, respectively.

The final significant difference between the two samples was in the proportion of respondents with *ownership of a garden*. The figures were 89 per cent for the Billesley sample and 70 per cent for the All Saints sample.

Non-significant differences between the two samples were found for the remaining twelve recreation-related variables. The greatest

282

differences occurred in respect of age, marital status, length of the actual working week, and ownership or regular use of a motor car. On *age*, the Billesley sample had a higher proportion of respondents aged 12–19 years than the All Saints sample—14 per cent compared with 6 per cent—while the reverse was true for respondents aged 20–29 years—14 per cent to 20 per cent. On *marital status*, there were more single persons in Billesley (21 per cent) than in All Saints (16 per cent), and less in the other two groups—married, and separated, widowed and divorced. On *the length of the actual working week*, Billesley respondents tended to work less hours than All Saints respondents: 50 per cent of the former worked less than 40 hours per week compared with only 38 per cent of the latter. Finally, 28 per cent of Billesley respondents had *ownership or regular use of a motor car*, compared with 20 per cent of All Saints respondents.

The effect of these differences in the socio-economic composition of the two sample populations was, broadly, to reduce the *volume* of recreation activity in the All Saints area to a level below that which might have been expected if the All Saints sample had been more nearly similar to that of Billesley. There did not appear, however, to be any significant differences between the two samples in the *nature* of relationships between activity patterns and the profile variables. Thus, for example, the nature of the relationships between type of school last attended and number of activities ever undertaken during 1968 tended to be the same for the two samples, although the numerical values for these relationships were different. In Figure 11, the diagrams (i) and (ii) show the relationship for each area between the proportion of respondents whose last school attended was a Primary, Elementary or 'Council' school and the number of activities ever undertaken during 1968. The diagrams (iii) and (iv) show the same information in respect of respondents whose last school attended was a Secondary Modern school. In both instances the pattern is the same in each area as we move from one group of activities to another. In diagrams (i) and (ii), the proportion of respondents participating in 1–2 activities is greater than the proportion participating in none; then there is a fall as the proportion for 3–4 activities is greater than for 1–2 activities; then, there is a rise again as the proportion for 5–9 activities exceeds that for 3–4 activities; and, finally, the pattern shows another fall again as those participating in 10 or more activities are less than those for 5–9 activities. In diagrams (iii) and (iv), the two patterns are again the same. What is different in both cases is the *scale* of the relationships. In each case, the proportion of respondents participating in nil, 1–2 and 3–4

283

activities is lower in Billesley than in All Saints, while the proportion participating in 5–9 and 10 or more activities is higher. Thus, the

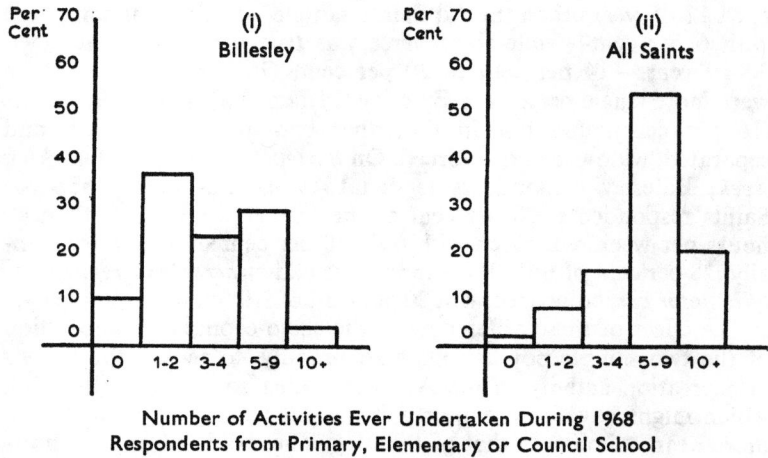

Number of Activities Ever Undertaken During 1968
Respondents from Primary, Elementary or Council School

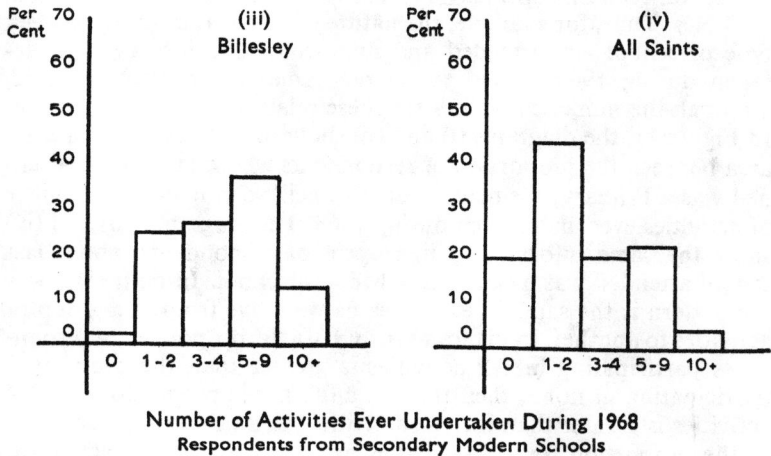

Number of Activities Ever Undertaken During 1968
Respondents from Secondary Modern Schools

Fig. 11. Width of recreation activity by type of school last attended

volume of activity tends to be higher in the Billesley area than in All Saints. The same kind of relationship was found for virtually all of the profile variables. Generally, when comparing the two samples

284

on specific groups within each profile variable against the number of activities ever undertaken during 1968, the *nature* of the relationship would be the same for both samples, but the *scale* would be different. Usually, more respondents in the All Saints sample would be in the lower numbers of activities (4 or less), while fewer respondents would be in the higher groups (5 or more activities). There were some exceptions to this pattern, but they were relatively few in number.

Comment

The pattern which has emerged from this analysis is one which precludes any unqualified statements about the nature and extent of basic (net) relationships between activities and opportunities. There would, of course, be no difficulties encountered in identifying *gross* activity–opportunity relationships. In fact, this has been done for some selected activities and opportunities within each area in Table 51. Problems do not arise in identifying such relationships, but in establishing the extent to which they are statistically significant: that is, the extent to which the former (activity) is a function of the latter (opportunity). The analysis has shown that, by and large, recreation opportunities are greater in the Billesley study area than in the All Saints area, especially in respect of opportunities provided by the City Council. It has shown, further, that the depth and breadth of recreation activity is generally higher among the Billesley sample than among the All Saints sample. But it has also shown that the socio-economic differences between these two sample populations are such that a greater depth and breadth of recreation activity is to be expected from the Billesley sample anyway. Thus, what we have is a situation in which both the socio-economic 'determinants' of recreation activity and the availability of recreation opportunities are greater in one area than in the other. This means that it would be impossible, without a more sophisticated statistical analysis, to infer that the greater volume and breadth of recreation activity in the former area is the result of the one factor rather than the other. Furthermore, as noted at the beginning of this chapter, the absolute numbers of respondents participating in most activities are too small to make meaningful statistical analysis possible. Thus, even if a more sophisticated approach were to be used—such as, for example, a multivariate analysis of the kind used in the Outdoor Recreation Resources Review Commission studies [40]—it is doubtful that it would succeed in establishing satisfactory functional relationships between activities and opportunities.

Table 51. *Participation in Selected Recreation Activities Related to Opportunity to Participate for the Two Study Areas*[1]

ACTIVITY	BILLESLEY			ALL SAINTS		
	Opportunities	*PI*[2]	*P2*[3]	*Opportunities*	*PI*[2]	*P2*[3]
Soccer	17	10	6	2	6	4
Cricket	9	5	*	0	4	1
Rugby	2	3	1	0	2	1
Tennis	14	8	2	16	4	2
Golf	3	8	3	0	2	*
Visit to youth club	2	8	2	1	1	*
Visit to community/church centre	9	5	2	5	9	5
Visit to pub/social club	11	52	29	22	58	44
Bingo	1	21	12	2	20	14
Gardening⁴	(i) 10 (ii) 525	63	39	(i) 2 (ii) 326	28	16

Notes:
1. Figures which are significantly different between the two areas, at least at the 5 per cent level of probability, are shown in italics.
2. *PI* = percentage of respondents that had participated in activity at least once during 1968.
3. *P2* = percentage of respondents identifying activity as one of the three undertaken most often during 1968.
4. Opportunities in respect of *Gardening* are of two kinds: (i) Allotments, (ii) Private gardens owned by persons in the sample.
* Means less than 1 per cent.

This last point can be illustrated by reference to the information in Table 51. What this shows is that, no matter which of the two (given) measures of recreation activity is used, participation is generally higher in the area which has the greater number of opportunities. There are three exceptions to this—tennis, visits to a community or church centre and bingo. But, for only two of the ten listed activities are any of the differences between the two areas statistically significant. For *Gardening*, the difference on both measures is significant at the 1 per cent level of probability. For *Visits to a pub or social club*, the difference on the *P1* measure is significant at the 1 per cent level. This last activity is the one which holds most interest, for it is the only one for which the functional relationship between activity and opportunity can be established with reasonable certainty. It has two characteristics that make this possible. Firstly, the absolute numbers of participants are large enough for the percentage differences between the two samples to be significant. Secondly, it is an activity for which opportunities were greater in the All Saints area than in Billesley. Thus, it is possible to argue that participation was greater among the All Saints sample, *in spite of* the fact that the socio-economic differences between the two samples would lead one to expect a higher rate of participation amongst the Billesley sample; and, therefore, that the probable cause of the higher participation in the All Saints area is the greater number of opportunities.

In conclusion, it must be acknowledged once again that this attempt to identify conclusively activity–opportunity relationships was unsuccessful. The details of the attempt have been presented here in order that other researchers might know how the attempt was made, the particular problems that were encountered, and the lines of reasoning involved. One other final point is, perhaps, worth making. It was the author's opinion that multivariate analysis techniques aimed at isolating the independent effects of the various profile characteristics in influencing recreation activity and, thereby, providing a basis for weighting the data for the All Saints sample, was not worth while in view of the absolutely small numbers participating in most activities. Further work might be undertaken, however, which would show this judgement to have been, if not erroneous, perhaps somewhat sweeping.

Part Four
Forecasting

Chapter 12

Some Major Problems of Forecasting

The history of recreation demand forecasting is one which has passed through four main stages—some optimistic in outlook, some pessimistic. During the mid 1950s it began to become apparent that it would be *necessary* to do something about planning for leisure. The removal of the last of the wartime and postwar rationing in the early 1950s and the evidence of increasing levels of participation in recreation pursuits in the United States were indicators of what was to come in Britain—although nobody in Britain in 1950 could be blamed for failure to foresee the growth of recreation activity, in both town and countryside, which was made possible by rapidly increasing levels of personal income and car ownership. But, once the trend was clearly recognized it became obvious that planning would be necessary to cope with potential developments. Moreover, planning implied some kind of forecasting; and, hence, there grew up a need for recreation demand forecasting. The first stage in the history of this forecasting was the initial reaction to this expressed need. It was almost one of despair—in Taylor's words, 'the phase when serious scholars said that it was something that could not be done' [134]. There were too many nonmeasurable causal factors, so that even if we could forecast the effects of the measurable influences, the results would be subject to such a degree of error as to make them of little or no practical value. This view was, however, rarely advanced in quite such dogmatic fashion and lasted only for a relatively short period of time.

It was soon followed by the second stage, the use of estimates: that is, the informed judgements of administrators, planners and other 'experts'. Such estimates, based upon a great deal of detailed information or experience, were, it was thought, the most credible forecasts that could be achieved. The problem with this was, of course, that estimates soon came to embody prospectives. No longer were the experts producing estimates of *what was expected to happen*. Instead, they were increasingly providing statements of *what ought to happen*. They had moved away from simple forecasting toward deterministic, or goal-oriented, planning. (This is not to suggest that such planning is illegitimate or unacceptable, but merely to say that it is something over and beyond forecasting.) Thus, the reaffirmation by the Ministry of Housing and Local Government in 1955 of the standard of six acres of sports pitches per thousand population in urban areas, first proposed by the National Playing Fields Association thirty years earlier, was essentially a statement of goals, not a forecast of needs. The inherent, often unconscious, belief was that reliable forecasting was impossible.

Both of the first two stages in this history can be seen, essentially, as pessimistic in outlook. The third stage was inherently optimistic. This was the use of extrapolation to predict the numbers of visitor-days that particular kinds of areas and facilities, such as National Parks, could be expected to attract in some given future year. Here, at last, was a scientific approach to forecasting—scientific, that is, in the sense that it was wholly based upon an objective mathematical system which excluded value judgement. In this sense, the extrapolations of visitor-days to particular kinds of recreation areas constituted the first, crude mathematical models for recreation demand forecasting. Optimism began to rise and, for the first time, serious scholars began to feel that the problem was not insoluble. Of course, Clawson, who was perhaps one of the earliest writers to employ extrapolation techniques, has indicated the weaknesses and limitations of such extrapolations [18]. The importance of these extrapolations, however, did not lie in their accuracy, but in the approach that they represented. Recreation demand forecasting was at last a respectable academic and scientific field of endeavour. The road to be travelled would be a long one, but at least it was clear what kind of road it was.

True respectability for the subject of recreation demand forecasting was only firmly established, however, with the fourth stage of development—the construction of prediction models. This is generally agreed to have begun with the work of the Outdoor Recreation Resources Review Commission between 1958 and 1962 [38], although there had been some general discussion of the applicability of such models before this period. The particular achievement of the O.R.R.C. study was, however, that it produced precise numerical forecasts of levels of participation in selected recreation activities by a process which involved the extrapolation of more than one variable. It employed a model which combined presumed causal variables in such a way that the interrelationships between them could be identified and account taken of them. Its importance lay in its recognition of the fact that there is rarely one single and 'correct' cause of any particular event or trend. There have been other, more sophisticated models developed since the O.R.R.C. study—in particular, the

292

simulation model employed in the *Michigan Outdoor Recreation Demand Study* [34]—but the O.R.R.C. model remains a landmark in the forecasting of recreation demand. We now knew not only the kind of road along which we were travelling, but also its direction.

It should be noted here, in passing, that the techniques employed in these last two stages of development—and, particularly, in the final stage—were not new in themselves. They were adopted—and adapted—from other areas of study where they had been more fully developed; for example, from traffic engineering and econometrics. What was new was the acceptance of the view that such techniques could be applied, with a fair expectation of success, to the forecasting of recreation demands.*

Recreation demand forecasting has therefore been through four main stages of development; from the phase where many scholars felt that it could not be done, through the stage of estimates (which were often really prospectives), on to the stage of extrapolations, and finally to the stage of prediction models. Numerous problems have been encountered during this development—which has all occurred in a remarkably short space of time—but one in particular has proved to be a major difficulty. This concerns the assumption that has had to be made, at each stage, concerning the relationship between past events or trends and the future. Essentially, each method of forecasting has had to assume that the future is in some way reflected by the past. Extrapolation is unique in assuming that the variable under consideration will continue to act in exactly the same way in the future as it has done in the past. Estimates and predictions utilize less rigid interpretations of this principle—the former permit a greater degree of subjective judgement while the latter allow for significant changes in the ways and extent to which past trends are assumed to continue into the future; both assume, however, that the future is, to some degree or other, reflected in the past.

It is difficult to see how some general assumption of this nature can be avoided—short of the inspired visions of prophets, sooth-sayers and clairvoyants. Moreover, there is no clear evidence to suggest that such assumptions are wholly unrealistic and that they provide a picture of the future which is totally unrelated to what actually happens. In the first place, it is clearly impossible for fore-casters to foresee, very precisely, developments which arise from no obvious existing base. All technological forecasting, for example, must be based upon a given existing technology. Forecasters may

* For a discussion of some of the techniques themselves, see Chapter 3.

speculate about the likely effects of revolutionary discoveries arising out of known research; but they cannot be expected to take account of the effects of chance discoveries or genius. Secondly, experience and empirical inquiry have shown that many present conditions are indeed derived from clearly identifiable and consistent past trends and that, therefore, the future *is*, in some way, reflected by the past.

It is not, therefore, the assumption about a consistent relationship between the past and the future which provides the major problem for the forecaster, but rather, the nature of that relationship. In the case of the (known) close relationship between *per capita* disposable income and *per capita* visits to National Parks in the United States, for example, the difficulty for the forecaster is to determine the extent to which the numerical value of the correlation between the two variables will remain constant or fluctuate in the future. It is a reasonable and valid assumption that levels of *per capita* disposable income will continue to influence *per capita* visits to National Parks. But will the scale of this influence increase or decline in intensity, or will it remain at approximately the same level?

Herein lies the crux of the forecaster's problem. Indeed, it represents the major difficulty faced by *all* of the social sciences, and not just recreation planning. Essentially, the concern is to discover whether there are any stable parameters, any constant relationships in the system, similar to those that can be found in mathematics and the physical sciences. For example, the area of a circle is always π multiplied by the radius squared. This is a relationship which is stable and constant in all situations, one which never deviates. The key question is whether there are any similar relationships in the social sciences; and, if so, what are the particular variables which give them? To date, we have no evidence with which to satisfactorily test this notion, let alone to prove or disprove it. Some crude indications can, however, be gauged from two recent recreation studies in the United States.

A major, nation-wide study of outdoor recreation activity in the United States was undertaken in 1960 by the Outdoor Recreation Resources Review Commission [39]. On the basis of the established relationships between levels of participation in selected activities and presumed causal variables—income levels, education, occupation, place of residence and age–sex—certain projections were made of the likely levels of participation in these same activities in 1976 and 2000 [41]. A second study of outdoor recreation activity was undertaken in 1965 by the Bureau of Outdoor Recreation [7], which included an

294

analysis of the levels of correlation between the same activities and presumed causal variables. The complete findings of this second study have not yet been officially published, but preliminary analyses enable certain general comparisons between the two studies to be made, which serve to illustrate the forecaster's dilemma.

The detailed method by which forecasts were made for 1976 and 2000 on the basis of the data for 1960 has been outlined in Chapter 3 and reference should be made to this or to the original report for the technicalities. What is of concern here is that the study established net relationships between levels of participation in selected recreation activities and each of five socio-economic characteristics: family income, education, occupation, place of residence and age–sex. These established relationships *were then assumed to remain constant throughout the period for which forecasts were being made*. It is this latter assumption which can be tested, to a limited extent, by the data obtained through the second survey in 1965.

In fact, when the data from the two surveys were compared, it quickly became apparent that there had been few substantial changes in correlations and, hence, that the assumption of constant co-efficients made in 1960 was generally accurate, at least for the relatively short period up to 1965. Nearly all of the correlations had different values in the two years, but most of the differences were within acceptable limits of statistical tolerance. In other words, they could have been, and probably were, the result of random sampling error. There were, however, some significant differences. Moreover, these differences operated in both directions. That is to say, not only were there some significant changes in the correlations between select-ed activities and particular classes of each socio-economic factor, but in some cases the value of the coefficient increased while in others it decreased. In the case of fishing, for example, the proportion of res-pondents in the income-group $8,000–$10,000 who had participated in the activity rose from 31 per cent in 1960 to 36 per cent in 1965. In contrast, the proportion of females in the age-group 18–24 years who had participated fell from 48 per cent at the former date to 43 per cent at the latter. Both differences were found to be statistically significant when subjected to the kind of test which was employed in the present study and which is shown in Chapter 6. A note of caution is, however, pertinent here. These calculations of statistical sig-nificance were made from the gross figures provided in the pre-liminary report of the 1965 survey. These figures were 'rounded' and cannot, therefore, be subjected to rigorous statistical testing. The purpose in citing them here has been to illustrate the ways in which the assumed 1960 correlations could have changed, not to suggest that the changes have been precisely of this particular order.

In summary, then, it is argued that the major problem for the forecaster is not his need to assume that the future is reflected in the past. Some assumption of this nature is essential if any kind of forecast is to be possible. Otherwise, one man's guess would be as good as another's. The key difficulty is, rather, to identify and justify the nature of the relationship which is assumed between past trends (or present values) and the future. The simple and rather crude comparison between the 1960 survey of outdoor recreation activity in the United States and the one undertaken in 1965 served to show, firstly, that the assumption of a constant correlation coefficient between selected activities and presumed causal variables is not *necessarily* accurate, even over relatively short periods of time, and secondly—and most important—that, if correlation coefficients do change, they can do so *in either direction*. The forecaster's problem is, therefore, to decide, first,whether or not the correlation between, say, swimming and income levels is likely to change significantly during the period for which he is required to forecast and, second, if so, in which direction. Indeed, it could turn out that the relationship is inherently unstable anyway, in which case this particular variable would have to be rejected as an input to the forecasting model in favour of either an entirely different variable or another variable operating 'behind' the particular unstable variable.

The problems deriving from the need to assume constant correlation coefficients between levels of participation in selected activities and their presumed causal variables are, in one sense, technical problems. The solution would appear to lie in the investigation, largely by means of empirical case studies, of ways of improving upon and refining the general assumption about relationships between past trends and the future. In another sense, however, this difficulty represents a more fundamental problem. It was suggested earlier that the history of recreation demand forecasting has passed through four main stages of development. It is, perhaps, time to move into a fifth stage. The main reason why so little is known about the nature of the relationship between past trends and the future is because little or nothing is known about the basic causes of recreation behaviour, the attitudes and aspirations of recreationists. All forecasting to date has been concerned with the behaviour patterns of people at recreation; no attention has been given to the determinants of behaviour—apart from the general presumption that behaviour is, in some way, a derivative of such factors as income level, standard of education, place of residence and age–sex. If however, we had better knowledge of the causes of recreation behaviour, it might be easier to quantify more precisely the nature of the relationship between past trends and future ones. Cullingworth [92] has posed the problem most dramatically: 'The inadequacy of extrapolations (and, indeed, all forecasts) is that they have traditionally dealt with results rather than causes—the number of births rather than the determinants of attitudes to family size; the number of individuals participating in a recreational activity rather than the motivations of recreationalists; the number of cars rather than the reasons why people buy and use cars.' Recreation demand forecasting has now reached the point at which it can afford to turn its attention to this problem. To continue the analogy begun earlier, we know the kind of road along which we are travelling; we know the direction of movement; it is now time to examine the vehicle in which we are riding.

Motivations have not, of course, been entirely neglected in recent recreation demand studies. The collection of data about the socio-economic profiles of recreationists has been undertaken largely because it was assumed that these motivate the behaviour of recreationists. Moreover, such characteristics can be readily reduced to numerical values and, hence, can be easily used as inputs to mathematical models. There is considerable doubt, however, as to the true extent to which these socio-economic characteristics motivate recreation behaviour. How far for example is the ownership of a motor car the result of various recreational (and social) attitudes and how far is it a cause of them? To what extent is recreation behaviour a result of social status and to what extent is it a cause, or defining characteristic, of such status? All that has been done to date has been to demonstrate that recreation behaviour is usually correlated with possession of certain socio-economic characteristics. It has merely been assumed, not proven, that the latter are the independent variables, the causes, while recreation behaviour is the dependent variable, the effect. Conceptually, however—and quite probably in practice also—the relationship could operate in either direction. Recreation behaviour could be the independent variable determining, say, social status.

But perhaps even more important than this possibility of a two-way relationship between recreation behaviour and selected socio-economic characteristics is the need to take account of the effects of attitudes and aspirations upon recreation behaviour. Some general account has been taken of these in strategic recreation planning in Britain, but they have received no specific attention. Thus, for example, there has often been a general assumption in municipal recreation planning that, with greater affluence among working-class people, their recreation habits and behaviour will approximate towards that of professional and middle-class people: 'what the middle classes do today the working classes will do tomorrow'. The few studies that have been made of this subject suggest, however, that this assumption is too simple, that the relationship is more complex than this. This assumption, like those made in respect of the relationships between recreation behaviour and socio-economic characteristics, fails to get behind behaviour patterns to investigate the attitudes, hopes, fears, and aspirations that motivate those behaviour patterns.

It is, of course, a fairly simple exercise to identify the need to take account of attitudes and aspirations in forecasting recreation demands. It is much more difficult to devise a method for incorporating data about these characteristics within a predictive model. Ellis and others [131] at the University of Waterloo, Ontario, are currently experimenting with an approach to this based upon three inter-related models: a *psychological needs* model, a *social-role* model, and a *social-institutions* model. The first of these models would attempt to take account of the attitudes and aspirations of recreationists, the second would incorporate their socio-economic characteristics, while the third would examine institutional aspects of recreation behaviour. In terms of the present discussion of attitudes and aspirations, the psychological needs model is the most relevant. This is taken directly from psychological science and recognizes five basic categories of human need: bio-somatic (such as food and shelter), safety, love and affection, esteem, and self-actualization. Ellis postulates that all attitudes and aspirations in respect of recreation will reflect one or more of these basic needs. Hence, it is to psychological science, concerned with the study of needs, their expression and interrelationships, that we must look for a satisfactory means of incorporating attitudes and aspirations within a predictive recreation model. Ellis's multiple model has not yet been fully constructed or tested, but it represents, potentially, the most promising method yet proposed for incorporating attitudes and aspirations into the forecasting process. The major difficulty lies, of course, in the quantification of these attitudes and aspirations. A knowledge of which of these influence recreation behaviour provides a better understanding of behaviour patterns themselves. But, although a better understanding will be welcome and, even, enlightening, it may not help forecasting very much unless the revealed causal attitudes and aspirations can be quantified for inclusion in a mathematical prediction model. On the other hand, even though one suspects that these variables will be inherently unquantifiable, it does not follow that the attempt to identify them is merely an academic extravagance. They may be of particular help in policy-making; that is, in determing *what* recreation opportunities should be provided, rather than how *much*.

That we need to take account of attitudes and aspirations is becoming increasingly obvious. At one time it was probably sufficient to utilize only data about socio-economic characteristics in forecasting. When a considerable part of a man's life and effort is devoted to satisfying his bio-somatic and safety needs, the scope for aspirations to affect his recreation behaviour is limited. He, generally, must take whatever recreation he can get. As these primary needs are increasingly satisfied, however, attitudes and aspirations start to play a greater role in determining behaviour. This point has been particularly well made by Desmond Morris [133]: 'You could say that man does not live by central heating alone. It isn't enough to give people basic security and comfort. This is obviously a vital part of the battle. But to think you're home and dry when everyone's got hygiene, medical care, central heating, education, schools, hospitals, and all the rest of it is desperately short-sighted, because you've left out the question of the human brain.' Morris notes that many people are surprised that intelligent young men and women choose to live as hippies, gypsies or tramps in preference to the many obvious benefits that modern society offers them. He continues: 'I don't find it at all extraordinary. It seems to me an incredible indictment, because by rejecting what society has to offer they must be getting something which makes up for all the lost comforts. And what they are getting is a sense of adventure and a sense of smashing the routine.' In this case, attitudes and aspirations have resulted in the rejection of all but the very basic bio-somatic and safety needs in favour of love and affection and self-actualization. In other cases, attitudes and aspirations would be reflected in, say, an increased desire for love and affection, or esteem, or self-actualization, which is expressed through various different kinds of recreation (and other) behaviour.

In addition to the need to incorporate data about attitudes and aspirations within a predictive recreation model, there is also a problem which arises from the need to take account of the effects of policy decisions upon future behaviour. In assuming constant correlation coefficients between selected recreation activities and the presumed causal variables for the forecasting period, the forecaster is also implicitly assuming a fundamentally unchanged supply, or opportunity, situation. Yet it is highly unlikely that this will be so. Of course, it is possible to incorporate an item within the forecasting model which makes allowance for some change in the opportunity factor—as indeed the O.R.R.R.C. study attempted to do. But such an item usually takes account only of the direct influences upon opportunity. There are, however, many indirect influences at work. In the case of swimming, for example, it is a relatively simple technical exercise to determine the present correlations between levels of participation and each major causal variable, including opportunity. These correlations can then be assumed to remain constant throughout the forecasting period, while the values of the independent causal variables change. But there are other extraneous variables which may cause the values of the correlations themselves to change. In this particular case, levels of participation in swimming are a function not only of such variables as income and age–sex, but also of *ability to swim*. People who cannot swim will not do so, and such people constitute a relatively large proportion of the total population at the present time. This situation will change substantially, however, in the near future, since we now have an educational policy which encourages all schoolchildren to learn to swim and provides time during the school curriculum for them to do so. The proportion of the total population in twenty years time which is *able* to swim will be significantly higher than the present proportion, a change which is likely to have some effect upon the numbers who *choose* to swim for recreation purposes.

This example of the effects of policy decisions upon recreation behaviour is a fairly simple and rather obvious one. Others, however, will be more subtle and less readily identifiable. The problems that such effects pose for the forecaster are twofold: firstly, to identify the likely effects and, secondly, to take account of them in making his forecasts. In the first case, it is obvious that such effects will be easier to identify for the near future than for the medium or long-term future. The shorter is the forecasting period, the more likely it is that such effects can be identified and incorporated within the model. In the longer forecasting period it will be more difficult both to identify such effects and to take account of them in the prediction process.

This leads, in fact, to a consideration of what is, perhaps, the most difficult problem in forecasting at the present time—a difficulty which applies not only to recreation demand forecasting, but to almost all branches of social, economic and technological forecasting. This concerns the period for which forecasts should be attempted. It also, inevitably, involves a consideration of the relationships between forecasting and planning, between *what is expected to happen under certain assumed circumstances* and *what it is intended should happen under similar or other circumstances*. The difference lies, essentially, in the degree of control which can be exercised over the key causal variables. Forecasting is non-deterministic; it attempts to define what will happen under given conditions. Planning is goal-oriented; it attempts to make something happen by controlling and manipulating particular conditions. Inevitably the two processes become linked, and even interwoven. This is particularly true in the long term, when the ability to control and manipulate major causal variables is much greater. Both processes are concerned with the future, but the two approaches are radically different. The distinction has been described particularly well by Kahn [132]. In forecasting, 'one looks at an existing situation, selects certain tendencies that one thinks of as important or relevant, and extrapolates. If desired, one can then look at various policy measures which might affect these projections to see how they might change the result.' In goal-oriented planning, on the other hand, 'one first sets up some future context, world or scenario which one wishes either to achieve or to avoid and then asks what sequence of events might lead to the realisation of this goal'. In recreation, as in any other subject, it is imperative that the decision-maker should be clear in his own mind as to which of these two processes he is really applying.

In general, it is probably realistic to say that forecasting, in the sense that it has been defined above, is unlikely to be a satisfactory exercise for a period of more than about ten years ahead. The opportunities for extraneous factors to influence events and developments tend to multiply rapidly beyond this period. In particular, the opportunities to manipulate variables through policy decisions are much greater. In technological forecasting, for example, there are certain relatively inflexible constraints upon production which facilitate short-term forecasting. It takes about ten years, for example, for a new process to move from the first discovery in the research laboratory to large-scale use in production; first the process will need to be thoroughly tested, then the industry will need to be 'tooled up' for production, and the potential market explored. Sometimes, this procedure may take less than ten years, but usually it takes longer. Thus, it is a general principle of technological forecasting that any major innovation which is expected to be in operation in industry in, say, ten to fifteen years time, must be in existence, at least in the laboratory, at the present time. Beyond a period of about fifteen years ahead, however, this requirement becomes progressively less valid until it disappears altogether. Similar constraints operate in other sectors of forecasting. In education, for example, a radical change in the approach to secondary schooling, such as the introduction of the Comprehensive system, takes at least five years to produce its first effects and much longer to be fully effective.

The suggested figure of about ten years is, of course, an arbitrary one, and, in some cases, it may be possible to forecast with a fair degree of confidence for a longer period ahead, while in other cases, ten years may seem to be too long. The important point is not the precise period for which forecasting is possible, but rather, what is to be done about the longer period, for which some general indication of possibilities is required. It is here that the concept of *alternative futures* can be of value. The purpose in forecasting alternative futures is not to predict what will happen under one set of probable conditions, but to offer a range of possible happenings under a range of possible conditions with varying degrees of probability. It is this kind of long-term forecasting which has developed rapidly in recent years and which is exemplified by the work of Kahn and Wiener at the Hudson Institute in New York [95]: 'And what is central, therefore, to the present future studies is not an effort to "predict" the future, as if this were some far-flung rug of time unrolled to some distant point, but the effort to sketch "alternative futures"—in other words, the likely results of different choices—so that the polity can understand the costs and consequences of different desires.' Alternative futures, therefore, occupy a point somewhere between forecasting and planning on the methodological scale. They attempt to show what is expected to happen under each of a range of different assumed conditions. These alternative expectations then provide the basis for a goal-oriented choice. In this way, what is expected to happen under a particular set of conditions (forecasting) becomes what it is intended should happen (goal-oriented planning) when one alternative future is chosen in preference to the others.

In concluding this chapter, it is worth repeating some of the reasons why we attempt to forecast at all. Essentially, forecasting is necessary because ours is increasingly a planned society: planned, that is, in the sense that we attempt not simply to accept change as an inevitable consequence of time, but rather, to control change so as to achieve specified ends. In an age of intense and increasing competitive demands for land and natural and human resources for a variety of purposes—housing, industry, education, transportation, health, and so on—the need for planning is obvious. Moreover, planning implies not only a consideration of alternative uses for resources, but also alternative times for these uses. No resource is inexhaustible over time—not even Man himself. Planning necessarily involves commitments over time; and the latter, equally clearly, necessitate some kind of forecasting. Colburn [130] has made this relationship particularly well: 'A Planner must, in sequence; determine the present status of affairs relevant to the field for which he is planning; attempt to determine what the future course of events may be in the absence of planning and implementation of its action programme; determine the desirable and undesirable characteristics of these trends; and finally develop a program of action which would reshape the trends towards the desirable ends.' Forecasting, for whatever period ahead, is merely a technique which attempts to illustrate what can be expected to happen to one or more dependent variables when certain independent, or causal, variables behave in particular ways. The technique may be improved in any number of ways; in recreation demand forecasting, for example, by incorporating within the process certain key variables, such as attitudes and aspirations, which were previously omitted. But it remains a technique, or process which is essentially an aid to planning. In making forecasts, we are not attempting to determine what the future will be; for no future is predetermined. Rather, a forecast states what is expected to happen in the absence of any major policy decisions to the contrary; or, in the case of alternative futures, if particular policies are put into effect.

Part Five

A Strategy for the Provision of Recreation
Facilities

by A. J. Veal

Chapter 13
The Theory

This part of the report differs substantially from the remainder in that it provides an illustration of a theory for the provision of recreation facilities, rather than a wide-ranging examination of particular research problems. It has arisen largely from the belief that, at some stage during the research, breadth should be sacrificed for depth, in order to show how surveys fit into the complete process of decision-making. What was envisaged was a theory, or series of models, which could be used by local authorities—and other bodies wishing to provide recreation facilities—as a basis for determining the optimum location of a proposed new facility of a given kind. The section has three chapters: the present one, which outlines the theory; Chapter 14, which describes ways of collecting and analysing the data needed to test and use the theory; and Chapter 15, which presents an experiment already undertaken to test its validity.

Before describing the workings of the theory, however, it was thought worth while to outline briefly the basic stages in the decision-making process, which were considered to be appropriate to this kind of problem. These were fivefold: (i) the identification of policy needs; (ii) the development of the research methodology and theory; (iii) the gathering of data; (iv) the analysis of these data; and (v) the recommendations for policy. This structure differs from that outlined in Chapter 5 only on the number of stages in the research process that have been identified. The two outlines are wholly compatible, however; this structure merely amalgamates several stages of the previous one, while subdividing one stage. The reason for the existence of both can be sought from their contexts. The outline given in Chapter 5 is more appropriate to academic research, where the need is stronger for the independent identification of such matters as the nature of the problem, a statement of objectives and a consideration of alternative methods of presentation of the findings of the research. The structure outlined above is more appropriate to research undertaken directly for policy-making bodies, such as local authorities, where these issues can be considered under the single heading of the identification of policy needs. What follows is a brief outline of the activities to be undertaken at each of the five stages of this decision-making process.

The first stage—*the identification of policy needs*—requires the assumption that a body exists which is competent to take decisions and to act on the basis of them or, at least, to press for action to be taken. In most cases, this will be a local authority, although what follows will be applicable, in general, to commercial and voluntary organizations as well. The first requirement is, of course, that this decision-making body should determine exactly what it is that it wants or needs to know; and this must be related, to a large extent, to what it is able to do. Thus, for example, a local authority does not simply wish to know what are the recreation requirements of a particular area. It also wants to know which of these requirements it will have to provide itself, and how best it should go about providing them. These decisions will often reflect, in practice, what has happened in the past; but some flexibility should be maintained to allow for unseen possibilities and opportunities. Thus, a local authority might consider providing a dry ski slope even though it hasn't done so in the past.

Once the policy needs and possibilities are known, the research investigator is able to start thinking about *the alternative ways in which these needs can be met*. The needs, and the points at which action can be taken, become variables in his view of the real world. He must decide what factors or variables are important and how they are related: that is, he must try to understand how the real world works and how its workings can be affected by policy decisions. In a formal sense, therefore, a model—or a series of models—is built. This need not be a deterministic, quantitative model. It can equally be just a series of ideas about which factors are important in determining certain events, and why they are important. It is at this point that lack of data to confirm or disprove ideas or hypotheses may become apparent—which leads to a consideration of the next stage in the process.

This stage has been defined as *the gathering of data*, rather than simply a survey, because it needs emphasizing that surveys constitute only one of several possible sources of data about recreation. Having determined the nature of the data required, the form it should take and the ways in which it is intended to use it, it is possible to decide from what source or sources it should come and, hence, whether or not a survey is appropriate. Data from the Census and other official and unofficial sources should be fully investigated first, as well as data from previous surveys which may be relevant. This could suggest that a survey is not necessary, although in the majority of cases at present, it is likely that some kind of survey will be necessary to fill in the gaps in available data.

The fourth stage in the process—*the analysis of data*—should follow lines laid down during the development of research methodology and theory in stage two. Ideas and theories will be proved or disproved, and methods will be found to be useful or not useful. Obviously, in the light of the analysis, original ideas may have to be altered until meaningful results emerge. Once this has been achieved, however, the investigator can proceed to the final stage, *the policy recommendations*, which should be related directly to the original policy needs.

The remainder of this chapter is taken up with a discussion of the first two stages of this research and decision-making process, in relation to the problems encountered in deciding whether or not to increase the provision of recreation facilities within a particular area; and, if so, in what ways and in what places.

Identification of Policy Needs

The problem can be illustrated by the case of a body administering a homogeneous set of facilities in a given administrative area. Some examples of types of bodies and kinds of facilities could be as follows:

(i) *Public bodies*	Town parks
	Swimming baths
	Libraries
	Country parks
(ii) *Public or private bodies*	Games pitches and courts
	Golf courses
	Bingo halls
	Social clubs
(iii) *Commercial bodies*	Cinemas
	Public houses

Of course, in a real situation, the type of facility to be considered would be clearly indicated. At this stage, however, the concern is simply to keep the options open, and to take the opportunity to keep some generality of approach.

Organizations administering the kinds of facilities listed above have many problems. The one that is to be tackled here is that of expansion. Are new facilities needed? If so, how many? Where should they be located? And what use is likely to be made of them if they are provided? It is important to note that such questions can be asked in terms of the present (or, rather, the present planning period

—possibly up to five years ahead) or of the future. In most cases, decisions about the provision of new facilities should take as much account of the need to meet present unsatisfied demand as to satisfy the future growth of demand.

What is envisaged, therefore, is a situation where, in a defined area, there are a certain number of existing facilities of a given type. The body responsible for the provision of this facility knows the location of existing facilities, at least those which it owns itself. It is prepared to build new facilities or expand present ones (or press for funds to do so) if this is thought necessary.

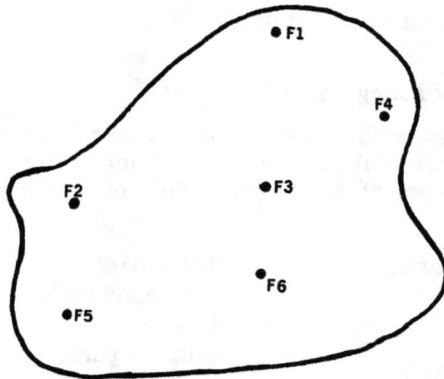

Figure 12. The distribution of recreation facilities in a hypothetical planning area

Formulation of Methodology and Theory

The first requirement is to understand the existing situation thoroughly. This can be represented diagrammatically as in Figure 12. This represents an administrative or planning area in which there are a given number (N) of facilities. All of these facilities may not be owned by the authority concerned, but they must all be located and taken into consideration. Thus, for example, a local authority will not necessarily own all golf courses within its area, but it cannot plan new ones without taking private clubs into consideration. Equally, cinema operators cannot plan new cinemas without taking into account the locations of competitors. This identification of the location of existing facilities represents the first gap to appear in our knowledge, and will have to be tackled in the next stage of the process.

310

For present purposes, the simplifying assumption is made that users of the facilities come only from within the planning area under consideration. Equally, it is assumed that people within the planning area cannot use facilities outside it. (These assumptions can later be removed.) It is then necessary to examine patterns of use of the facilities and to try to determine how the introduction of new facilities will affect these patterns.

Within the planning area there will be a given population, some of whom will make use of the facilities in question and some of whom will not. And of those who use the facilities some will use one particular facility and some will use another, while others may use several. If it were known what factors made people use the facilities and what factors decided which particular facilities they used, then it might be possible to decide how many people would use new facilities if they were provided. At this point it is necessary to put forward some ideas which might seem possible. Relevant factors can be divided into two groups: supply considerations and socio-economic factors.

In the closed system postulated above, if there were, for example, no swimming pools in the planning area, no one in the area would swim. If there was one swimming pool for every member of the population—everyone who wanted and was able to swim, could do so. It is quite likely that in the intermediate ranges of supply an increasing number of people would swim, as the number of facilities was increased, as illustrated in Figure 13. The saturation level is, of course, unlikely to be as high as one swimming pool per person.

Supply cannot simply be defined, however, in terms of the numbers of facilities available in the planning area. The accessibility of these facilities in relation to the people using them must also be considered. If people live a long way from the nearest available facility this is likely to prove a deterrent to use. Obviously, the regular, keen participant will not be deterred to the same extent as the casual user; but, depending on the mobility of the participant, and other factors to be discussed below, this is bound to affect the use made of facilities.

There is another aspect of supply which also warrants consideration. This is the 'attractiveness' of each individual facility. Newness, size, prices, car parking, and so on, are all relevant. Thus, it is likely that a user will be prepared to go further to use a facility which is attractive than one which is not: or he may even be induced to use the facility when he might not have otherwise done so.

To sum up, therefore, three causal factors can be identified under

311

the heading of supply: the numbers of facilities available; the location of these facilities; and their attractiveness. It is important to note that these factors are not merely the characteristics of supply; they are, rather, those characteristics which directly affect demand for, or use of, facilities.

Socio-economic factors relate directly to the members of the population. The way in which age, sex, class, income, and so on, affect the likelihood of a person's engaging in particular types of activity has been discussed fully in other parts of the report.* Such characteristics are all factors which will tend to affect a person's

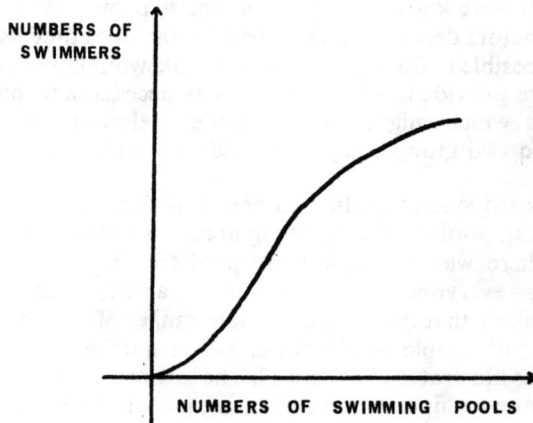

Figure 13. A hypothetical relationship between numbers of swimmers and numbers of swimming pools

desire and ability to participate in given activities. At a later stage, consideration can be given to ways and means of deciding which of these factors are important for different types of facility.

To aid in formalizing the above concepts, it can be supposed that the planning area is divided up into several smaller areas or zones numbered from 1 to n. If the planning area were as large as a country, these smaller areas could be local authority areas or counties. If the planning area were smaller, the sub-areas might be Wards or Parishes or Census Enumeration Districts. Completely arbitrary grid-square areas could even be used, but, from the point of view of availability of data and comparability with other studies, it is probably best

* See Chapter 9.

312

to use administrative or census areas. Each of these areas will contain a certain population and in each population there will be a certain number of users of the facilities under consideration.

These various concepts can now be defined in a form suitable for use in a model:

X_{ij} is a measure of the use made of facility j by residents of zone i, in a given period of time. The unit used might be person-visits per annum, or person-hours per annum, or total expenditure. In the subsequent discussion this quantity will generally be referred to as 'number of users'.

A_j is the attractiveness, or 'attraction factor', of facility j. There may be, in fact, several of these factors for each facility—say Q of them—$A_{1j}, A_{2j} \ldots, A_{Qj}$. These factors could reflect such things as the newness or size of the facility, prices charged (if any) and the availability of car parking.

D_{ij} is the distance of zone i from facility j. Distance might be measured in miles, as 'the crow flies' or by road, or in terms of time taken to travel from the zone to the facility, or in some combination of time and distance.

E_i represents one or more socio-economic characteristics of the population of zone i: it could be, for example, the number of females under 65 years of age.

P_i is the resident population of zone i.

There are assumed to be N facilities and n zones in the planning area.

X_{ij} is the dependent variable; that is, it is postulated that its value depends on the value of the other variables specified—the independent variables. Thus, the more attractive (A_j) a facility is, the more people will use it, or the more intensively they will use it. The further away (D_{ij}) a facility is, or the less accessible it is, the fewer people will use it or the less intensively they will use it. This is because of the deterrent effect of distance—the costs and inconvenience of overcoming it—and because at greater distances people are often less aware of the existence of a facility. The socio-economic structure of the population (E_i) will also affect participation rates, so that, for example, an area with a lot of old people will, other things being equal, tend to have fewer active sportsmen than an area containing a high proportion of young people. For some recreation activities, the income levels of the population may also be important, as will the overall total population (P_i) of the area.

The aim of this exercise is not just to note that these factors affec-

the numbers of users; but, by actually measuring them in particular situations, to find out precisely how they are related in a quantifiable way. The object is to produce a system whereby it can be said that 'if an area with given socio-economic and population characteristics (E_i, P_i) is a known distance (D_{ij}) from a facility with an established attraction factor (A_j), then it is possible to determine the numbers of people (X_{ij}) who will use that facility'. Once it is possible to make this statement for any type of area, for any distance and for any kind of facility, then it will be possible to make rational decisions about the location and appropriate size of new facilities. The formulation of a series of models to achieve this will be explained in the appendix to this chapter. Here, some of the criteria for the optimal location of facilities will be discussed, together with some of the situations in which the problem might arise.

Criteria for Optimal Location

A useful starting point for the discussion of criteria is that the authority or body concerned should so arrange its facilities that maximum possible use is made of them. There will of course be certain constraints on this. Probably the most important of these will be the costs involved. But other constraints may also be important, especially in the public sector. For instance, the stated policy of the providing authority might be that no one in the planning area should be further than a given distance from the nearest facility. In this case, the locations of the necessary minimum set of facilities can be determined with the help of a map, a ruler and a pair of compasses. But there will still be the problem of deciding the size of the facilities to be built; and rational decisions on this would be helped if it was possible to forecast the likely demand beforehand. Technical considerations will also be relevant. It might well be, for example, that certain facilities can only be built to a predetermined minimum or maximum size. Again, some activities give rise to traffic congestion or noise, which must also be considered.

The sort of theory being formulated here will not absolve the user from taking policy and technical factors into consideration. It will not provide a complete decision-making machinery. What it will do is reduce uncertainty on one very important aspect, namely the level of use to be expected of a new facility, in a given location.

It is quite likely then, that in a situation where a new facility is to be built, technical and policy considerations will eliminate many of the possible sites, and will give some order of priority to the remaining

314

ones. These latter sites can then be tested with the theory and an order of priority given on the basis of the results.

It should be remembered, however, that any new facility is likely to draw at least some of its users away from existing facilities. This will certainly need to be considered. But to see *how* it should be considered requires the identification of the kinds of organizations that might be involved in providing the new facility; for each will employ varying criteria. There are three basic kinds: firstly, an organization owning all facilities of the given kind in the area; secondly, an organization owning some but not all of these facilities; and thirdly, an organization owning only the new facility.

An organization owning all available facilities of the given kind will want to locate the new facility in such a way as to maximize the total use of all facilities, while ensuring that none of the existing facilities is adversely affected. The criteria for judging whether or not existing facilities have been adversely affected will vary, but would probably require some condition such as that use should not fall below a certain level dictated by technical or policy considerations. The implication is that *all* facilities have to be looked at in the planning process, not just the new one.

When an organization owns only some of the available facilities, interest will generally be in maximizing use of its own facilities only. But it may want to adopt a 'good neighbour' policy and try to ensure that its actions do not unduly affect the levels of use of facilities owned by other organizations. Even in the commercial field this may apply, if the body concerned is in favour of 'friendly' rather than 'cut-throat' competition.

An organization owning only the new facility will be in a similar position to the one owning a few. It will locate its facility so as to maximize possible use of it, but may nevertheless take care not to damage competitors unduly.

Another factor to be considered is the future—in particular, the future policy of the body concerned. Thus, if funds are to be available to increase facilities at regular intervals, then a plan for the location of facilities to be built over a period of, say twenty years could be formulated. The resultant pattern might be very different from, and better than, one resulting from the taking of entirely separate decisions on individual facilities. Looking that far ahead, it will also be necessary to take account of future population distribution and future values of E_i.

When more than one new facility is to be considered, the alternative plans become very numerous and hence the amount of work necessary to find the best one increases. Thus, if there are ten available sites and one facility to locate, the number of situations to be investigated is ten. But if three facilities have to be investigated the number of possibilities increases to 120.* With the aid of computerized models, however, this should present few problems. When facilities can be of more than one size or type the number of alternatives becomes even larger.

To summarize then, the major criterion for optimal location that the models to be developed in the appendix will employ is the level of use forecast for individual facilities or groups of facilities. The aim will be to find that location which maximizes this level of use, subject to given policy constraints.

* The choice of objects r at a time, from a body of n gives nCr choices.

$$nCr = n!/r!\,(n-r)!$$

In this case $_{10}C_3 = 10!/3!7! = 120.$

Appendix to Chapter 13

Detailed Specification of the Models

Although the ideas in this appendix are generally simple ones, their expression in mathematical terms may appear complex to those without a minimum mathematical background. It should be possible to get some idea of the basic concepts, however, without fully understanding all of the mathematics involved. The appendix describes the important process of transforming ideas and concepts into testable, usable mathematical forms.

1. *A Simple System*

In order to build up realistic formulations of the relationships between the variables X_{ij}, A_j, D_{ij}, E_i and P_i (defined on page 313) it is necessary to begin with a simplified, apparently unrealistic, system. In fact, it could well be that a simple system will more accurately reflect the real world than a complex one, which would show that either the real world is simpler than was thought, or that the more sophisticated concepts involved in the complex system are invalid. If it is supposed that all available facilities are homogeneous—so that they are all equally attractive to the user as far as price, amenities, 'image', and so on are concerned, and that all facilities are equally well served by public transport and roads, then the only characteristic which needs to be taken into account is the *distance* of the facility from the user's home. If users always go to the nearest available facility, it follows that each facility will have a clearly defined catchment area. Users do not use facilities outside the catchment area in which they live. (It is assumed, for the present, that users do not travel from places other than their homes, such as place of work or school.)

Considering the individual, therefore, it could be said that the *probability* (R) that an individual living within the catchment area will use the facility is inversely related to his distance from it. In symbolic terms:

$$R_n = aD_{nj}^{-b} \tag{1}$$

where a and b are constants and D_{nj} is the distance of individual n's home from facility j. For any zone containing P_i people, therefore:

$$\sum_{n}^{P_i} R_n = \sum_{n}^{P_i} D_{nj}^{-b} \tag{2}$$

The sum of the probabilities will give the number of people in the zone so that $\sum_{n}^{P_i} R_n$ is equal to X_{ij}. If it is assumed that $D_{ij} = D_{2j} = \ldots D_{Nj} = D_{ij}$, that is, that all inhabitants of the zone are considered to be the same distance from the facility, then from equation (2):

$$X_{ij} = P_i a D_{ij}^{-b} \tag{3}$$

Transposition of the P_i gives the *proportion* of the population using the facility:

$$X_{ij}/P_i = a D_{ij}^{-b} \tag{4}$$

In addition to (1) and (4) an exponential form can be put forward: Instead of (1):

$$R_n = c e^{-dD}nj \tag{5}$$

where c and d are constants, and hence instead of (4):

$$\frac{X_{ij}}{P_i} = c e^{-dD}ij \tag{6}$$

It could well be that the zones chosen for analysis do not all fall completely within one catchment area. There are two ways of overcoming this problem. If the zones are small in relation to the catchment areas the latter can be drawn so as to include whole zones, and the resulting error ignored. Alternatively, the populations of split zones can be divided in proportion to the areas falling in the catchment areas concerned. Again this will lead to error because of a probable unequal distribution of population within zones.

Equations (4) and (6) are the first, simple form of model, which could be tested, and possibly used, in decision-making. In a given planning area, catchment areas of facilities can be drawn on a map as long as the location of all facilities is known. Within any one catchment area (or, indeed, in several) data can be collected on numbers using the facility, distance travelled, and population of zones. Taking logarithms of equations (4) and (6) yields equations as follows:

$$\log (X_{ij}/P_i) = \log a - b \log D_{ij} \tag{7}$$

and

$$\log (X_{ij}/P_i) = \log c - dD_{ij} \tag{8}$$

These are equations which, with data as described above, would be amenable to linear regression which would test the appropriateness of the models (that is the 'goodness of fit' of the data to the equations) and provide estimates of the parameters (a, b, c and d).

It should be pointed out that if such a model were tested and found to be satisfactory in statistical terms, this would not indicate necessarily that the assumptions behind the model were true, but only that, within the limits set by statistical considerations, the complicating factor could be ignored. But, the more simplifying assumptions that there are attached to a model, the more cautious the user must be.

To illustrate the use of this simple model in the sort of decision-making process outlined in the main part of the chapter, it is necessary to introduce a term for the number of users of one facility. This is the sum of the users from each of the zones in the catchment area of the facility. This quantity will be termed X_j and is defined by:

$$X_j = \sum_i^{nj} X_{ij} \qquad (9)$$

where n_j is the number of zones in the catchment area of facility j.

If a hypothetical new facility were introduced to the system in a given position it would be possible to draw the new set of catchment areas. Only those facilities whose catchment areas had been reduced in size by the new facility would be affected. The number of zones in their catchment areas (n_j) would be reduced. X_j for these facilities would also be reduced accordingly. But for the new facility, the level of use could be estimated by substituting the known values of P_i, D_{ij}, a and b or c, and d in equation (7) or (8) (whichever had been shown by the testing process to be most appropriate), and then the resultant values of X_{ij} summed as in equation (9). The estimated use of all facilities (denoted by X) is equal to the sum of the users of individual facilities:

$$X = \sum_j^{N} X_j \qquad (10)$$

The values of the X_j's and of X can be calculated for all possible locations of the new facility. The optimal location is then the one which gives the maximum level of overall use (X) as long as none of the levels of use of individual facilities (X_j) falls below 'acceptable' levels.

A similar process is followed when more than one new facility is introduced at a time.

2. Heterogeneous Population

(a) Multivariate Approach

It was originally postulated that the probability that an individual would use a facility was a function only of the distance he lived from the facility. But the individual may have personal characteristics which will also affect this probability. Thus, if a person is old he is unlikely to engage in athletics, and if he is poor he is unlikely to engage in motor-racing. It can be supposed that there a certain number (K) of these characteristics (E), which are considered to be relevant. Where the characteristics are not expressed in numerical form (for example, sex or type of job), they may be converted into dummy variables; (for example, E_{n1} could be the dummy variable for 'male' and E_{n2} for 'female'; a male will have value 1 for E_{n1} and 0 for E_{n2}, while a female will have 0 for E_{n1} and 1 for E_{n2}). Then an equation can be written as follows:

$$R_n = q_0 D_{nj}^{-b} + a_1 E_{n1} + a_2 E_{n2} + \ldots + a_k E_{nk} \qquad (11)$$

Again, summing over all individuals in a zone yields:

$$\sum_n^{P_i} R_n = X_{ij} = a_0 \sum_n^{P_i} D_{nj}^{-b} + a_1 \sum_n^{P_i} E_{n1} + a_2 \sum_n^{P_i} E_{n2} + \ldots + a_k \sum_n^{P_i} E_{nk}$$

$$= a_0 P_i D_{ij}^{-b} + a_1 P_i E_{i1} + a_2 P_i E_{i2} + \ldots + a_k P_i E \qquad (12)$$

The detailed interpretation of the E_i depends on the original form. For instance if E_{n3} is the age of individual n, then $\sum_n^{P_i} E_{n3}$ is equal to P_i multiplied by the average age of the population of the zone. If, say, E_{n2} is the dummy variable for females, then $\sum_n^{P_i} E_{n2}$ gives the number of females in the population which is equal to P_i multiplied by the *proportion* of females in the population.

Transposition in (12) again gives the proportion of the population using the facility:

$$X_{ij}/P_i = a_0 D_{ij}^{-b} + a_1 E_{i1} + a_2 E_{i2} + \ldots + a_k E_{ik} \qquad (13)$$

Again, the exponential form is possible, although it cannot be derived directly from the individual's equation. The logarithmic transformation is:

$$\log (X_{ij}/P_i) = a_0^{-bD} ij + a_1 E_{i1} + a_2 E_{i2} + \ldots + a_n E_{ik} \qquad (14)$$

And, again, this provides a testable model. In the case of (13), because of the additive nature of the equation, it is not possible to take logarithms and get a direct solution for b from the regression equation. Instead, it will be necessary to substitute different values for b by trial and error or iteration until a best fit of the data is obtained.

The process for finding the optimum location of a new facility using these models is similar to that described for the simpler form.

(b) *Disaggregative Approach*

There is, however, another aspect of the heterogeneous population which needs consideration. In addition to the idea that, say, an old person may be inately less likely to engage in certain leisure activities,

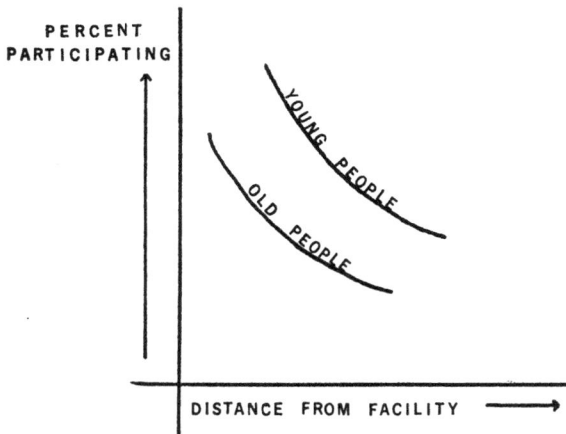

Figure 14. Hypothetical distance–use relationships for Assumption 1

it may be that, if a person is old, distance is more of a deterrent. Equally, to a young person, or to a wealthy person, distance may be less of a deterrent. This phenomenon would be reflected in a different value of the exponent b for different groups of the population. This can be represented diagrammatically. First, the idea that old people of different types are inately more or less active participants is illustrated in Figure 14. In this case the curves, though at different distances from the origin, are parallel. Second, the idea that, in addition, distance may affect the two groups differently is shown in Figure 15. Here the curves are not parallel, the proportion of old people participating falls more rapidly as distance increases.

L

To cope with this it will be necessary to have a separate equation for each group of the population. For practical reasons it may be necessary to limit disaggregation of the population to one axis only, but conceptually division along several axes would be better. Thus, if the data source for zone population characteristics were the Census, then, for example, the number of people in each age-group is known, and the number of car-owners and non-car-owners is known, but the number of car-owners and non-car-owners within each age-group is not known. The latter information would be available only from special surveys.

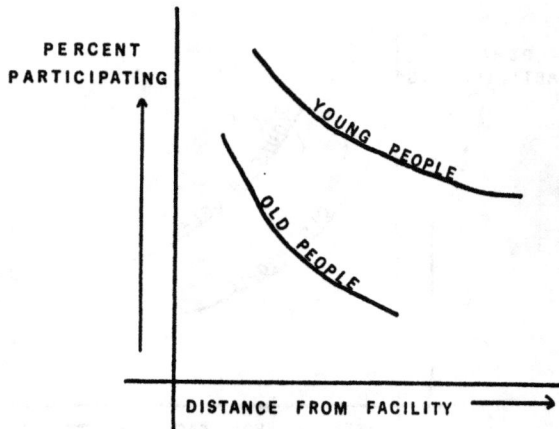

Figure 15. Hypothetical distance–use relationships for Assumption 2

The models in this case will be similar to those in equations (4) and (6) with the difference that there will be a separate equation for each group of the population thought to be significant. Each group equation will be expected to have different parameters.

The limitation on this type of model is that disaggregation of data will result in smaller numbers of observations for estimating each equation. The extent to which disaggregation can be pursued, therefore, will depend on the available total sample size with which the model is to be tested.

There may be a case for combining the multivariate approach and the disaggregative approach. Thus, one might have two separate equations, one for males and one for females. But the rest of the

322

relevant variables—age, income, education, and so on—would be included in these equations.

Using this form of model, the procedure for optimal location of new facilities becomes a little more complex. The catchment areas for each group of the population are identical, and still based on distance only, so that the new catchment areas resulting from additional facilities can be delineated as before. But the level of use of facilities must be calculated separately for each population group and then summed to obtain totals. The procedure for comparison of alternative sites is then exactly as before.

3. *Heterogeneous Facilities*

So far, consideration has been given to a single proposition—that distance alone will decide which facility a potential user will go to. This leads to an easy delineation of catchment areas. Within these catchment areas, consideration was first given to a straightforward gravity model; this was then extended by the introduction of additional variables relating to the population, either in a multivariate or disaggregative approach. At each stage testable models were produced. It is now intended to develop the concepts further and to consider not only the characteristics of the population, but also those of the available facilities. These characteristics are of many kinds, such as prices charged (if any), availability of refreshments, the number of alleys in a bowling centre, the size of a swimming-bath, the availability of car parks, and so on.

(a) *The Utility Function with Homogeneous Population*
It can no longer be said that distance alone will decide which facility the user will go to. The decision will now be taken on a combination of distance and other factors, such as those mentioned above. Suppose there are Q attraction factors for each facility: A_{1j}, A_{2j}, $A_{3j} \ldots A_{Qj}$. Then for any position on the map, distant D_j from facility j, there will be a 'utility' function which will describe the attraction of facility j at that point. The attraction of a facility will be proportional to the various attraction factors, and inversely proportional to distance. In linear form:

$$U_j = u_0 D_j + u_1 A_{1j} + u_2 A_{2j} + \ldots + U_Q A_{Qj} \tag{15}$$

where the u's are constants, and u_0 is expected to be negative. For simplicity, it will again be assumed that the population is homogeneous, so that the same utility function applies to everyone.

Brief mention should be made here of the method by which equation (15) can be calibrated. The method most appropriate is that of discriminant analysis.* This statistical process takes two 'populations' (in this case the users of two different leisure facilities) and the characteristics which are believed to distinguish them (in this case the D's and A's), and chooses coefficients (the u's) of a linear function of the characteristics (such as equation (15)) which best distinguishes the two populations. This process could be applied to selected pairs of facilities, probably ones with contiguous catchment areas, and, hopefully, the sets of coefficients would be similar. If not, the particular form of the utility function may need to be changed; for example, additional attraction factors may need to be introduced. Small differences in sets of coefficients obtained from different pairs of facilities may be accommodated by using the average value obtained. Once the coefficients in (15) have been found, all available facilities, including any hypothetical new ones, can be placed in order of preference for each zone in the area. In this way catchment areas can be drawn, since a zone will fall in the catchment area of the facility with the highest value of U_j.

Within the catchment areas so described, the original models as in equations (4) and (6) will still be applicable with one major difference; the parameters for each facility will tend to be different reflecting the overall differences in level of use, resulting from differences in attraction factors. In order to be able to specify parameters for any hypothetical new facilities it will be necessary to relate the parameters to the attraction factors of the existing facilities.

(b) *The Utility Function with a Heterogeneous Population*
Again, heterogeneity can be tackled in two ways: by a multivariate or disaggregative approach. The multivariate approach would add socio-economic variables to the utility function and again to the generative functions operating within catchment areas, as in equations (13) and (14). As with a homogeneous population, however, the parameters of the equations within catchment areas would differ from facility to facility.

The disaggregative approach would involve separate utility functions of the type given in equation (15), for each population group. These utility functions, which might even include different

* See Fisher, R. A., 'The Use of Multiple Measurements in Toxonomic Problems', *Annals of Eugenics*, **7**, 179 (1936); and Quarmby, D. A., 'Choice of Travel Mode for the Journey to Work', *Journal of Transport Economics and Policy*, Vol. **1**, No. 3, September 1967.

sets of attraction factors, would reflect the differing response of the groups to distance and attraction factors, and would result in different catchment areas for each group. Within these catchment areas, equations (4) and (6) would be applied. Again, the drawback with this sort of approach, apart from its increasing complexity, lies in the increased quantity of data necessary to test it.

4. *The Probability Approach*

Probability has so far been used simply in relation to the *generation* of users of facilities; that is, it has been argued that 'the *probability* that a particular person will participate in a given activity is a function of certain factors'. Huff suggests, however, in connection with shopping centres, that probability can be used to describe the *distribution* of users among available facilities.* Thus, the probability that a user will go to one particular facility is equal to the attraction of that facility relative to all available facilities. This results in users from one zone, in effect, distributing themselves amongst all available facilities; the numbers going to each facility being proportional to their relative attractiveness. This does away with catchment areas.

As Huff points out, the validity of a model which is used merely as a tool and is not based on human behaviour can be questioned. That is why, in the formulation of the models discussed above, the starting point has usually been the individual, with aggregation into groups following. The justification for the use of probability in a shopping model is that the attraction factors usually involve such measures as the total floor space or the variety of shops in each shopping centre. The individual shopper thus relates these factors to the probability that he will be able to find the commodities he needs on a particular trip. There could be similar applications to the leisure field. The individual planning a holiday may, on the basis of certain characteristics, decide that one resort is more likely to offer a 'good time' than another. But where facilities are more homogeneous—for example, swimming baths, or football pitches—and the individual has more knowledge of what to expect when he gets there, the probabilistic approach will be less appropriate. Bearing in mind the list of types of facility with which this study is primarily concerned, this approach (with the possible exception of country parks) seems hardly relevant.

* D. L. Huff, 'A Probabilistic Analysis of Shopping Center Trade Areas'. *Land Economics*, February 1963.

5. *Dropping the Assumption of a Closed System*

It has been assumed so far that the planning area is a closed system, that people outside the area are not able to use facilities within it, and that people living in the area are not able to use facilities outside it. Although this may well be the pattern *de jure* or *de facto*, in some cases it will not be. What happens to the systems discussed above if this assumption is removed? There are several possibilities.

If the amount of 'overlap' were small or if there appeared to be no net gain or loss of users by the planning area concerned, then, once this had been established, it could be ignored in the calculations. Alternatively, the catchment areas could be extended outside the planning area. The extraterritorial areas could be taken into account to determine overall user patterns, but be excluded for decision-making processes. A third alternative is to treat the 'outside world' as one extra zone from which, or to which, a standard net number of users would be gained, or lost, respectively.

6. *Inclusion of Non-Home-Based Trips*

So far it has been assumed in the models that all journeys to use facilities take place from home. Thus, socio-economic characteristics of zones have referred to the socio-economic characteristics of the resident population. For some types of facility this assumption might not be wholly appropriate. In particular, trips based on place of work or school could be important. This would be particularly important in the case of swimming baths or parks located close to a large factory or office complex.

To include working and school population in the models would raise data collection problems (daytime population is available in the census for complete local authority areas only). But if these could be overcome, working and school population could be accounted for by either adding them to the population figure (and perhaps subtracting the number working and going to school outside the area) or by including them as additional variables in the multivariate approach or as additional population groups in the disaggregative approach.

Further sophistication could be achieved by performing the analysis separately for daytime and evening where this was appropriate.

7. *Summary of Relevant Models*

We began by considering a homogeneous population faced with a homogeneous set of facilities. This resulted in delineation of catchment areas and, then, within catchment areas, the setting up of user-generation equations (4) and (6).

When the assumption of homogeneity of population was dropped, two approaches became possible: the multivariate approach, in which socio-economic characteristics are included in one equation with the distance variable; and the disaggregative approach in which groups of people of different types were dealt with in separate equations. The resultant models were formulated in equations (11), (12), (13) and (14). When the assumption of homogeneity of facilities was dropped, attraction factors were added to distance in the generative equations. Again, heterogeneity of population was dealt with in both the multivariate and disaggregative approaches. The resultant models were similar to equations (13) and (14), but the utility function (15) was used to determine catchment areas.

8. *Testing the Models*

Before a model can be used for forecasting or decision-making it must be tested against the real world—first, to see that it adequately describes the real world and, secondly, in order to find values for the parameters (such as b, $a_0 \ldots a_k$ and $u_1 \ldots u_Q$ in the above models).

Models have been established above relating numbers of users of facilities to distances, socio-economic factors and attraction factors of facilities. Are these variables, in fact, related in the way postulated? The only sure way to answer this question is to measure them and see. It is likely that, in different situations involving different sorts of facility or different types of area, the appropriateness of the models will differ, as will the values of the parameters.

As indicated before, it will not be possible here to test the models in all or even several situations. For various practical reasons, the testing will be applied to public libraries which, though they serve non-leisure functions to a certain extent, nevertheless have many practical features which make them ideal for the purpose. This will be further discussed as the experiments are described, in the following chapters.

Chapter 14

Data Collection for the Experiments

In Chapter 13, selected questions of recreation planning policy were considered and a theory developed as a potential means of tackling them. The present chapter outlines the ways in which the data were obtained to use as inputs in an operational test of the theory.

One of the initial aims of this whole project was to investigate the value of collecting data by means of surveys at recreation sites as an alternative to surveys in households. This was done primarily by means of a review of previous research in recreation and the social sciences generally, which is summarized in Chapter 1. The primary concern in the present chapter is to illustrate the use of such site surveys as a means of securing the necessary data to test theoretical concepts and, hence, to show their value as tools in the planning process. It was readily apparent that, in order to test the kind of theory advanced in Chapter 13, it would be necessary to know the residential distribution of a considerable number of the actual users of the particular kind of facility being examined. It is clear that on-site data collection is particularly appropriate for securing such information.

Essentially, the required information consists of the numbers of users travelling to a facility from different distances and from within different zones for which overall population characteristics are known. In addition, we would need to know the time taken by each user, or group of users, to travel to the facility and the frequency or intensity of use. The data about travel time could be used either as an alternative to the data about distance, or in addition to it. There were, also, various practical constraints operating during the planning of the experimental studies, which severely limited the choice of the type of facility to be considered. These have been outlined briefly in Chapter 4 and resulted in the choice of public libraries for the case studies. The main considerations in making this choice were, firstly, that public libraries existed in both of the areas where the household surveys were taking place (and, although the exact nature of any relationships between the two experimental studies was not foreseen, it was felt that such relationships could well be developed as the studies progressed); secondly, public libraries are used continuously throughout the day, so that economic use could be made of interviewers and it would not be necessary to resort to the use of self-administered questionnaires (as might be the case with, say, cinemas); and thirdly, since interviewing was to take place in the winter months, attention would have to be devoted to the effects of the weather (interviewing in public libraries would not be affected by adverse weather conditions).

Although, strictly speaking, the results which follow apply only to public libraries, the techniques used, with some modifications, can be applied to any of the types of facility discussed in the previous chapter. There would seem to be little point in discussing in detail the modifications appropriate to each type of facility. Such a discussion would be of relatively little value without experience of the various types of facility, and this was not obtained in this study. The present work is by no means conclusive even on public libraries, especially since it has not been possible to follow through the initial findings into a complete planning exercise. The full implications of the relative success of this experiment in applying the gravity concept to a leisure situation are that further research and exploratory planning exercises are needed both with libraries and other leisure facilities, in order to explore the full possibilities of this concept as a tool in leisure planning. On the other hand, there is no doubt that the experiment was relatively successful and that it has provided us with useful experience of the applicability of this kind of model to leisure planning situations.

Collecting the Data

In the case of public libraries a ready source of information on the residential distribution of borrowers lies in the lists of users and their addresses which most libraries keep. This source does not, however, provide information on the frequency of use or the period of time taken to travel to the library. Also, the *type* of source is not usually available for other kinds of facility, such as swimming pools. It was decided therefore, not to use this information, but to rely solely on survey data. (It is admitted, however, that in a 'real' situation this ready source of information should be used in the first place, at least for the pilot work). When this type of survey is being planned, the length and content of the questionnaire affect the way in which it is administered, and vice versa. It is often difficult therefore to relate the exact process through which the two aspects of the study were formulated. In this case, however, the physical constraints of organization were very real, so it is perhaps as well to begin by describing this aspect.

Two interviewers were stationed at each library entrance. Users were stopped as they entered the library and asked if they would mind being interviewed. When they had finished interviewing one person, the interviewers were instructed to stop the next person to enter the library. In this way interviewing was conducted at a fairly even rate and in a relatively unbiased manner throughout the period of the survey. Where users entered the library together, there was a tendency for the more forceful member of a couple or group (sometimes perhaps the husband at other times, the wife, for example) to be interviewed, so that some bias may have crept in here. There was really no way of checking that interviewers did not avoid certain 'types' of people, although they were specifically warned against doing this.

Although interviewers were interviewing at a steady rate throughout the day, the sample drawn was necessarily unbalanced because of the varying rates at which people enter the library at different times in the day. Thus almost *all* of the persons who used each library during the morning and early afternoon—mainly housewifes and elderly people—could be interviewed. But, during the lunch period, late afternoon and evening a smaller *proportion* of users would be interviewed, since the total numbers of persons using each library would be very much greater during these periods. This kind of disproportionate scale of interviewing can, of course, be corrected by weighting the value of the interviews carried out during any particular period according to the total numbers using the library during each period. Figures of the total numbers of users were obtained by counting the total numbers of people entering each library during fifteen minute periods throughout the day. In this way, it was possible to calculate the proportion of users interviewed during any given fifteen-minute period, since the time of interview was entered on each questionnaire. It was then a simple task to weight the findings during the analysis in order to simulate a constant proportionate sample.

In a period of two and a half days, 450 interviews were obtained at one library and 350 at another. This represents between four and six interviews per hour per interviewer.* This is, of course very productive compared with the known results of household interview surveys —although we have no direct comparison for a questionnaire of similar length and kind.

It was decided to pilot the questionnaire first, as a means of checking its design and the question wording. The key question was the one which asked from where the user had come. Since information

* Including the person who was simply counting total numbers of users as an interviewer.

on the populations of zones derived from the census was to be used, it was thought that the home address would be the most important. But, if a large proportion of people were coming from or going to work or school, then industry and schools might prove to be important generators of use, so we checked on this too. Also, if people were on their way from one place to another when they called at the library (this would not happen as much with other types of facility like golf courses or swimming pools), the distance travelled *to the library* would only really be the distance that they had gone *out of their way* in order to visit it; hence, the inclusion of a question for these people which asked: 'How long would it have taken you to go directly to your destination without calling at the library?'

The pilot survey had revealed that there was relatively little seasonal variation in the patterns of use of each library, so the question on this topic was modified slightly in the questionnaire that was used in the final survey. The information obtained in response to this question—'How often do you come here?'—was converted into a single measure—'visits per annum'—for purposes of coding and analysis.

Questions about the numbers of books borrowed and the borrowing of books for friends were included with a view to their possible use as an alternative measure to 'numbers of users' and 'visits per annum'. Thus, the unit of measurement could be, at its simplest, 'numbers of users from each zone'; a more complex version could be 'visits per annum from each zone'; and more complex still would be 'numbers of books borrowed per annum from each zone'. The first measure could be used for general planning purposes; the second would be of interest in the planning of such items as car parking and access; and the third alternative would be useful in planning the size of the library in terms of stocks of books held.

The profile questions were kept to a minimum—firstly, to simplify the analysis and, secondly, to keep the questionnaire as short as possible. They covered only four items: age of the respondent, his marital status, number of persons in the family or household, and occupation of the head of household. The latter information was required in order to place the user in a particular socio-economic group.

A final question, about other leisure pastimes, was asked partly out of curiosity and partly because it was thought that it might be interesting to compare the responses to this with some of the data obtained from the household interview survey.

In addition to the information obtained from respondents, the

Census Enumeration District in which the interviewer lived was later identified (at the same time as the address was found and the distance travelled recorded) and the code number of the E.D. was recorded at the end of the questionnaire.

The information from each questionnaire was transferred to one punched card for analysis. Most of the questions were precoded in the questionnaire. As can be seen from the questionnaire itself, all of the information was recorded in fifty columns—which was perfectly satisfactory, since a normal punched card has space for eighty columns of information.

In the same way that data collection problems and theoretical considerations interact on the design of the experiment and in particular the questionnaire, so these things are affected by the analysis to be carried out. Although the collection of the data has been dealt with separately in this chapter, it must not be thought that it was not, at the time, influenced by the analysis to follow. These influences, and at times the lack of them, should become apparent as the analysis is described in the next chapter.

Chapter 15

The Experiments

This chapter will provide an overall description of the characteristics of the data obtained from the two site surveys, together with an outline of the basic analysis performed and a discussion of the extent to which the findings support the theory advanced in Chapter 13. It will conclude with a brief consideration of the implications of the findings for policy-making and for future research.

The Survey Data

Approximately 750 interviews were completed at the two libraries, 618 of which were found to be usable for the analysis. The rejects resulted mainly from cases where the address of the respondent was not given, or where the address that was given could not be located on the city map. Since distance and zone of origin, or Enumeration District, were to be the key variables, questionnaires without this information had to be rejected. In other cases, where individual questions had not been answered, the questionnaire could still be included within the total, these particular respondents being classified as non-respondents on the individual questions. The basic data obtained are shown in Table 52, in two forms: first, the raw data; second, the raw data weighted to compensate for variations in interviewing rates. The effects of the weighting are, in fact, relatively small. Only the data used in the subsequent analyses are presented in the table.

The Analysis

The first analysis to be carried out was an even simpler exercise than that implied by equations (4) and (6) in the Appendix to Chapter 13. The aim was to test the gravity concept at its most elementary level. Each library was imagined to have concentric rings around it, each ring being 0·1 miles wide. The number of users per square mile was calculated for each ring to give the values of X, the distance of the rings from the library giving the corresponding values of D. Then X was regressed against D. This gave correlation coefficients of $-0·77$ for the suburban library (Billesley) and $-0·82$

333

Table 52. The Site Surveys—Basic Data

| | RAW DATA | | | | WEIGHTED DATA | | | |
| | Yardley Wood (suburban) | | Handsworth (inner urban) | | Yardley Wood (suburban) | | Handsworth (inner urban area) | |
	No.	per cent	No.	per cent	No.	per cent	No.	per cent
Total Sample	248	100·0	370	100·0	246·6	100·0	368·4	100·0
Sex: Male	136	54·8	195	52·7	136·7	55·5	200·2	54·3
Female	112	45·2	175	47·3	109·8	44·5	168·2	45·7
Mode of transport to library								
Foot	131	52·8	199	53·9	125·5	50·9	195·5	53·0
Bus	12	4·8	105	28·5	11·6	4·7	102·5	27·8
Bicycle	5	2·0	6	1·6	3·6	1·5	7·3	2·0
Motor cycle	4	1·6	5	1·4	3·7	1·5	6·4	1·7
Car	95	38·3	53	14·4	101·0	41·0	55·7	15·1
Other	1	0·4	1	0·3	1·2	0·5	1·1	0·3
Distance of origin from library								
Up to ¼ mile	41	16·5	86	23·2	40·9	16·6	86·7	23·5
Over ¼ up to ½ mile	65	26·2	82	22·2	62·6	25·4	84·7	23·0
Over ½ up to ¾ mile	67	27·0	70	18·9	66·6	27·0	66·2	18·0
Over ¾ up to 1 mile	29	11·7	68	18·4	27·0	11·0	64·7	17·5
Over 1 mile	46	18·5	64	17·3	49·5	20·1	66·1	18·0
Nature of origin								
Home	214	86·3	266	71·9	210·0	85·2	258·1	70·1
School	14	5·7	46	12·4	16·5	6·7	47·8	13·0
Place of work	13	5·2	42	11·3	12·1	4·9	46·8	12·7
Other	7	2·8	16	4·3	8·0	3·2	15·6	4·2

Was journey to library direct?								
Yes	217	87·5	316	85·4	218·8	88·7	317·8	86·3
No	31	12·5	54	14·6	27·7	11·3	50·6	13·7
Time of journey to library								
0–4 minutes	59	23·8	74	20·0	59·0	23·9	73·8	20·0
5–9 minutes	84	33·9	95	25·7	87·9	35·6	98·7	26·8
10–14 minutes	45	18·1	89	24·1	42·6	17·3	84·6	23·0
15 + minutes	60	24·2	110	29·7	57·1	23·2	109·8	29·8
No reply	0	0·0	2	0·5	0·0	0·0	1·5	0·4
Distance of destination								
Up to ¼ mile	45	18·1	84	22·7	43·6	17·7	83·4	22·6
Over ¼ up to ½ mile	69	27·8	75	20·3	68·5	27·8	78·3	21·3
Over ½ up to ¾ mile	66	26·6	66	17·8	63·1	25·6	66·8	18·1
Over ¾ up to 1 mile	30	12·1	75	20·3	34·4	14·0	72·8	19·8
Over 1 mile	38	15·3	70	18·9	36·8	14·9	67·0	18·2
Nature of destination								
Home	206	83·1	289	78·1	205·9	83·5	297·2	80·7
School	12	4·8	26	7·0	10·9	4·4	21·1	5·7
Place of work	13	5·2	31	8·4	11·2	4·5	27·5	7·5
Other	17	6·9	24	6·5	18·5	7·6	22·6	6·1
Was journey from library direct?								
Yes	235	94·8	276	74·6	237·4	96·3	285·0	77·4
No	13	5·2	94	25·4	9·2	3·7	83·4	22·6
Time of journey from library								
0–4 minutes	59	23·8	63	17·0	60·5	24·5	58·8	16·0
5–9 minutes	83	33·5	90	24·3	88·4	35·9	95·3	25·9
10–14 minutes	47	18·9	102	27·6	43·0	17·5	101·6	27·6
15 + minutes	59	23·8	115	31·1	54·6	22·1	112·6	30·6

335

Table 52. (continued)

| | RAW DATA | | | | WEIGHTED DATA | | | |
| | Yardley Wood (suburban) | | Handsworth (inner urban) | | Yardley Wood (suburban) | | Handsworth (inner urban area) | |
	No.	per cent	No.	per cent	No.	per cent	No.	per cent
If origin and destination different, time of journey								
0–2 minutes	3	1·2	0	0·0	3·8	1·5	0·0	0·0
3–5 minutes	5	2·0	5	1·3	6·9	2·8	4·6	1·3
6–14 minutes	10	4·0	18	4·9	9·8	4·0	19·9	5·4
15+ minutes	21	8·5	38	10·3	22·3	9·0	42·6	11·6
Not applicable	209	84·3	309	83·5	203·7	82·6	301·2	81·8
Frequency of visits								
12 or less p.a. (once a month or less)	71	28·6	83	22·4	70·1	28·4	84·0	22·8
13–26 p.a. (once a month–once a fortnight)	83	33·5	102	27·6	89·0	36·1	103·6	28·1
27–52 p.a. (once a fortnight–once a week)	65	26·2	105	28·4	56·1	22·8	107·0	29·1
Over 52 p.a. (more than once a week)	29	11·7	80	21·6	31·2	12·7	73·7	20·0
Number of books borrowed per visit								
Less than 3	73	29·4	99	26·8	66·7	27·0	102·1	27·7
3	114	58·1	226	61·1	151·7	61·5	220·9	60·0
Over 3	25	10·1	33	8·9	24·0	9·7	34·7	9·4
No reply	6	2·4	12	3·2	4·1	1·7	10·7	2·9

Whether books borrowed for friends																
Always	63	25·4		56	15·1		64·8	26·3		48·3	13·1					
Sometimes	72	29·0		52	14·1		71·1	28·9		51·8	14·1					
Never	112	45·2		259	70·0		109·4	44·4		265·8	77·2					
No reply	1	0·4		3	0·8		1·2	0·5		2·5	0·7					
Number of books borrowed for friends																
Less than 3	59	23·8		44	11·9		57·0	23·1		44·8	12·2					
3	44	17·7		49	13·2		46·8	19·0		43·1	11·7					
Over 3	27	10·9		15	4·1		27·3	11·1		12·3	3·3					
No reply or not applicable	118	47·6		262	70·8		115·4	46·8		268·1	72·8					

for the urban one (Handsworth). These values are highly significant, indicating a strong negative association between distance and density of users. When log X was regressed against D, the correlation coefficients were -0.88 and -0.80 respectively, an increase for one library and a decrease for the other.*

Thus far, the concept seemed to work. But the usefulness of the idea in planning depends on its being applied to small areas or zones; that is, the planner must be able to forecast the numbers of users expected from any given zone in the catchment area of a hypothetical facility. The next step, therefore, was to use the information with respect to Census Enumeration Districts. These areas usually contain a population of approximately 2,000 persons, although they vary considerably around this figure. Their areas may also vary considerably—from, perhaps, thirty acres in a dense urban residential area to several hundred acres if parks or industrial areas are included. In the case of the library which was situated in the inner urban area there were 44 E.D.s in its catchment area (that is, users came from 44 E.D.s around the library). In the case of the suburban library, the number of Districts was 29.

For the next stage of the analysis the number of users from each E.D. (X) was regressed against the distance of the E.D. from the library (D), as measured by the *average* of the distance travelled by the users from the E.D. This gave correlation coefficients of -0.79 for the suburban library and -0.53 for the urban one. The suburban library, therefore, shows an improvement (though not a significant one) in its index with the use of E.D.s, whereas the urban library shows a distinct drop in value. Throughout the analysis the results pertaining to the inner urban library are less consistent than those for the suburban library. No doubt this can be explained by the complexity of residential patterns within the inner urban area. In the suburbs the population is more evenly spread and, at least in the area surrounding the library, less inroads are made on the area by railway property and large-scale industry, both of which tend to impede movement. This disappointing result from the urban library was maintained when the same data were used, but with log X regressed on D. The correlation coefficients were then -0.76 for the suburban library and -0.46 for the urban one. However, this comparatively low figure for the urban library is still significant at the 1 per cent

* The sign of the coefficient indicates the *nature* of the relationship. The *absolute* value of the coefficient indicates the *strength* of the relationship. It is therefore legitimate to talk of, for example, -0.88 being *greater than* -0.77. The reference is, and will be in the rest of the chapter, to the absolute value.

level, indicating that it is 99 per cent certain that the two variables are correlated.

It was only after this point in the analysis that the equations formulated in the Appendix to Chapter 13 were put to the test. The number of users for each E.D., as a percentage of the total population of the E.D. (given by the 1966 Census), was regressed against the distance of the E.D. from the library. With the proportion of users represented by X and the distance represented by D, this formulation is given in equation (4) in the Appendix to Chapter 13. Since E.D.s vary in population, an improvement in the correlation coefficients might have been expected as a result of the introduction of population proportions into the equation. This, however, was not the case. For the suburban library the coefficient was now -0.77 and for the urban one, -0.48. And when log X was used (equation 8) the coefficients were -0.75 and -0.36, respectively. The surveys were, of course, undertaken in October 1968, whereas the population figures relate to 1966 when the Census was carried out. In the inner urban area where much of the property was privately rented, and where there was also some redevelopment, the population figure could be expected to have changed significantly during the intervening period. The other point to bear in mind is that the 1966 Census was itself only a 10 per cent sample Census, and the statistical error expected in small-area data at this level is considerable. Data from a complete Census would be more satisfactory.

The correlation coefficients so far obtained are shown in Table 53. Before proceeding further with the analysis, however, it will be useful to assess the results obtained so far in terms of their potential value for future planning of leisure facilities generally.

The regressions of the number of library users as a proportion of the E.D. population against distance gives the following parameters for equation (4);

For the Suburban library,

$$X/P = 0.006 \ D^{-1.6} \qquad \text{(A)}$$

For the Urban library,

$$X/P = 0.0002 \ D^{-0.9} \qquad \text{(B)}$$

The results for the two libraries are clearly very different. The effect of distance on the proportion of users is much greater in the case of the urban library. The reasons for these differences have a direct bearing on the usefulness of the model in planning. The answer could lie in the additional variables discussed in Chapter 13. In particular, the

339

low use made of the urban library (relative to the population in the catchment area), as signified by the low coefficient 0·0002, could be explained by the socio-economic characteristics of the population of the catchment area. The attractions of the libraries themselves might also be important. Although libraries cannot compete on price, there may be subtle differences in the quality of services offered, although this would be difficult for the non-user to detect. What are probably more important as attraction factors are the built-in advantages and

Table 53. *The Initial Correlation Coefficients*

	VALUES OF THE COEFFICIENTS	
	Suburban Library	*Urban Library*
Concentric Rings		
No. of users per sq. mile (*X*) × Distance of ring (*D*)	−0·77	−0·82
Log of No. of users per sq. mile (log *X*) × Distance of ring (*D*)	−0·88	−0·80
Enumeration Districts		
No. of users (*X*) × Distance of E.D. (*D*)	−0·79	−0·53
Log of No. of users (Log *X*) × Distance of E.D. (*D*)	−0·76	−0·46
No. of users as a proportion of the population (*X/P*) × Distance of E.D. (*D*)	−0·77	−0·48
Log of No. of users as a proportion of the population ((Log *X/P*)) × Distance of E.D. (*D*)	−0·75	−0·36

disadvantages of the locations of the libraries. Thus, the suburban library stood on its own, was fairly obvious from the road and had ample parking facilities. This was not the case with the urban library, which had no car park, was lost in a complex of local authority buildings and may not have been known by those living farther away. This issue of 'awareness' and some ways of dealing with it are discussed by Maw [139]. There are many interesting and important issues here which could only be explored analytically if data were available for two facilities with contiguous catchment areas, as discussed in Chapter 13.

The results so far indicate that, provided the differences in the equations for the two libraries can be explained, the approach might be usefully employed in planning contexts. Thus, if the planner had available data on the population of Enumeration Districts in the area where new libraries were proposed, by utilizing the distances of the E.D.s and their population, in turn, in equation (A) or (B), estimates of the numbers of users expected over a three-day period (the period of the survey) could be obtained. This would be useful in comparing alternative sites. Estimates of annual use could be obtained by 'grossing-up' the figures for the three-day period.

As indicated in Chapter 13, further development of the model involves the introduction of E.D. data in addition to population size, such as the age–sex structure of the population and its socio-economic composition. But, rather than attempt this at this stage, the other developments mentioned in Chapter 13 were tested. These were the use of other measures of use besides 'numbers of users', and the use of 'time' instead of distance.

The first formulation was 'frequency of visit' against distance: instead of counting the numbers of users emanating from each concentric ring, or E.D., the numbers of visits per annum were counted. As indicated in Chapter 14, each user's 'frequency of visit' was converted into a 'visits per annum' total, so this exercise was easily performed. The resultant correlation coefficients were as shown in Table 54. These coefficients exhibit the same pattern, in terms of their relative sizes, as the earlier ones. They are all, however, lower than the corresponding coefficient when number of users was the criterion. As mentioned previously, the relationship between the number of visits recorded in the period of the survey (what we have called the number of users), and the total number of visits in a year would normally be found through knowledge of the total number of visits per annum from other sources. In this way a gross total would be known. There is a chance, however, that with varying sizes of catchment area, a more general model would be obtained by employing the users' own estimates of frequency of visits. This would be particularly true if stated frequency of visit is actually related to distance travelled for individuals. The indications from the present survey are that users living at the farthest distances from the library make the least number of visits. Few of the users who live more than a mile away visit the library more than once a week. Equally, few of those who live less than a quarter of a mile away make visits less than once a month. The pattern is similar for both libraries. This is, obviously, a finding which could apply to many kinds of recreation facility. It is also one which is important in forecasting demand, since it means that facilities with spatially large catchment areas will tend to have lower *average* visiting rates. The variable 'visits per annum', though in most ways similar in its operation to 'numbers of users', requires more consideration, especially in its application to hypothetical facilities with varying catchment areas.

Similar considerations apply when 'books borrowed per annum' is used as the dependent variable. The equivalent variable in the case of other facilities would obviously be different: for example, 'person-hours' would be used in the case of swimming pools and, probably,

TABLE 54. *Correlation Coefficients Using Visits per Annum*

	CORRELATION COEFFICIENTS	
	Suburban Library	*Urban Library*
Concentric rings		
Visits per annum × Distance	−0·70	−0·79
Log of visits per annum × Distance	−0·85	−0·78
Enumeration Districts		
Visits per annum × Distance	−0·74	−0·39
Log of visits per annum × Distance	−0·72	−0·36
Visits per annum per head of population × Distance	−0·72	−0·35
Log of visits per annum per head of population × Distance	−0·71	−0·29

'person-rounds' in the case of golf courses. The correlation coefficients obtained when this measure was used show a similar pattern but are, generally, lower than with 'numbers of users'. And again, the relevance of this particular formulation for planning purposes really depends upon whether or not the number of books that users say they borrow at a time varies with distance. This latter relationship is not as clear as was the case with 'visits per annum'. In the case of the surburban library the number of books borrowed is not related to distance travelled; in the urban library it is.* In some circumstances, then, it could be that the number of books borrowed is entirely neutral as far as distance travelled is concerned, so that

* For the suburban library chi-squared is 5·7, for the urban one chi-squared is 22·3. The latter is significant at the 1 per cent level.

total borrowing requirements could be obtained from forecasted numbers of users simply by multiplying by a constant factor—the average number of books borrowed. In other circumstances, however, the number of books borrowed would have to be treated as a variable in its own right, related to distance in a similar way to visits per annum.

Attention can now be directed away from a consideration of alternative measures of 'use' toward an alternative measure of 'distance'. An initial analysis was again performed using concentric rings around each library, but on this occasion they were 'time-rings'; that is, users were grouped on the basis of the (stated) period of time taken to travel to the library. The rings were one minute 'wide'. When

TABLE 55. *Initial Correlation Coefficients Using Time*

	CORRELATION COEFFICIENTS	
	Suburban Library	*Urban Library*
Concentric 'Time' rings		
No. of users × Time	−0·75	−0·77
Log of No. of users × Time	−0·73	−0·70
Enumeration Districts		
No. of users × Time	−0·07	−0·05
Log of No. of users × Time	−0·23	−0·06
No. of users as a proportion of population × Time	−0·07	−0·08
Log of No. of users as a proportion of population × Time	−0·24	−0·08

Enumeration Districts came to be used, the journey time from each E.D. was estimated as the average of the journey times of all of the users from the E.D.—a similar technique to that used for distance. Table 55 gives the correlation coefficients obtained. These show much lower values than heretofore for the E.D.s. However, the relatively high coefficients for the concentric rings would indicate that the variable is a valid one, although it may need considerable sophistication of the model to render it useful in planning, where zones of the Enumeration District type would have to be used. It is suspected that one of the main drawbacks in using time as a variable is the difficulty of obtaining accurate data about it. In the case of distance, interviewees were asked for their addresses, and the distance was subsequently measured on a map. The only error would, therefore, lie in the difference between the straight line distance, as measured on a map, and the length of the actual route travelled by the users. In the case of time, however, unless the surveyor is prepared to travel each route by the appropriate mode, and time the duration of the journey, the judgement of the interviewee must be relied upon. And, as suggested in Chapter 14, this may be erratic: one person's 'five minutes' may be another person's 'ten'.

For the present experiment, therefore, the use of 'time' in place of 'distance' does not appear to be a worthwhile exercise. For the record, however, regressions using 'visits per annum' and 'books borrowed per annum' against time have been performed. The results give a similar pattern to that obtained for 'number of users' against time. If anything, the coefficients are generally lower—to the extent that two of them have positive values!

Comment

Clearly, there is much more that can be done with the data obtained from the two site surveys; and some suggestions will be made for further work in the final chapter of this report. But, for now, it is worth taking stock of the implications of the rather basic analyses that have been outlined above. It is reasonably accurate to say that the basic ideas and concepts of the theory have been borne out by the analyses. In addition, every indication has been given that the inclusion of the more sophisticated elements of the theory—the attraction factors and the socio-economic variables—would support this claim, rather than refute it. Further development of these ideas, both through more sophisticated analysis (using our own and other data) and by application to other types of facility, is obviously indicated. In the meantime, the analysis has shown that the gravity model concept has as much potential value for recreation planning as it has for transportation and other planning fields.

In a wider sense, the experiment has illustrated the potential for recreation research which is more than just descriptive and informative. The kind of model employed here could prove immensely useful in helping to formulate decisions about whether or not to provide new facilities and, more directly, where to locate new facilities. It is along this track that recreation research must travel if it is to remain relevant to the problems of a real world, and is not to become merely an academic extravagance.

344

Epilogue

An epilogue is defined in *Webster's Dictionary* as 'a concluding section that rounds out the design of a literary work'. It is doubtful that the author had in mind a work such as this one when he used the adjective 'literary'. Yet the sense of the definition is highly appropriate to what it is intended should be encompassed in this final chapter. The purpose is, indeed, to provide a concluding section that will round out the design of the research that has been reported here. It is important, however, to note exactly what is conveyed by the use of the term 'rounding out'. To round out the research requires much more than a mere summary of what is contained in the remainder of the book. It should involve not only a recitation of major findings, but also an evaluation of them; not only an account of the objectives of the research which were achieved, but also a statement of those objectives that were not achieved. Such a rounding out of the research should also include any suggestions for further work that stem from what has been accomplished. The present chapter will attempt to do all of these things under three broad headings. The first—the *Summary*—will consist of a statement of what the research has achieved, together with an account of its failures. The second— the *Comment*—will include a consideration of the potential value of the research for planners, and a discussion of the extent to which the investigator would carry out the research differently if he were free to repeat it. The final section—the *Suggestions for Further Research*— represents the author's recommendations for priorities in further research.

Summary

Much has been achieved through this research. The methodological review of recent recreation (and other) studies was, in one sense, the most productive part of the whole study. It provided the research team with a comprehensive knowledge of recent and current recreation research which few other investigators have ever been able to acquire. It led us to the realization that many of the methodological problems encountered in recreation studies are not unique, but have often been experienced—and overcome—in other fields of social research. Above all, it enabled the team to identify those problems which clearly warranted priority in our own research and, hence, to define the precise objectives to be pursued in the experimental studies. Perhaps the importance that was attached to the methodological review may be best illustrated by reference to the amount of time spent on it: out of a total period of thirty-two months spent on the study, ten months were devoted to the review of previous and current research.

At least in a general sense, the first of the experimental studies achieved its main purpose—the formulation of a set of guidelines for use in future studies. The joint use of interviews and self-administered questionnaires in the household and activities survey demonstrated that this can, indeed, be a useful method of increasing the size of a sample without a proportionate increase in costs. The method could be particularly valuable for use in local and subregional studies where the distances that interviewers will have to travel in order to collect self-administered questionnaires will not be prohibitive. The time budget diary studies showed that the major methodological problems associated with their use—in particular, the difficulties of coding and analysing 'free responses'—can be successfully overcome; and that, when they are, this method of collecting recreation data can aid in the formulation of planning and management policies in a way that questionnaire surveys cannot. The cluster and factor analyses demonstrated that the notion that people can be grouped into 'recreation types' on the basis of the kinds of activities in which they participate is a valid one—even if much more work will have to be done before such a concept will be readily usable in the formulation and implementation of planning policy. Finally, the analysis of profile data against the 'depth' and 'breadth' of respondents' recreation activity made possible the identification of the main socio-economic characteristics that are correlated with recreation behaviour.

Of course, this first—and largest—of the experimental studies was in no way an *unqualified* success. Despite the acquisition of nearly twice as many questionnaires through the joint use of interviews and self-administered questionnaires as could have been expected through the use of interviews alone, the total numbers of respondents were still often inadequate to permit a detailed analysis of minority recreation activities to be carried out. And despite the success of the cluster and factor analyses in identifying some stable recreation groups, there is much more that needs to be done before we can be sufficiently confident of the validity of such groups to use them in the determination of planning policies. Again, while the analysis of profile data did provide a sound basis for the formulation of guidelines for the collection and analysis of such data in future studies, it is clear that further work will be necessary to refine these. In particular, there is a need to measure the possession of these characteristics against other indicators of recreation activity besides 'breadth' and 'depth'.

But though there may be qualifications, it can reasonably be argued that the household and activities survey achieved most of its main purposes. There was, however, one objective which it failed completely to achieve—the identification of consistent activity-opportunity relationships. To do this, the data about participation in recreation activities obtained from the survey had to be related to the data about opportunities derived from the inventory of facilities in the two survey areas. This constituted the second of the experimental studies.

The inventory of recreation opportunities in the two study areas was, itself, a partial success. For, while it was fairly clear that the inventory had failed to identify *all* opportunities, it did demonstrate that a considerable volume of information about opportunities can be obtained from a demand survey. This approach is, however, only likely to be useful for local studies, where the proportion of residents covered by the survey can be relatively large; and, hence, where there is a reasonable chance that all major facilities will be identified by at least one respondent. It is doubtful that the method would be very successful for studies on a regional and subregional basis, unless the sample sizes were to be, relatively, very great. The second part of this experimental study—the attempt to identify consistent activity-opportunity relationships—was almost wholly unsuccessful. The reasons for this have been discussed in the relevant chapter, but it is worth noting here that the cause of this failure lay primarily in the inadequacy of the data rather than in a weakness of the method. Further work with this approach, drawing upon our experiences, could perhaps yield more useful results.

There is no meaningful sense in which it can be held that the third of the studies was either a success or a failure; for it was not really an experimental study in the way that the others were. It was not concerned with research methods and techniques, but with 'the data which are the raw material of these technical processes'. It was discursive in kind, not analytical, It is believed, nevertheless, that the study has been of great value. It showed, for example—through the crude comparative analysis of the two national recreation surveys of 1960 and 1965 in the United States—that the assumption of a constant correlation coefficient between recreation activities and presumed causal variables is not *necessarily* correct, even over relatively short periods of time, and, more important, that if coefficients do change, they are likely to do so in either direction—upwards or downwards. But though this crude analytical work was useful, the main purpose of the study was to focus attention upon some of the problems that arise from the *concept* of forecasting rather than from the forecasting *process* itself. This it has done.

The last of the experimental studies—the construction of a theory for the provision of recreation facilities and its subsequent testing— was an undoubted success. The basic ideas and concepts of the theory were borne out by the two case studies. It is true that the analyses that were undertaken for these two cases were of a fairly basic kind, but they gave every indication that a more sophisticated analysis would support the validity of the theory. There is little doubt that the study has shown that the gravity model concept is potentially as valuable for recreation planning as it has been shown to be for transportation planning.

Comment

In attempting to consider the worth of a completed research project, it is a valuable exercise for the investigator to consider in what ways he would change the design of the research if he were in a position to re-start the project. Such an exercise is particularly appropriate in the present case because of the broad and rather vague terms of reference that were set for the study, which meant that it could have developed along any one or more of several lines. With the benefit of hindsight, a better research scheme than the one actually employed might be identified.

One point, in fact, emerges very clearly when this kind of exercise is applied to the present study. This is that the study was too wide in its scope and too ambitious in what it tried to achieve. The study was planned to be completed in a period of two years: financial and other resources were available only for this period of time. Yet any one of the four experimental studies alone really required this length of time to be pursued thoroughly. The methodological review of recent and current research by itself took ten months to complete, about 40 per cent of the time allotted for the whole study. In a very real sense, then, the project sacrificed depth for breadth. This was the result of a deliberate decision, taken on the basis of the findings of the methodological review. And it is doubtful that, given the chance to

348

reconsider, any other approach would have been adopted instead. Certainly some differences would be apparent. For instance, it is unlikely that an attempt would have been made to measure activity-opportunity relationships. For it is now obvious that this is too complex a problem to be undertaken merely as a small part of a study which has many other purposes. In general, however, it is likely that the project would be handled in much the same way as it has been.

The review of previous studies had indicated that the greatest need was for relatively unsophisticated answers to some urgent and pressing methodological problems of a fairly basic kind. What was required was a set of guidelines for future research which would ensure comparability among different studies. And since these guidelines were necessary for a number of items—time budget diaries, profile data, 'recreation types' and so on—it was conceded that, given the limited resources, the emphasis would have to be on breadth rather than depth. There was, however, one line of research where, largely because of the particular interests and expertise of one member of the research team, it was decided to examine a methodological problem in some depth—the application of the gravity model concept to an urban recreation planning problem.

But though the study has, in general, emphasized breadth rather than depth, this does not mean that it has little or no potential for use in the formulation and implementation of planning policies. The experiment with the joint use of interviews and self-administered questionnaires demonstrated a method for obtaining recreation data from large numbers of respondents at an *absolute* cost which is not appreciably greater than would be incurred for a straightforward interview survey, and at a *cost per respondent* which is considerably below this. This could be of immense value for local studies where financial resources for data collection are often very low. The success in constructing a satisfactory scheme for the coding and analysis of the time budget diaries means that the latter can now be seriously considered for use in regional studies, where the unique kind of information which they provide—especially about the relationships between recreation and other activities—could be useful in the setting of regional planning policies. The analysis of 'recreation types', when further refined and validated by correlation with socio-economic groups within the population, could provide the planner with a much-needed flexibility in his operations. The concept of *substitutability* between activities is one which will open a whole new dimension for the urban and regional planner faced with seemingly ever-increasing demands upon severely limited land and water

349

resources. The identification of those profile characteristics which are most closely correlated with recreation activity not only means that comparability between future studies will be much easier to achieve; it also means that the inputs to forecasting models can be refined. For the first time, there is a strong likelihood that the results of a study carried out in a city such as Birmingham can be directly and immediately compared with those derived from a study in, say, Newcastle upon Tyne. Finally, of course, the application of the gravity model concept to a specific recreation planning problem has shown that this kind of research is capable of being directly useful for formulating planning decisions.

It is not contended that the research outlined here will be directly useful to the planner in the sense that it provides a wholly objective system of decision-making. We have not created a formula, or set of equations, for which the planner merely has to enter the appropriate values and wait until the decision as to what to do emerges at the other end (although the gravity model comes fairly close to this!). What the study has demonstrated is, rather, the potential for recreation research which is more than just descriptive and informative. The findings of the study will need refinement and further investigation before they can be expressed in precise mathematical formulae: and some will never be capable of such expression. For planning is not a science amenable to entirely objective calculation: it also involves values, tastes and preferences. But a greater amount of objectivity than is presently apparent is clearly desirable, and many of the findings of this research, when further substantiated, could provide this. Thus, for example, the time budget diary studies could play an important role in the construction of a strategy for the planning of recreation opportunities of the kind outlined in Table 44. Essentially, therefore, the present research represents a step along the road towards greater definition and refinement of the tools available to the planner in his task of providing satisfactory recreation opportunities for the whole community.

Suggestions for Further Research

In making suggestions for further research stemming from the experiences and findings of this project, it will be useful to take a broad twofold approach: firstly, to consider what further research can be undertaken by utilizing the very extensive volume of data collected in this study; and secondly, to indicate areas of research where further work will require the collection of additional data.

This distinction is particularly valuable because, generally, the most expensive and time-consuming part of a study lies in the collection and coding of the necessary data. If, therefore, suitable data are already available for a particular projected analysis, then the costs of obtaining useful results, in both time and money, will be considerably reduced.

The first analysis that might be undertaken with the existing data is to repeat the various tests that have been already made, but with weighted data. All of the statistical tests for the household and activities survey so far have been carried out with the raw data. This is not very unusual; nor is it thought to be a significant source of error in the findings. It would be useful, however, to check the findings by applying the same tests to the data after the latter have been weighted to compensate for differences in the success rates of interviewers and for non-response—since some evidence is available about the characteristics of non-respondents to the activities questionnaire (though not to the household questionnaire). As well as being a useful check upon the findings of the present analysis, such a further analysis might also tell us a great deal about the effects of bias.

Considerable further work could also be done with the time budget diaries. The emphasis here was on the construction of a satisfactory system for the coding and mechanical handling of the data; but no attempt was made to fully analyse the diaries themselves and, thereby, to identify exactly the kinds of data that can be obtained from diaries that survey questionnaires cannot provide. A further analysis of the diaries would also help us to obtain a more precise definition of the time–distance constraints upon the use of available recreation time, which, in turn, could be employed in the construction of a classification of recreation opportunities with direct planning potential.

There is obviously much more work that needs to be done with the concept of 'recreation types', and most of this, at least initially, can be done with the existing data. The most immediate need is for the correlation of the different cluster and factor groups with the socio-economic characteristics of the sample population, especially with those characteristics which were found to be closely correlated with the 'breadth' and 'depth' of respondents' recreation activity. Such an analysis would serve both to test the validity of the cluster and factor groups and to check the strength of the correlations between recreation activity and particular profile characteristics. A second line of inquiry would be the determination of 'types' based upon depth of recreation activity rather than breadth: that is, the

351

application of cluster and factor analyses to the data about *activities undertaken most often* by respondents. Perhaps this could be done in terms of 'volume of participation', by incorporating the frequency of participation in this most common activity.

Further work can also be undertaken with the profile data from the present study. First, the validity of the profile characteristics themselves could be further ascertained through the use of other tests besides chi-squares; for instance, Spearman, Kendall or Kruskall–Wallis tests where appropriate. Second, the relevance of the groups into which the data were divided for analysis could be refined. The test used here was to relate these groups to *average activity rates*, amalgamating these groups where differences appeared to be not significant. A more sophisticated approach statistically, however, would be the application of a chi-squared or other test on *each set of two groups*.

There is not a great deal of further work that can be done on the problem of activity–opportunity relationships with the data available from the present study. It might be worth applying a multivariate analysis to the data in the hope that this will enable the effects of the differences in socio-economic characteristics between the two areas to be isolated from the effects upon recreation activity arising from differences in opportunities. Given the other inadequacies of the data, however, it is doubtful that such an approach would be very useful.

Finally, there is much that could yet be done with the data from the site surveys. The most obvious need here is for the continuation of the tests of the gravity model concept by the inclusion in the analysis of the socio-economic data about the library users. The model was tested only in its simplest form, and there is considerable scope for refinement. A further analysis of this kind should be given very high priority in future work because of the model's direct applicability to the decision-making process in planning.

All of the suggestions for further research so far have been aimed, in effect, at improving and refining the work that has already been tackled here. There is some scope, however, for entirely new work utilizing the data obtained from the present study. The most obvious project would be to analyse the actual responses obtained from the household and activities survey in the way that would normally be done for other surveys. This might tell us a considerable amount about, for example, relationships between the activities that respondents undertook most often and those which they stated they would most *like* to undertake; that is, between actual behaviour and aspirations. Such an approach, if carried through carefully, might provide some useful indications of how activity patterns could change in the immediate future with given changes in socio-economic parameters.

We come, finally, to a consideration of future research that can only be undertaken with data obtained from sources other than the present study. There appear to be three priorities here: first, a further and complete study of activity–opportunity relationships; second, the construction of a forecasting model for use at least at the national and regional levels; and third, the application of the gravity model concept to other kinds of recreation facilities.

The first of these studies would probably best be undertaken by the use of *before-and-after* surveys rather than by trying to compare socially homogeneous areas which have very different recreation opportunity structures. The approach would be, first, to select an area in which a major new recreation opportunity was in process of development. A survey would then be carried out before the development was complete and again after it was in full operation. Then, hopefully, it would be possible to identify changes in recreation patterns stemming directly from the provision of the new opportunity. This approach was considered and rejected in the present study because it requires the investment of considerable resources over periods of several years. It was always conceded, however, that this was probably the most satisfactory way of tackling the problem. The lack of success of the alternative method used in the present study has, if anything, reinforced this view.

The second study—the construction of a forecasting model for use in national, regional and, ultimately, local studies—could use as its starting point the review of previous forecasting studies outlined in Chapter 3 and the discussion of problems in Chapter 12. But, though there is an urgent need for such a model, it should be recognized that it is unlikely to be of great practical use until we have definitely established which socio-economic characteristics play the greatest part in determining recreation activity. It is also likely to be much more useful when it can be applied to well-founded groups of activities, or 'recreation' types.

The need for the third study is obvious. The application of the gravity model concept to the problem of providing and siting new libraries demonstrated a tool which, with but a little refinement, can be directly utilized in the planning process. It seems fairly obvious, therefore, that the applicability of the model to other kinds of facilities—for example, swimming pools, sports stadia and golf courses—should be thoroughly and rapidly examined.

It is obvious that the volume of research suggested here represents

M

the investment of a considerable sum of money. It is equally obvious that this amount of money is unlikely to be available at one time. In concluding this account, therefore, it will be useful to indicate the relative importance of the suggested projects. The order of priorities, as I see it, is as follows:

1. The refinement of the gravity model.
2. Further analysis of the cluster and factor groupings.
3. Further validation of the recreation-related profile data.
4. Application of the gravity model to other kinds of recreation facilities.
5. Construction of a forecasting model.
6. *Before-and-after* studies of activity–opportunity relationships.
7. Further analysis of the time budget diaries.
8. Analysis of the data from the household and activities survey.
9. Investigation of the effects of non-response in creating bias.

Other investigators will no doubt have their own orders of priorities. This ranking stems directly from my experiences with the present study. Perhaps it can provide a useful basis for the formulation of a programme of recreation research.

Bibliography

A. RECREATION STUDIES

1. British Broadcasting Corporation, *The People's Activities*, Audience Research Department, 1965.
2. British Travel Association, *Home Holiday Survey*, published annually.
3. British Travel Association, *Survey of Whitsun Holiday Travel, 1963*, duplicated report.
4. British Travel Association, *August Bank Holiday Survey, 1965*, duplicated report.
5. British Travel Association—Peak Park Planning Board, *Peak District National Park Survey, 1963*, summary report + study reports.
6. British Travel Association—University of Keele, *Pilot National Recreation Survey—Report No. 1*, 1967.
7. Bureau of Outdoor Recreation (U.S.A.), *The 1965 Survey of Outdoor Recreation Activities*, U.S. Department of the Interior, 1967.
8. Burton, T. L., *The Classification of Recreation Demands and Supplies*, University of Birmingham, Centre for Urban and Regional Studies, Research Memorandum No. 1, 1967.
9. Burton, T. L., 'Holiday Movements in Britain', *Town and Country Planning*, Vol. XXXIII, No. 3, March 1965, pp. 118–25.
10. Burton, T. L., 'Caravan Sites for Holidaymakers', *Town and Country Planning*, Vol. XXXIV, No. 2, February 1966, pp. 113–19.
11. Burton, T. L., *Windsor Great Park: A Recreation Study*, Wye College Studies in Rural Land Use, No. 8, 1967.
12. Burton, T. L., *Outdoor Recreation Enterprises in Problem Rural Areas*, Wye College Studies in Rural Land Use, No. 9, 1967.
13. Burton, T. L. and Fulcher, M. N., 'Measurement of Recreation Benefits—A Survey', *Journal of Economic Studies*, Vol. 3, No. 2, July 1968, pp. 35–48.
14. Burton, T. L. and Noad, P. A., *Recreation Research Methods*, Centre for Urban and Regional Studies Occasional Paper No. 3, 1969.
15. Burton, T. L. and Wibberley, G. P., *Outdoor Recreation in the British Countryside*, Wye College Studies in Rural Land Use, No. 5, 1965.
16. Central Council of Physical Recreation, *A Preliminary Analysis of the Non-Residential Use of the Crystal Palace National Recreation Centre*, 1965.
17. Chapin, F. S. and Hightower, H. C., *Household Activity Systems—A Pilot Investigation*, University of North Carolina Urban Studies Research Monograph, 1966.

355

18. Clawson, M. and Knetsch, J. L., *Economics of Outdoor Recreation*, Johns Hopkins Press for Resources for the Future, 1966.
19. Coppock, J. T., 'The Recreational Use of Land and Water in Rural Britain', *Tijdschrift Voor Econ. En Soc. Geografie*, Mei–Jun 1966.
20. Cracknell, B., 'Access to the Countryside as a Factor in Planning for Leisure', *Regional Studies*, Vol. 1, No. 2, 1967, pp. 147–61.
21. Cullingworth, J. B., 'Planning for Leisure', *Urban Studies*, Vol. 1, No. 1, May 1964, pp. 1–25.
22. Cullingworth, J. B., *The Classification of Recreational Activities*, unpublished paper, 1965.
23. Dower, M., 'Fourth Wave: The Challenge of Leisure', *Architects Journal*, January 20, 1965.
24. Dumazedier, J., *Toward A Society of Leisure*, Free Press, 1967.
25. Greater London Council, *Surveys of the Use of Open Spaces—Vol. 1*, Research Paper No. 2, 1968.
26. Hammond, E. C., *Survey of Visitors to Wye and Crundale National Nature Reserve*, Nature Conservancy, unpublished paper, 1965.
27. Hampshire County Council—Mass Observation Limited, *Village Life in Hampshire*, 1966.
28. Hole, V., *Children's Play on Housing Estates*, National Building Studies Research Paper 39, H.M.S.O., 1966.
29. Hunt, A., *A Survey of Scottish Tourism*, Government Social Survey, 1966.
30. Industrial Society, The, *Holidays: Current Practices and Trends*, Information Survey and Report Series No. 134, September 1966.
31. Jephcott, P., *Time of One's Own*, University of Glasgow Social and Economic Studies, Occasional Papers No. 7, 1967.
32. London Borough of Brent, *Survey of the Sports Interests of School Leavers in Brent*, Planning and Research Department, 1965.
33. London Borough of Brent, *Survey of Sports Clubs in Brent*, Planning and Research Department, 1966.
34. Michigan Department of Conservation, *Michigan Outdoor Recreation Demand Study*, Technical Report No. 6, 1966 (in 3 volumes).
35. National Opinion Polls Limited, *Major County Cricket*, 1966.
36. Nicholls, D. C. and Young, A., *Recreation and Tourism in the Loch Lomond Area*, University of Glasgow, 1968.
37. Norfolk County Council, *Report on the Norfolk Holiday Industry*, County Planning Department, 1964.
38. Outdoor Recreation Resources Review Commission (U.S.A.), *Outdoor Recreation for America*, Summary Report + 27 Study Reports, U.S. Government Printing Office, 1962.
39. Outdoor Recreation Resources Review Commission (U.S.A.), *National Recreation Survey*, Study Report No. 19, U.S. Government Printing Office, 1962.
40. Outdoor Recreation Resources Review Commission (U.S.A.), *Participation in Outdoor Recreation: Factors Affecting Demand*

Among American Adults, Study Report No. 20, U.S. Government Printing Office, 1962.

41. Outdoor Recreation Resources Review Commission (U.S.A.), *Prospective Demand for Outdoor Recreation*, Study Report No. 26, U.S. Government Printing Office, 1962.

42. Outdoor Recreation Resources Review Commission (U.S.A.), *Projections to the Years 1976 and 2000: Economic Growth, Population, Labour Force and Leisure, Transportation*, Study Report No. 23, U.S. Government Printing Office, 1962.

43. Proctor, C., *Dependence of Recreation Participation on Background Characteristics of Sample Persons in the September 1960 National Recreation Survey*, Appendix A to O.R.R.R.C. Study Report No. 19.

44. Robinson, J. P. and Converse, P. E., *Sixty-six Basic Tables of Time–Budget Data for the United States*, Draft Report, University of Michigan Survey Research Center, 1966.

45. Sports Council, *Planning for Sport*, Central Council of Physical Recreation, 1968.

46. Wager, J. F., *The Public Use of Ashridge*, duplicated report, 1964.

47. Wager, J. F., 'Outdoor Recreation on Common Land', *Journal of the Town Planning Institute*, Vol. 53, No. 9, November 1967, pp. 398–403.

48. Wolfe, R. I., 'Perspective on Outdoor Recreation: A Bibliographical Survey', *Geographical Review*, Vol. 54, No. 2, April 1964, pp. 203–38.

Initial Appraisals of the Regional Sport Councils

49. Technical Panel, East Midlands Sports Council, *Recreation in the East Midlands—An Initial Appraisal of Major Facilities*, 1967.

50. North East Advisory Council for Sport and Recreation, *Provision for Sport and Recreation in the North East*, 1965.

51. Northern Advisory Council for Sport and Recreation, *Water Sports in the Northern Region*, North Regional Planning Committee, 1967.

52. Northern Advisory Council for Sport and Recreation, *Public Swimming Baths in the North East*, North Regional Planning Committee, 1966.

53. Northern Advisory Council for Sport and Recreation, *Survey of Golf Facilities*, North Regional Planning Committee, 1967.

54. West Midlands Sports Council Technical Panel, *Regional Recreation*, 1967.

55. Greater London and South East Sports Council, *Sports Facilities: Initial Appraisal—Volume 1*, 1968.

56. Eastern Sports Council, *First Appraisal of Major Facilities and Field Games*, 1967.

57. South Western Sports Council, *Initial Appraisal of Major Facilities*, 1967.

58. County of Lancashire, *Survey of Existing Facilities for Sport and*

Physical Recreation—Preliminary Report, County Planning Department, 1967.

59. County of Cheshire, *Recreation in Cheshire: Survey of Existing Facilities for Sport and Physical Recreation—1. Preliminary Report*, County Planning Department, 1967.
60. The Sports Council for Wales, *Major Sports Facilities—An Initial Appraisal*, 1967.
61. Yorkshire and Humberside Sports Council, *Sports Facilities—An Initial Appraisal*, 1967.
62. Southern Sports Council, *Major Sport and Recreation Facilities—A First Appraisal*, 1967.

B. SOCIAL RESEARCH METHODS

63. Atkinson, J., *A Handbook for Interviewers*, Government Social Survey, H.M.S.O., 1967.
64. Bechhofer, F., *Data on Occupations With Special Reference to Locality Studies*, Papers of the British Sociological Association Working Party on Comparability of Data, Set 1, Paper 5, unpublished paper, 1968.
65. Chapman, D., *Age, Sex, Marital Status, Birth Place*, Papers of the British Sociological Association Working Party on Comparability of Data, Set 1, Paper 1, unpublished paper, 1968.
66. Clausen, J. A. and Ford, R. N., 'Controlling Bias in Mail Questionnaires', *Journal of the American Statistical Association*, Vol. 42, No. 240, December 1947, pp. 497–511.
67. Festinger, L. and Katz, D., *Research Methods in the Behavioural Sciences*, Staples Press, 1954.
68. Gittus, E., *Income*, Papers of the British Sociological Association Working Party on Comparability of Data, Set 1, Paper 4, unpublished paper, 1968.
69. Gray, P. G. and Corlett, T., 'Sampling for the Social Survey', *Journal of the Royal Statistical Society*, Series A, Part II, 1950, pp. 150–99.
70. Hancock, J., 'An Experimental Study of Four Methods of Measuring Unit Costs of Obtaining Attitudes Towards Retail Stores', *Journal of Applied Psychology*, 1940.
71. Kish, L., *Survey Sampling*, Wiley and Sons, 1967.
72. Kluckhohn, F. R., 'The Participant-Observer Technique in Small Communities', *American Journal of Sociology*, Vol. 46, No. 3, November 1940, pp. 331–43.
73. Moser, C. A. *Survey Methods in Social Investigation*, Heinemann, 1958.
74. Parten, M. B., *Surveys, Polls and Samples*, Harper and Row, 1950.
75. Reuss, C. F., 'Differences Between Persons Responding and Not Responding to a Mailed Questionnaire', *American Sociological Review*, Vol. 8, No. 4, August 1943, pp. 433–8.

76. Sawyer, H. G., *The Meaning of Numbers*, Speech given to the American Association of Advertising Agencies, 1961.
77. Seitz, R. M., 'How Mail Surveys May be Made to Pay', *Printer's Ink*, 209, 1944.
78. Shevky, E. and Bell, W., *Social Area Analysis*, Stanford University Press, 1955.
79. Shuttleworth, F. K., 'A Study of Questionnaire Technique', *Journal of Educational Psychology*, Vol. 22, No. 9, December 1931, pp. 652–8.
80. Sletto, R. F., Pretesting of Questionnaires', *American Sociological Review*, Vol. 5, No. 2, April 1940, pp. 193–200.
81. Stacey, M., *Family and Household*, Papers of the British Sociological Association Working Party on Comparability of Data, Set 1, Paper 3, unpublished paper, 1968.
82. Szalai, A., *Instruction Manual of the Time Budget Research Project*, unpublished paper, 1965.
83. Watson, R., 'Investigations by Mail', *Market Research*, 5, 1937.
84. Webb, E. J. *et al.*, *Unobtrusive Measures: Nonreactive Research in the Social Sciences*, Rand McNally, 1966.
85. Weinberg, A., *Education as a Key Variable*, Papers of the British Sociological Association Working Party on Comparability of Data, Set 1, Paper 2, unpublished paper, 1968.
86. Weir, R. H., *Language in the Crib*, Mouton, 1963.
87. Yates, F., *Sampling Methods for Censuses and Surveys*, Griffin, 1960.

C. GENERAL REFERENCES

88. *Birmingham Post Year Book and Who's Who 1968–1969*, The Birmingham Post, 1968.
89. Centre for Urban and Regional Studies, University of Birmingham, *The Work of the Centre*, Occasional Paper No. 4, 1969.
90. *City of Birmingham Abstract of Statistics No. 12*, City of Birmingham Central Statistical Office, 1969.
91. *City of Birmingham Development Plan*, 1960.
92. Cullingworth, J. B., *The Politics of Research*, Inaugural Lecture at the University of Birmingham, 1968.
93. Dankert, C. E. *et al.*, *Hours of Work*, Harper and Row, 1965.
94. Government Social Survey, *Young School Leavers*, H.M.S.O., 1968.
95. Kahn, H. and Wiener, A. J., *The Year 2000*, Macmillan, 1967.

D. DISCUSSIONS AND CONSULTATIONS

96. Cannell, C., Survey Research Center, University of Michigan, U.S.A. (Methods of Data Collection.)
97. Chapin, F. S., Center for Urban and Regional Studies, University of North Carolina, U.S.A. (Time-Budget Studies and Activity Systems.)
98. Clawson, M., Resources for the Future Inc., Washington, D.C., U.S.A. (Techniques of Projection.)

99. Converse, P. E., Survey Research Center, University of Michigan, U.S.A. (Time-Budget Studies.)
100. Coppock, J. T., Department of Geography, University of Edinburgh. (Methods of Data Collection.)
101. Griffiths, I., Department of Physical Education, University of Manchester. (Methods of Data Collection.)
102. Hammer, P., Center for Urban and Regional Studies, University of North Carolina, U.S.A. (Time-Budget Studies and Activity Systems.)
103. Hemmens, G., Department of City and Regional Planning, University of North Carolina, U.S.A. (Methods of Data Analysis.)
104. Hightower, H. C., Center for Urban and Regional Studies, University of North Carolina, U.S.A. (Time-Budget Studies and Activity Systems.)
105. Law, S., Planning Department, Greater London Council. (Methods of Data Collection and Analysis.)
106. Mueller, M., Survey Research Center, University of Michigan, U.S.A. (Methods of Data Analysis.)
107. Nicholls, D. C., Department of Town and Regional Planning, University of Glasgow. (Methods of Data Collection.)
108. Ramprakash, D., General Register Office. (Methods of Projection.)
109. Sillitoe, K., Government Social Survey. (Methods of Data Collection and Analysis.)
110. Sutherland, A., Planning Department, City of Newcastle upon Tyne. (Methods of Data Collection.)
111. Willmott, P., Institute of Community Studies. (Methods of Data Collection and Analysis.)

E. PROJECTION OF RECREATION-RELATED VARIABLES

112. United Nations, *General Principles for National Programmes of Population Projection as Aids to Development Planning*, ST/SOA/ Series A, 38, New York, 1965.
113. United Nations, *Methods for Population Projections by Sex and Age*, ST/SOA/Series A, 25, New York, 1956.
114. Cox, P. R., *Demography*, Cambridge University Press, 1959.
115. Schneider, J. R. C., *Local Population Projections in England and Wales*, Population Studies, Vol. 9, July 1956.
116. Economic Trends No. 139, May 1965: *Projecting the Population of the U.K.*
117. General Register Office, *Registrar-General's Quarterly Return for England and Wales*.
118. General Register Office, *Quarterly Return of the Registrar-General for Scotland*
119. Isard, W., *Methods of Regional Analysis*, Massachusetts Institute of Technology Press, 1960.

120. Freeman, Fox, Wilbur Smith and Associates, *The West Midlands Transport Study*, 1967.
121. Boudeville, J. R., *Problems of Regional Economic Planning*, Edinburgh University Press, 1966.
122. Organization for Economic Co-operation and Development, *Techniques of Economic Forecasting*, Paris, 1965.
123. *The National Plan*, Cmnd. 2764, H.M.S.O., 1965.
124. W. Beckerman and Associates, *The British Economy in 1975*, National Institute of Economic and Social Research, Cambridge University Press, 1965.
125. Mogridge, M. J. H., 'The Prediction of Car Ownership', *Journal of Transport Economics and Policy*, Vol. 1, No. 1, January 1967, pp. 52–74.
126. Tanner, J. C., 'Forecasts of the Future Numbers of Vehicles in Great Britain', *Roads and Road Construction*, September 1962; and 'Comments on Forecasting Car Ownership and Use', *Urban Studies*, Vol. 3, No. 2, June 1966, pp. 143–6.
127. Ministry of Education, *Higher Education*, Report of the Committee on Higher Education (The Robbins Report), Cmnd. 2154, H.M.S.O., 1963.
128. Department of Education and Science, *Statistics of Education*, H.M.S.O., published annually.
129. Outdoor Recreation Resources Review Commission (U.S.A.), *Projections To the Years 1976 and 2000: Economic Growth, Population, Labour Force and Leisure, and Transportation*, Study Report No. 23, U.S. Government Printing Office, 1962.

F. ADDITIONAL REFERENCES

130. Colburn, W. H., 'A Practitioner's Critique', in *Predicting Recreation Demand*, Michigan State University, Recreation Research and Planning Unit, Technical Report No. 7, 1969, pp. 36–50.
131. Ellis, J., private correspondence.
132. Kahn, H., 'World Futures', *Science Journal*, October 1967, pp. 121–5.
133. Morris, D., 'Boredom: The New Blight', *Sunday Times Weekly Review*, November 2nd 1969.
134. Taylor, G. D., 'History and Techniques of Recreation Demand Prediction', in *Predicting Recreation Demand*, Michigan State University, Recreation Research and Planning Unit, Technical Report No. 7, 1969, pp. 4–13.
135. McQuitty, L. L., 'Pattern Analysis—A Statistical Method for the Study of Types', in Chalmers *et al.*, *Labor Management Relations in Illini City*, University of Illinois Press, 1954.
136. Harman, H. H., *Modern Factor Analysis*, University of Chicago Press, 1967.
137. Stevens, S. S., 'On The Theory of Scales of Measurement', *Science*, 103, 2684, June 7th 1946.

138. Siegel, S., *Nonparametric Statistics for the Behavioural Sciences*, McGraw-Hill, 1956.
139. Maw, R., 'Construction of A Leisure Model', *Official Architecture and Planning*, 22, 8, August 1969.
140. Stamp, L. D., *The Land of Britain: Its Use and Misuse*, Longmans Green, 3rd edition, 1962.

Index

For Product Safety Concerns and Information please contact our EU
representative GPSR@taylorandfrancis.com
Taylor & Francis Verlag GmbH, Kaufingerstraße 24, 80331 München, Germany